LORDS OF SMASHMOUTH

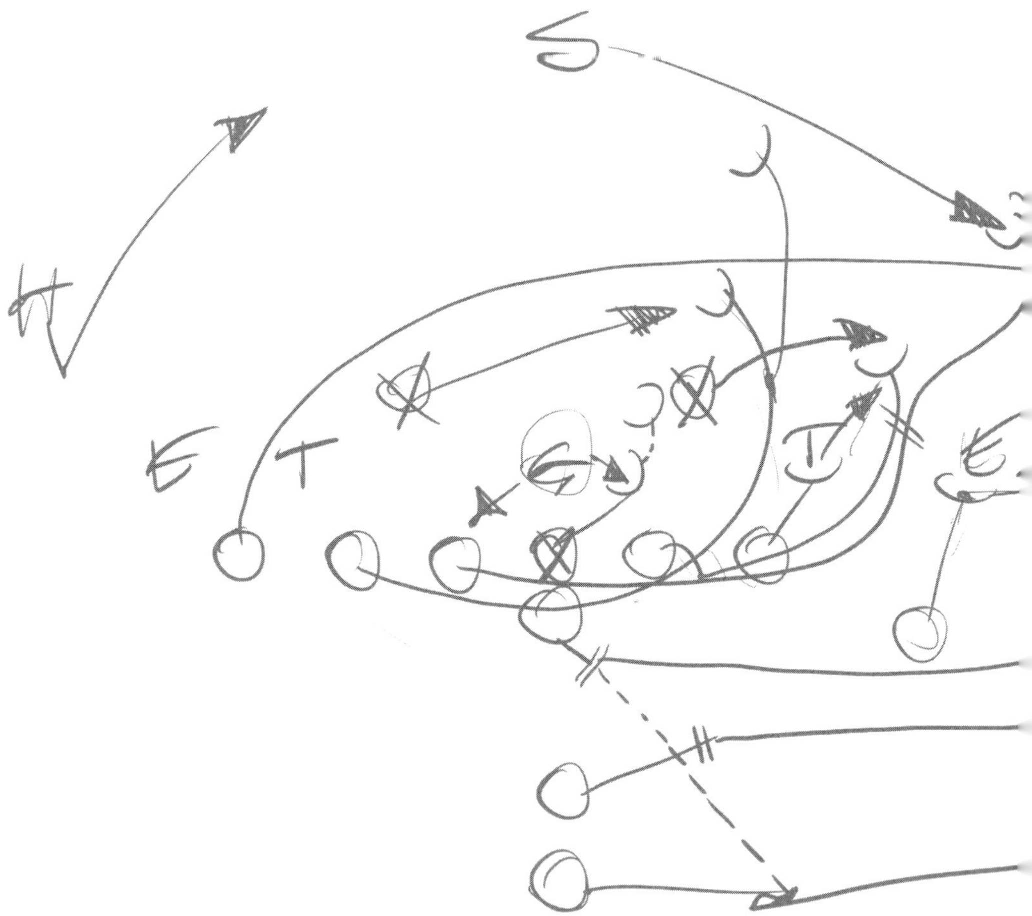
S
H
E
T
E

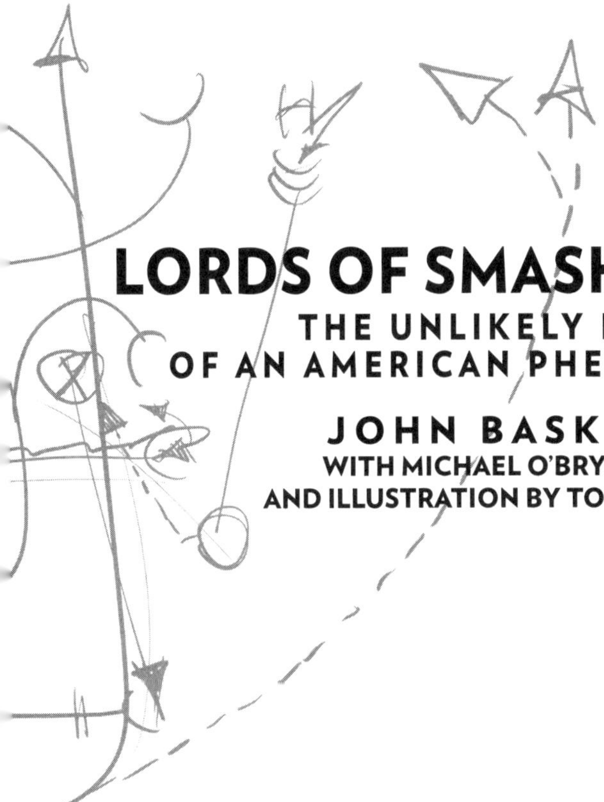

LORDS OF SMASHMOUTH

THE UNLIKELY RISE OF AN AMERICAN PHENOMENON

JOHN BASKIN

WITH MICHAEL O'BRYANT

AND ILLUSTRATION BY TODD KALE

ORANGE *frazer* PRESS

Wilmington, Ohio

ISBN 978-1949248-524

Orange Frazer Press
37½ W. Main St.
P.O. Box 214
Wilmington, OH 45177
Telephone: 937.382.3196 for price and shipping information.
www.orangefrazer.com

Art direction: John Baskin
Cover design: J Porter
Cover art: Greg Storer, (Ohio State tight end, 1975-1977)
Illustration: Todd Kale

Ohio State-Michigan program courtesy the College Football Hall of Fame, Atlanta, Georgia.
"University Days" excerpt from *My Life and Hard Times* by James Thurber.

For additional Thurber information see *www.ThurberHouse.com* and *www.JamesThurber.org*.

Library of Congress Control Number: 2021912379

First edition and printing

For Lonnie, best man

"Every Saturday afternoon during the football season, while a scarlet-jerseyed quarterback of Ohio State University barks signals on the field, 425,000 additional quarterbacks in Columbus and another eight million throughout the state are sure to think, at some point during the game, that each of them could do a better job. By Monday morning, the traditional time for quarterback sniping, these millions of signal callers will have replayed the game several times over in their own minds, and will then start replaying it in groups. Along about Wednesday or Thursday the coming Saturday's game will come up for discussion, and all of Ohio will decide in advance just how that one ought to be played."

— Robert Shaplen, *Sports Illustrated*, October 24, 1955

ACKNOWLEDGMENTS

Academic sports historians Kurt Edward Kemper, Michael Oriand, Raymond Schmidt, and Murray Sperber for their inestimable work and synthesis; The Public Library of Cincinnati and Hamilton County (its staff and especially its online resources); Mike Brown; the Colvilles, Jim, Jackie, Meaghan & Ryan; Colleen Goodhart, Denison University Digital & Archival Projects; Michael Graham (as good at editing as at sportswriting); Ken Gray; Sasha Griffin, Denison University Archivist & Special Collections librarian; the undying spirit of Woody Hayes (still in the house); Bill Kimok, Ohio University Archivist and Records Manager; Tim Lichtenberg; Halle Mares, Archives Program Assistant, The Ohio State University, University Libraries Archives; Rod Russell; sportswriters Chuck Culpepper, Bob Hunter, David Hyde, Bill Livingston, Bill Rabinowitz, and Mark Rea (who provided valuable reportage, as well as superbly sharp proofreading); Kent Stevens, historian, the College Football Hall of Fame; special thanks to Lori Styler of the Barbara Hogenson Agency; Lonnie Wheeler, the forever classy sportsman (and boon companion); and Nancy Zimpher.

CONTENTS

V.
Postscript—297

PREFACE

I.

I ARRIVED IN OHIO FROM THE CAROLINAS JUST DAYS AFTER THE 1969 ROSE BOWL, the new special assignments writer for the *Dayton Daily News* and unprepared for the unending water-cooler conversations about Ohio State, replete with tales of an eccentric Columbus character who seemed to have no last name, being referred to only as "Woody." This was, of course, the benighted dark ages before social media and the transmission of every errant thought, and thus I had somehow missed knowing who Woody Hayes was. Given the reverence of my new colleagues for him, I thought that perhaps he had founded the school. I quickly saw that I was an outlander and must study this new territory.

Football in the Carolinas was not monolithic as it was in Ohio where the Colossus of Columbus, on the breakwater of the Olentangy, towered over the entire state. We had a dozen Division I teams—and colors—to choose from, and our own assortment of characters. For instance, my northern colleagues did not know who Frank Howard was, surely an act of sacrilege in South Carolina. Not know the Bard of Barlow Bend? (That was the Alabama flyspeck village where he was from, describing his leave-taking as "walking barefoot on a barbed wire fence with a wildcat under each arm.")

Howard had been at Clemson as long as anyone could remember, endearing himself to the university's followers with such homespun witticisms as "I had a lot of offers to go to other schools, but I turned them all down because Clemson was the only place I could bum chewing tobacco from the professors." Once, driving through backroads Georgia to see a recruit, he was pulled over for speeding. It was during the Depression, so the fine was only three dollars. "I'm in kind of hurry," Howard said, "so don't stop me when I come back through here in about an hour." And handed the officer six dollars.

Howard, according to his own account, was given a look by Ohio State before Woody was hired. He didn't pursue what interest there might have been because he was sure the University wouldn't approve of his tobacco-chewing. "I didn't know if those Yankees could understand Southern talk," he went on to say, "and I wasn't sure my cook would go with me."

Clemson is still a small town, its population nearly doubled by students, although back in the mid-century when a sportswriter came down to cover a Clemson–Boston College game, he was less captured by the game than by the fact that he was bitten by a mule who stuck its head out of a downtown livery stable.

As a fledgling sportswriter for the *Greensboro Daily News* in North Carolina in the 1960s, I shared an intimate moment with Coach Howard, having been apprenticed to one of the old hands, an amiable fellow named Gene Warren who'd been sent to cover the Clemson–UNC game. UNC won handsomely, 29–0, and Gene and I headed from the press box to the postgame press conference.

"Just watch me," Gene said, then he collared the coach.

"Coach Howard," he said, "what was the turning point of the game?"

Coach Howard looked eminently pained, then he said to Gene, "Son, that's the goddamned dumbest question anybody's ever asked me."

For Gene's sake, I pretended I wasn't watching.

Once in the north and trying to get myself up to cultural speed, I took my clues from a colleague on the *Dayton Daily News* staff, Ben Kline, a quietly sardonic fellow whose claim to fame had been that he had been an Ohio State marching band drum major where one of his signal moments was being lectured in front of the entire band—and over the PA system—because he'd attempted a back bend during the playing of *A Mighty Fortress is Our God*. Ben did his best to acquaint me with the customs and rituals attached to Ohio State football, and I did my best to understand the Ohio compunction to create little scarlet-and-gray museums in every basement. Being naturally suspicious of any activity involving so many people acting in concert, it took time for me to fully appreciate what had been wrought years before in the frontier outpost that was Columbus, Ohio.

Ben first conveyed to me the status of Woody Hayes, the panjandrum of Ohio State who had already bronzed the school's football reputation (as well as his own), and that the university's orbit is gravitational, pulling all of Ohio toward it. Ben's favorite anecdote was of Woody on the plane trip to Illinois lecturing his team. He was holding Abraham Lincoln up as an exemplar of hard work and diligence, and he said what a great defensive end Lincoln would have been with his toughness and long, rangy reach. The players became so incited, Ben said, that an offensive tackle yelled out, "I can TAKE Lincoln, Coach!"

My arrival coincided with an Ohio State era that wouldn't be paralleled until Urban Meyer became the University's coach some forty years in the future. The Ohio State football program was constantly in front of the population, and Woody, with his nearly three-decade tenure was the last of the colorfully idiosyncratic old-school coaches. The fans were thus watching both the present and the past at the very same moment.

And even the non-fan took note of Hayes's burning passion and the abiding drama of his teams (which was often more on the sidelines and less on the field). In one eight-year stretch, Ohio State contended for the national title every year but one. An inveterate article filer and note-taker, I began to pay attention, for in those days there weren't many books on Ohio State football. (There *was* Robert Vare's best-selling *Buckeye* in 1974 that the *Denver Post* said was "a telling story of contemporary American civilization." It irritated Woody so much he accused the author of being "a plant from That School Up North.") Otherwise, the reporting was, by and large, found in the state newspapers with occasional visits by the East Coast cognoscenti.

Over time, my one dedicated file drawer became ten; my sports library grew exponentially as well. It was a hobby, yes, but with an eye to understanding the phenomenon. For it was surely that. Ohio State had begun, literally, in a pasture three-and-half miles from the corner of Broad and High with small prospects and athletics not even an afterthought. Football had actually been around in the Midwest for some time, in one fashion or another, but to small effect. (The Cincinnati *Commercial Tribune* along about 1828 fulminated against street urchins breaking out windows with their "foot balls," and at another early moment a skull was found in an Ohio City cellar, apparently used as a football before it was inadvertently kicked into the basement.) As for athletics on the Ohio State campus, there was a bit of baseball, some tennis (the governor let the players use the court at the mansion), and even less football, which might feature a hundred boys on the field in something resembling a prison riot.

Early in the twentieth century there was an entirely unlikely—but epochal—sports-related moment from which all other such moments derived. It came when a small group of like-minded men with the apparent ability to see into the future devised plans for a stadium so large it would hold three times the largest crowd that had previously seen an Ohio State game. If one looked at the plan as a business proposal, it was so fanciful as to appear the work of an illusionist. It was a pipe dream, pigs in flight, a blue moon, a fancy. Except it wasn't. It was the first step in a master plan that, in effect, converted that pasture along High Street into the wealthiest, most successful college football program in the country.

How did it happen? Not exactly like you think. Because there were always bear-market teams and missed opportunities. Jack Wilce lost an early national championship, and so did Francis Schmidt. Woody lost more than one. (The process was, of course, largely what Jim Tressel, far into the future, reminded everyone: on any given Saturday half the teams in America lost.) The trajectory, though, was ever upward. There were backward moments but they were just that: *moments*.

On the threshold of placing my sports library into a university archive, Michael O'Bryant, who'd co-edited two editions of the

Ohio Almanac with me (and survived), and I decided to look through the Ohio State material and see what we might make of it. The result is an attempt not to extol the grandeur of the program—glaringly obvious and done repeatedly— but to suggest how it all happened and what its various manifestations (and those of its people) meant.

If the thinking is particularly keen, it probably came from Michael; the irony is mostly mine. We hope the voluminous detail, as well as the patent vitality of thc program itself, will leaven our presence. The careful reader might look at it as a kind of antidote to the more customary offerings, unlike those that have gone before, and so a kind of sorting out in which we suggest a few alternate summations.

No matter the perspective, the story of Ohio State football is one of America's extraordinary sports stories. This book, then, is for the extraordinary fan.

—John Baskin

II.

For most of my life, Ohio State has had one of the most successful programs in college football. Born in the Basketball Kingdom (Kentucky), I didn't grow up an OSU fan. I was raised in the city-state of Cincinnati—the corner of Ohio where OSU's shadow is smallest. But it's hard to spend any time in the state and not be aware of the shadow cast by OSU football. While my friends went to the Mid-American Conference schools that seem to orbit Columbus, OSU was where our doctors and dentists went but not us small-towners out among the cows and cornfields.

It may have been 1968 when perceptions began to change. We had gone off to school or Vietnam as the farms we grew up with were replaced by housing developments and strip malls and—nearby—Kings Island. Tractors disappeared from our school parking lot, and the opening of rabbit season was no longer an unofficial school holiday.

It was also a time when the Buckeyes won the national championship and one of its stars came from another small school—Lockland. Images of Mike Sensibaugh picking off passes and stopping O.J. Simpson on the goal line during the Rose Bowl resonated with us. It was like one of us, or at least someone from our small school background, could make it at the big school. Soon it seemed as if everyone was going to OSU: friends, family, and eventually my old high school football coach who made it on staff as an assistant. My sister married the captain of the hockey team and a generation later my niece played tennis there.

I REMEMBER GAMES I ATTENDED FROM MORE THAN FORTY YEARS AGO, particularly the Ohio State-Michigan ones, and more clearly than I remember weddings and most funerals. In 1977, I sat in the middle of a pocket of empty Ohio Stadium seats (the hockey team had practice and the players couldn't use their tickets) as Oklahoma's Uwe von Schamann quieted 88,000 Buckeye fans with a 41-yard field goal. I was a few feet from Bo Schembechler in 1986 as he brought his team onto the field, oblivious to the Ohio Stadium abuse. In 1987, I saw a fist-pumping Earle Bruce, fedora intact, hoisted on the shoulders of his players in his last appearance as coach in the Big House. In 2002, I sat in Paul Brown Stadium watching passes slide just off the fingers of Bearcat receivers, and I missed seeing Michael Jenkins catch a Craig Krenzel pass in the Purdue end zone because the crowd rose up in front of me. In 2014, I saw Cardale Jones replace an injured J.T. Barrett on the road to another national championship. Sometime during that period I began to wonder, "Why Ohio State?" How did one of college football's greatest programs grow out of the fields north of Columbus and what was its impact?

Because of the tribalism around college football, it's difficult to clearly evaluate any school's relative position in the sport, but one place is at the College Football Hall of Fame in Atlanta. It may be where the story of college football is best told. Despite coming late to the spectacle and spending a couple of decades toiling in the cornfield conference with other Ohio colleges, Ohio State quickly moved into the big time and secured its place in the Hall.

This vagabond hall-and-museum was originally planned for Rutgers University, existed for a time at Kings Island, Ohio, then moved to South Bend, Indiana, before finally landing in downtown Atlanta, across from the Olympic Park.

For OSU fans barreling down I-75 to Margaritaville, it's worthy of a stop, and a good place to get a feel for Ohio State University's place in football history. The first thing that strikes a visitor is the three-story Helmet Wall of over 760 college football helmets. Looking closely, the visitor will notice that at the center is a gray Ohio State helmet with its customary scarlet stripe down the middle This should seem appropriate to all Buckeye fans, most of whom see OSU as the center of the football universe. By buying a ticket and registering one's school as Ohio State the helmet will light up, giving notice to all that a Buckeye is in the house.

It's mainly through the Hall's display of objects that puts OSU in the context of college football. Archie Griffith's helmet is on display while Chic Harley's waits in the wings. A visitor can find an Earle Bruce's fedora (as well as a headband with "EARLE" scrawled on it), and a Woody Hayes block O hat. Ohio State's legacy can be seen in Francis Schmidt's playbook, as well as Sid Gillman's copy of Schmidt's plays. Behind the scenes are Woody Hayes's scarlet jacket and the sweater vest Jim Tressel wore when he won the national championship. They are lying in storage, awaiting a turn on stage. The Hall also acknowledges OSU with its display of Script Ohio with two mannequins, one wearing a band director's uniform, the other a uniformed sousaphone player. But most of all, OSU's place is found in the story and film that features each of the twenty-five inductees associated with Ohio State football.

As with the Hall, this book attempts to put context into the story of the programs and individuals, examining the development of Ohio State football and its place in the national picture. You can describe a player, coach, or idea in yards and wins, or you can look at the same thing and try to determine its influence. If you want a book to tell you the greatest players, plays, or games of Ohio State football those books have been done. Our approach is to take a topic or idea connected to the OSU football program and see where it leads us. That place may take us far, but we always attempt to return to Columbus. It's a unique program with a unique story. We hope you might see OSU football in a way you've never seen it before.

—Michael O'Bryant

LORDS OF SMASHMOUTH

Section One
Prologue

In May of 1890, it wasn't headline news when Ohio State made its formal entry into the ranks of American collegiate football. There, its rag-tag team of largely self-coached fellows caught a train out of Columbus's Union Station and headed off into athletic immortality. That, as every true Scarlet-and-Gray fan knows, was the game against Ohio Wesleyan and a 20–14 win—the school's first.

It wasn't easy to get to this moment, and it wouldn't be easy to get beyond it, because Ohio State was a Johnny Football-come-lately. Michigan, for instance, was playing football in 1879, only a decade after the Princeton–Rutgers game that history calls the first American football game (although it probably wasn't, being more soccer than anything else), and in 1894 Michigan beat Cornell, the first time any of the upstart Westerners had beaten an Eastern power. Ohio

State, that same year, was playing Antioch and losing to such grid virtuosos as Wittenberg and Western Reserve.

In time, Ohio State would make up for its tardy start, but to understand why it took so long, it helps to know what the game itself was like, and why, at the outset, it was an Eastern game. First of all, most of the Ivy League schools were at least a hundred years older than Ohio State. And, second, football in America was known as "association football," that is, it was essentially soccer.

The Americans, though, perhaps in keeping with the more rough-hewn elements of Manifest Destiny, wanted a strapping, wholly muscular, red-blooded pastime. Boston schoolboys, for instance, liked rugby, the game described in detail in Thomas Hughes's classic, *Tom Brown's School Days*, which may have been how rugby crossed the Atlantic. (If so, it gave the lie to the notion that literature never harmed anyone.)

The Bostonians soon became "hot and ruddy from football," as Tom Brown put it, which meant rugby, and their numbers infiltrated Harvard. When the dust of the Civil War had settled, and the eastern schools were organizing themselves around association football, Harvard would have none of it. It had its own rules—"the Boston Rules," which allowed running and was therefore moving away from soccer. These Bostonians liked the multiplied action, or to quote Thomas Hughes again, "What would life be without fighting, I should like to know? From the cradle to the grave, fighting, rightly understood, is the business, the real, highest, honestest business of every son of man."

In 1874, Harvard played Canada's McGill University in three games, one of them under its own rules. The second game became known as the first American rugby game—and the precursor to the modern game we watch today, or, as the player-historian Michael Oriard called it, "the Great American epic in knickers and canvas jackets." What came of those games was running with the ball. Another year or two, and Harvard's refusal to bend to association football rules had changed the direction of the game.

On the day of the Ohio State–Ohio Wesleyan game in the spring of 1890, the twelfth man on the field was Walter Camp himself—the Yale man known as "the father of American football." He was the unseen but omnipresent official, although no one present knew exactly what Camp intended. So the captains huddled with the officials and tried to figure out Camp's rulebook, and the game followed the account of an earlier one in Cincinnati, in which "several attempts were made to establish a debating society."

The game was played without pads, no headgear, but, in all probability, with a line of scrimmage, which Camp had pushed into the emerging rules a decade before. (It was considered "The most important incident in the evolution of the game," the moment that separated American football from rugby.) At least one Buckeye was wearing painter's overalls and an old jumper padded with blanket scraps. The team locker was George Cole's dorm room, and Cole later described their playing strategy as: "Anything went but brass knuckles…."

Ohio State managed an easy 14–0 lead before Ohio Wesleyan began to take advantage of its physical superiority and tied the game at 14–14. Then Caesar Morrey, the OSU halfback who was also president of his senior class, took a pitch from quarterback Jo Jo Large and raced to the goal line where Ohio State had first-and-goal. Two wedge plays later, the fledgling team had won its first game, 20–14.

That was it, actually, for the entire 1890 season, which would consist of four losses in the fall, one of them a lopsided exhibition against the Dayton Athletic Club, which fielded a team with ringers from schools such as Yale, Princeton, and Michigan, and they beat Ohio State 50–0. (They'd just beaten Ohio Wesleyan almost as bad and, in addition to being big and rough, the Daytonians further offended the Wesleyan lads by serenading them with vulgar after-dinner songs.)

It was still an elemental game, and although champion sprinter Frank Rane waxed his mustache anew for the Wooster game, he and his teammates lost 64–0. Wooster's best player was also its dirtiest—a big Native American named Tyndall, who played with such marked incivility that *The Lantern* wrote afterward that Wooster should "send him back to his reservation."

Ohio State then lost to Denison and Kenyon, although by narrower scores, and the season—along with several more to come—marked Ohio State's infancy. The trend of looking to Wise Men from the East would continue for twenty-two years, through ten coaches, all of them Ivy Leaguers, with one exception when in 1906 the university hired Albert Herrnstein, a Chillicothe guy who'd played at—where else?—Michigan. (He was famed for scoring six touchdowns in 1902 against Ohio State in Michigan's 86–0 shellacking, and perhaps the hire was seen as a way to reverse-engineer his previous damages.)

By the time Harry Vaughn, a former Yalie, left Columbus in 1911, American football was firmly established in the Midwest. Ohio State never again looked east for coaching talent (not in the twentieth century, anyway). The Eastern dynasty would win national titles through the 1920s, but the balance of power was beginning to shift; Ohio State would soon be among the elite. And—unlike the Eastern schools—it would stay there.

> He was like some sort of fictional character who had walked off the pages of a screwball novel. He was either a brilliant coach or an insane imposter.—Brett Perkins, biographer

Football's crazy uncle

The offense begins—the legend of Francis Schmidt

THE MODERN ERA OF OHIO STATE FOOTBALL BEGAN IN LATE FEBRUARY OF 1934 WHEN A TALL FELLOW wearing a bow tie stepped off the train at Union Station in Columbus, his barely contained persona merely an intimation of the commotion he would visit upon the town throughout the rest of the decade. Francis Schmidt had arrived from Texas, complete with a Western bravado that extended to his offense, which offered flamboyant possibilities not seen in respectable football, and certainly not in Ohio.

This unusual coaching outreach was a credit to the OSU brain trust, who recognized accurately its dilemma: Jack Wilce's early teams had transformed OSU from a football Hooverville into a recognized power. But now, as one historian wrote, "the Buckeyes were caught in the inescapable cycle of shifting talent." Wilce's teams did not excel in the 1920s, and the Buckeyes were still playing Kenyon and Wittenberg. Taking note of empty seats in the stadium, the athletic department was nervous. The noise outside Ohio Stadium was beginning to seem louder than the crowd inside.

It wasn't just the won-lost record, either; it was the style of play that decreed football a game of field position, with games often reduced to punting contests and teams punting on second or third downs. Scoring was down, passing still a novelty. In 1933, teams averaged a feeble 12 points a game, down a touchdown from the decade before. The Depression was even getting to football.

The school wasn't desperate yet, but the midnight oil was burning in the athletic offices. Ohio State's athletic director, Lynn St. John, looked first at the Big Ten, which wasn't illegal but frowned upon. It was, as Schmidt's biographer Brett Perkins pointed out, "akin to finding a new spouse by dating your friends' wives." It also proved embarrassing: St. John was twice rejected and caught trolling his own conference. Then there was the Machiavellian backstory, in which St. John surreptitiously arranged to export OSU's present coach, Sam Willaman, to Western Reserve. (Willaman's five winning seasons were considered middling—in his 7-1 season of 1933, he'd still lost to Michigan—thus setting in perpetuity the precedent for how one must win at Ohio State.)

After all that, St. John looked farther afield. Football was now a national game, and while there was some regional parity, the Southwest had caught many an eye by playing a brassy, crowd-pleasing game in which the ball was actually thrown. Then thrown again. Ohio State particularly needed "crowd-pleasing." While offensive nonconformity made a lot of coaches nervous, Ohio State, to its credit, liked it. And took a long look at its most obsessed practitioner, the gloriously eccentric Francis Schmidt.

Nobody knew exactly why Southwestern football had taken this imaginative leap. Some said it was the geography, as if so much open space demanded novelty to occupy it. Schmidt's biographer said it was perhaps simply a reflection of the Southwest's traditional maverick independence, "particularly in Texas," he said, "where even the cattle walk with a swagger."

Whatever it was, Schmidt was its exemplar. His offense was an outrageous display "of shovel passes, sweeps, power thrusts, long passes, traps, laterals, power, and quick passes over the middle." Some even contend that Schmidt was first to use the I-formation.

Or as Perkins noted, "Nobody had explored the theory of excess like Schmidt had."

That style of offense was mostly lost on the rest of the country, but at Ohio State in the 1930s, Schmidt had the talent and the stage to go national with his razzle-dazzle. Columbus, Ohio, might have been the perfect place to revolutionize the sport—even if the sport didn't immediately know what had happened to it. Schmidt was aided by a propitious bit of timing when, a few days before Ohio State started talking to him, the rules committee reduced the size of the ball to near its modern specifications. Hash marks came into being, too, which meant teams could run to the sidelines without being trapped (before, the ball was played from wherever it had been whistled dead). Good omens for Schmidt.

Ohioans should have felt some premonition when Schmidt first arrived in town for interviews. There, at the old Deshler-Wallick Hotel, Schmidt got down on his hands and knees and demonstrated formations on the hotel floor, using pocket change. He was offered a three-year contract, unprecedented at OSU, but such contracts were being used increasingly around the country to secure the best coaches. And while Schmidt had been successful in the Southwest, his boys could just as well have been playing in China for what the people in Columbus knew about them. A Southwestern sportswriter tipped off the folks in Columbus. "You're in for the thrill of your life," he said. And so they were.

First, there was his personality. "He radiated a folksy, tumbleweed pomposity," said biographer Perkins, "with enough slang and humor to make him likable and enough swearing to deem him unforgettable." Then there was his game. His first two seasons fulfilled nearly all expectations—he went 7–1 both seasons, and in 1935 won a share of OSU's first Big Ten title in fifteen years. He beat Michigan his first four years, outscoring the Wolverines 114–0.

No one knew quite what to make of him, so they came out to see for themselves. His offense ran seven formations, and his

> "He was a zealot, full of excitement, confidence, and quirks—a cross between John the Baptist and Nero.—Brett Perkins, biographer

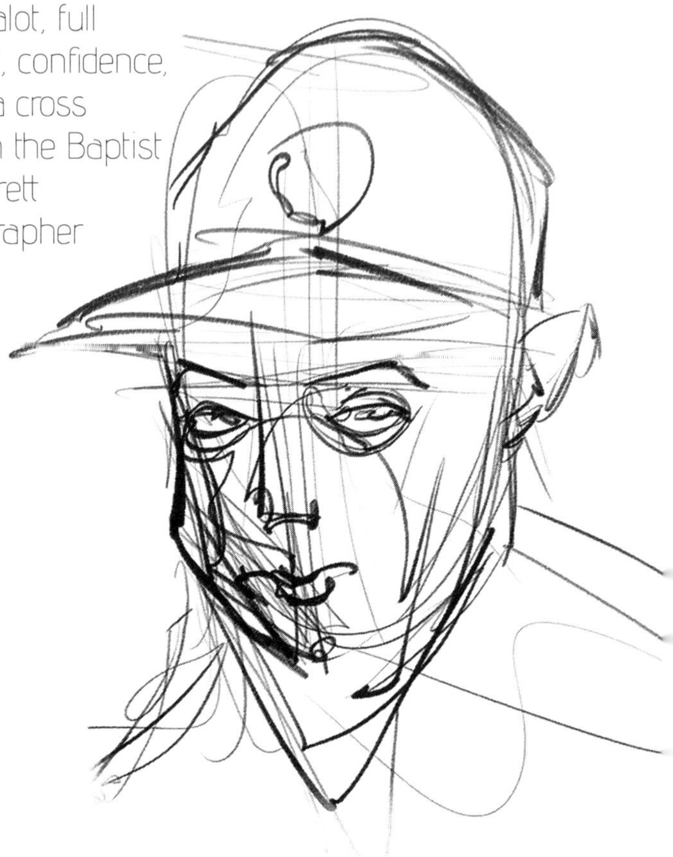

playbook, which he guarded as though it were one of the original Gutenberg Bibles, contained ultimately over five hundred plays. (Most coaches had twenty-five or thirty.) Schmidt had so many, and they were so complex, that he spent as much as 80 percent of his team's practice time teaching them, at the expense of his defense and fundamentals.

The writer Jerry Brondfield called him "a bow-tied, tobacco-chewing, hawk-faced, white-haired, profane practitioner of the football arts—modern football's first roaring madman on the practice field and the sidelines, and so completely zonked out on football that legend ties him to the greatest football story of the twentieth century."

Schmidt was so eccentric that he made Woody Hayes look like a country pastor. If Francis was at home on Fifteenth Street diagramming plays and happened to spot one of his players on the street, he'd open the window and yell for the player to come up. God knows when he'd get out again. One of his players saw him on campus, dreamy with his diagrams, walking through flower beds. And once into the side of a building. His plays, scribbled on random pieces of paper, even stuck out of the cushions in his Cadillac.

"He was a little crazy," said Tom Kinkade, one of his players. Some think he may have suffered from hypomania, which is linked to bipolar disorder.

In 1935, though, he was at the top of his game. That year, he described one of his new plays, run off a fake punt. The quarterback, Tippy Dye, took the snap and tossed an eight-yard shovel pass to end Sam Busich, who ran four or five yards. Then Busich lateraled to Art Boucher, who ran for another five. Next, Boucher pitched *another* lateral to Dye, who ran for 25 yards. Francis was delighted. "Did you ever see a man throw a forward pass," he said, "and then go on and take a lateral beyond the line of scrimmage on the same play?" No one had, it seemed.

That spring, Jesse Owens electrified the sporting world at the Big Ten meet in Ann Arbor when he set three world records and tied a fourth. One of them was a 9.4 in the 100-yard dash, speed that Schmidt noticed. At the Big Ten coaches' meeting, he said Jesse was going to play halfback for him. "We have a play in which Owens takes a lateral at full speed—his own copyrighted speed—and then broad jumps into the end zone," he said.

Not to be outdone, Elmer Layden, the Notre Dame coach, who was playing OSU that fall, said that if Owens started the Notre Dame game, he'd equip both his ends with motorcycles.

The ensuing game was the pinnacle of Schmidt's time at Ohio State. It might have been the pinnacle of his career. Ohio State was undefeated, headed for the national title, and the ensuing game would gain legendary status as one of the greatest football games ever played. A 1950 poll of football writers called it "The Game of the Century." It probably wasn't, but which other one was? What we had, of course, was the development of football's myth-making abilities keeping pace with the development of football's offense.

That 1935 game was a sellout, with over 81,000 in the Horseshoe, and scalpers were said to be getting $50 for a ticket, the equivalent of something like $[illegible]000 today. (That one game's attendance was nearly half of the entire attendance in 1932, the year before Schmidt arrived, when just 167,218 fans turned out—the lowest figure since the stadium had been built.) Officials in 1935 said they could have sold 200,000 tickets. And maybe so; not a lot was going on in Columbus in the deeps of the Depression.

The game demonstrated an unfortunate side to Buckeye Nation: many of its partisans saw the Notre Dame–Ohio State game as a contest between those who were Catholics and those who weren't. There was a plague of "nativist sentiment" abroad in the land, and while many thousands of Catholics saw Notre Dame as the physical manifestation of their faith, many who *weren't* Catholic saw it as the poisonous embodiment of a spiritual contagion. The *Dispatch* reported that twenty-four trains transported Fighting Irish fans to Columbus, including the entire student body. They were met with hostility and "anti-Catholic taunts," and the Irish footballers were received by "an audience of fifteen thousand anti-Catholics serenading them with jeers."

Lynn St. John, the Ohio State athletic director, thought it was a kind of Catholic hooliganism and pointed out that Ohio State had as many Catholics on its squad as did Notre Dame, noting that OSU's Catholic faculty and students rooted for Notre Dame. Ohio State administrators were unnerved by such zealotry and considered it a threat to the cohesion of their campus. So in the end, despite two great games (and two difficult Ohio State losses), big box office, and national press, the rivalry would not be renewed until 1995.

Schmidt had been worried about Notre Dame's aerial game, but his Buckeyes picked off three Notre Dame passes in the first half, and Ohio State took a commanding 13–0 lead into halftime. Then the crucial decisions. Notre Dame's Layden, wanting his best players to be fresh for the final quarter, started his second team when the second half began. (There was no free substitution in 1935; the rules allowed substitution only at the turn of the quarters.) No one scored in the third quarter, and Schmidt, also wanting a fresh team, pulled most of his starters and sent in the second team to play the final quarter. But now it was Notre Dame's first unit against Ohio State's second team.

Everybody knows what happened: Notre Dame scored three times in the final quarter, pulled out an 18–13 upset, and in Columbus that winter, hindsight was a cottage industry. Schmidt replaced his best backs in the fourth quarter, they complained; he stuck with a seven-man line on defense when Notre Dame was throwing all over the stadium; his punt strategy was amiss. Even the ghost of Knute Rockne was somehow involved.

The irony was that Notre Dame did it by throwing the ball. It was the Irish in the air, not Schmidt. How could such a thing happen? Passing set up the first score, followed by two touchdown passes. The last one was by a halfback named William Shakespeare, the son of a Staten Island firefighter who claimed descent from the real bard, even though the papers reported that William had flunked sophomore English. (He was known around the college, of course, as "The Bard of South Bend.") After the win, one of the radio announcers said, "I always said Shakespeare had a pair of rosary beads and a bottle of holy water in his back pocket." Another reported that in the game's last fifteen minutes, rosary beads across America sounded like castanets, and it was all a terrific story.

Afterward, the most interesting thing: Ohio State was, at last, one of the aristocrats. It had *arrived*. And its moment occurred even as it lost. Ohio State was playing a great team—a *peer*—and when aristocrats play, there is no loss of status. Being an aristocrat means you'll still be around—and you'll be back. Now everyone knew that, and in no small part because of Francis Schmidt.

He beat Michigan the next two years, but he never had another team like his 1935 one. Then he lost to Michigan three straight times, and he was through. But the notion of aristocracy held: even as Schmidt's mediocre 1940 team, his last, went 4–4, the

Horseshoe's home attendance averaged over 60,000 fans. Ohio State was also no longer playing schools such as Kenyon and Wittenberg.

The beauty of hindsight is that we get to second-guess the gods. The 1935 Notre Dame game might have revealed Schmidt's fatal flaw, which was his lack of organization. Players had long been dismayed at his coaching practices. He was so paranoid, for instance, that his playbooks were edited for the individual players, who saw only their particular assignments. They never knew what was going on around them, and they never saw the larger picture.

When Paul Brown first met Francis, he was appalled. Even he couldn't see exactly what Schmidt was doing. "There was no attention to detail," Brown said, "the equipment was second-rate, and the strategy was too complex without taking into account Schmidt's teaching methods." Brown was bothered by Francis's longshoreman language, too, which gave the university problems because someone always had to steer visitors out of earshot. (Schmidt was invariably apologetic, although after the fact: "Who did I cuss today?" he'd ask his players. "Who do I have to apologize to?")

It was some kind of irony that Schmidt elevated Ohio State into the first rank of America's teams—and himself into a kind of football immortality—then was replaced by Brown, the anti-Schmidt. Said Schmidt's biographer: "The darker side of Schmidt's obsession would unfold over the next few years, proving that the open-game movement was not sustainable without a practical foundation. Football would heed this lesson."

As for the new aristocrat, Ohio State had hired the ultimate organizational man. And he was everything Francis was not.

"...It wasn't like Grange or Harmon or anybody else. It was a kind of cross between music and cannon fire, and it brought your heart up under your ears.—James Thurber on Harley with the ball

Creation story

How a farfetched idea becomes an American epic

IF FRANCIS SCHMIDT WAS THE FIRST OF THE UNIVERSITY'S COACHING LEGENDS—WHICH, BASED SOLELY on his impetuous personality, he surely was—he assumed that mantle largely because the school's *first* legend had already been bypassed by history. While everyone remembered Chic Harley, John W. Wilce was merely one of those indeterminate names that occupy campus buildings, in this case, the university's student health center. Few recall today that Wilce was the innovator who ushered in Ohio State's first great football era.

He arrived in Columbus in 1913, one of two major university events that year, the other being Ohio State joining the Western Conference (soon to be known as the Big Ten). In hindsight, the accidental nature of fate often appears as genius, and so it was with Wilce. He arrived by way of an unlikely set of circumstances that wouldn't be duplicated in Columbus. First, he wasn't much older than his players. Second, he didn't have much more experience than they did. He came out of Wisconsin where he'd been a three-sport star and an All-Western fullback, and when he arrived, Ohio State was still a backwater football school whose last coach had left for a job in public recreation. (And the university's first two choices for the vacancy had turned down the position.)

In short order, Wilce became the program's infinite spirit, an understated man with advanced maturity, especially in one so young. More academician than jock, he must have perplexed his more recognizably macho colleagues. (He did, however, paint his locker room bright red to "inspire his meat eaters.") But as *Time* magazine pointed out later, he did more than anyone to give Columbus "a permanent football mania." If he wasn't part of the athletic department's grand design, he made it appear as though he was. After him, it was no longer an impossible notion that the sons of Ohio farm boys and factory workers might one day constitute their own aristocracy. It was, indeed, a driving notion, and it appealed to a growing audience who quickly assumed their own place in it.

Then in 1916—that bellwether season—Ohio State went undefeated. Not much had been expected of the season, for the football program was still beneath the consciousness of even most Ohioans. Wilce pronounced his team's prospects no more than "fair." He'd lost six players to graduation, one had dropped out to become a farmer, and several of his freshmen were ineligible.

There was one bright omen, though it was little noted at the time: OSU's 1915 freshman team had scrimmaged the sophomores and beaten them 49–0. The freshmen were led by a cross-town scatback from East High who may have weighed all of 160 pounds yet gave the school its first sense of size. On his first day in an OSU uniform, Chic Harley ripped off a 75-yard run against the varsity, a portent for his university tenure.

As a sophomore in 1916, he led a dramatic one-point win over Illinois in Champaign—overseen by a hearty knot of Buckeye supporters numbering fewer than two hundred—followed by another eye-opener with Wisconsin. The Wisconsin coach, Paul Withington, was so certain of victory in Columbus that he left his team in the hands of his assistants and went off to scout Minnesota. Thus he did not see the iconic run that encapsulated the Harley years at OSU—an 80-yard scoring run that beat the Badgers, 14–13. While Harley's legend grew throughout his three seasons at OSU, none better exemplified how dramatically Harley could change a game.

With eight minutes left, he took a punt at the 20, cut diagonally across the entire field, picked up a block by Shifty Bolen, and streaked past the deep backs to score. The *Dispatch*'s Russ Needham tried to describe his running style: "He would drive you mad with his deliberation. 'Why, oh, why,' you'd scream at yourself, 'doesn't he hurry?' But that wasn't the Harley technique. He'd loaf along hoping to string out his field of tacklers so he could meet them one by one. If he could, he was gone…."

Harley's physical talent was accompanied by an uncanny patience for following his blockers, then using a change of pace that allowed him to explode through the secondary. It is something coaches are still trying to teach backs today. "No single tackler ever brought Harley down in the open field," Needham wrote. His style was such that his physical grace was transmitted to the fans as pure emotion; one of his old East High teammates, Joe Mulbarter, watching Harley's 80-yard run in the final seconds against Wisconsin, became so affected he burst into tears.

The hometown crowds, who had been galvanized by his prep exploits, followed him to the university where he became America's premiere breakaway back. Old Ohio Field held about 5,000, and Harley tripled the crowds, who climbed nearby trees for a look. He was a will-'o-the-wisp runner whose dramatic style gave birth to OSU's lineage of great backs.

Before the season was out, it was as though an entirely new species, hitherto unknown, had been discovered in the middle of Columbus. It was the American Big Time Footballer, found pastured on old Ohio Field as if it had just arrived. Now, under Wilce's firm tutelage and the local import Harley, the OSU footballer could no longer be overlooked. So began the quality of oversight—by media and fan alike—that would expand exponentially throughout the century. This season began the divine notion that Ohio State

> His dazzling change of pace running at East High left tacklers bereft of oxygen and hundreds of schoolchildren forgot their play and lined the practice field to watch him.

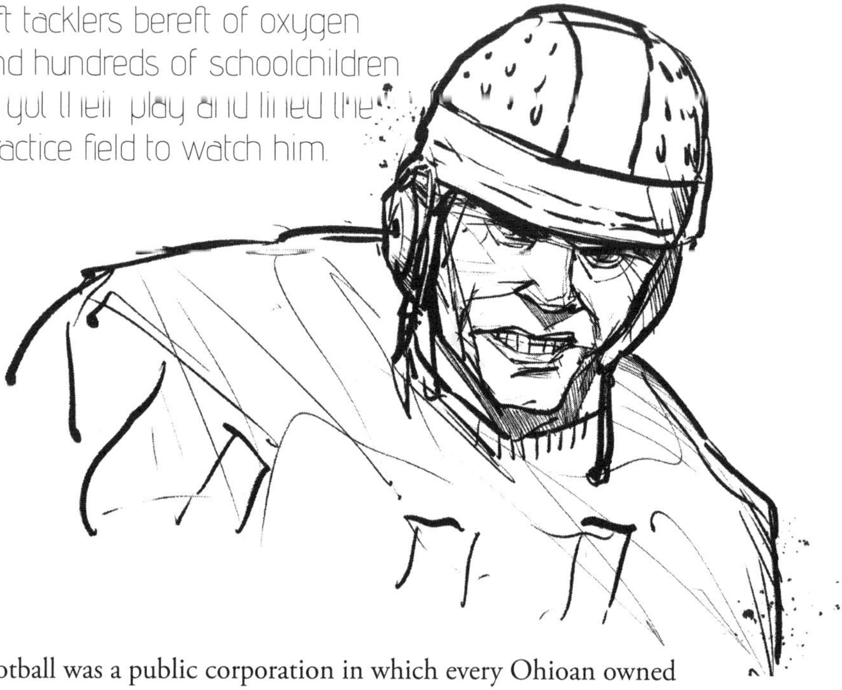

football was a public corporation in which every Ohioan owned stock—as well as the right to exercise his or her options, including the license to paint one's basement scarlet and gray and criticize at full volume every move each coach and player would ever make.

After Ohio State's 23–3 win over Northwestern for its first undefeated season and its first conference title, the *Dispatch* ran a Jesus-Comes headline so large it took up a third of the page. Ohio State football was now big. It would never again be small.

THERE WERE FOUR UNBEATEN, UNTIED COLLEGES IN 1916; TWO OF THEM, Pittsburgh and Army, were listed as co-champions. There was Ohio State, blinking unaccustomedly in the limelight, and then there was the tiny Presbyterian school, Henry Kendall College (soon to become the University of Tulsa), which upset the Oklahoma Sooners and astonished onlookers with such offensive innovation as "the tower play," whereupon the Kendall passer tossed the ball to a player sitting on the shoulders of a teammate. (It was quickly outlawed.) The originator was Kendall's assistant coach, an unusual fellow named Francis Schmidt, who would in time bring his extraordinary set of mind to Ohio State. About that, more anon.

Ohio State's program had taken a leap in stature, but it was not yet in the national conversation, nor were the players quite the heroic figures they'd soon be. Chic Harley became famous just before America's Golden Age of Sports, during which the wider audience would probably have made him a household name. Five years later, he would have become part of our national memory, in the manner of Red Grange and The Four Horsemen of Notre Dame.

The Eastern elites were now in a slow decline, and as Michael Parrish wrote, "the center of gravity in the college sport shifted from the old-stock Americans of the Ivy League schools to second-generation Irish, Italians, and Slavs who played for universities, many of them public, in the Midwest and on the Pacific Coast."

The decline of Eastern football came from its own success, as the Eastern footballers taught a generation of Midwesterners how to play the game. By the time Harley came to Ohio State, it was clear the Ivy Leaguers had done their job. The quality of play (and coaching) had improved to the point that Midwest players could compete on a major college level. Any lingering doubt of Eastern superiority on the field was put to rest with games such as Centre—a little Kentucky school of 300 students—beating the national champion Harvard in 1921. Still, it was a slow passing.

Chic Harley was both beneficiary and benefactor of this change. He no longer had to go to the East Coast to achieve attention. Conference affiliation, bringing with it a stronger schedule, gave Harley the stage where his spectacular performances brought Walter Camp to him—and made him a three-time All-American. The attention pushed the team onto the national stage.

While Harley gave OSU a taste of being in the national spotlight, the school needed more. One player could not put the school permanently into the national picture. The school had to break out of its provincial scheduling, jettison its in-state rivals, and attract prestigious teams in intersectional games. As much as anything, scheduling was important in enhancing the football team and the university's image. Sorry, Kenyon and Oberlin. Goodbye, Wittenberg. So long, Ohio Wesleyan.

On November 24, 1917, in a rare intersectional game, Wilce's favored Buckeyes and the Auburn Tigers battled to a scoreless tie, unleashing Southern sportswriters in a paroxysm of overcooked metaphor not seen since the war (or as it was known in the local parlance, "The Wahr," usually enunciated in two syllables).

The South was just emerging on the national scene as a distinct football region, and intersectional contests such as this one were just beginning to be seen as more than a college football game; it was reported in the context of the Civil War—a clash of cultures. Even northern writers got into the act, the *Columbus Dispatch* reporting that "No more picturesque game was ever played in the Southland on a battlefield where North and South fought again."

The war had ended a mere half-century or so before, and as events proved, would be fought for at least another half-century. What better immediate place than the gridiron? As it turned out, righteous indignation is quite the motivator: Auburn was not only playing a team of Northern aggression—and one that, thanks to Chic Harley, had become a team of some national note— it was playing for the honor of its homeland.

The Ohio State–Auburn game was largely responsible for the narrative that would play out in the South all the way to the next war. It was a narrative saying the South was a beleaguered country whose station in life had come about by oppression, and every game between it and the Northern teams was—to paraphrase that notable Prussian athletic director, von Clausewitz—"merely the continuation of war by other means." (Two Alabama historians posited in 1981 the theory of what they called "the Confederate temperament," influenced mightily by the influx of Celts from Ireland and Scotland. One of the historians, Forrest McDonald, said the Celts were always the meanest. The Southerners are naturally violent, he said, football was the South's idealized replay of the late war, and Bear Bryant was the South's Robert E. Lee.)

The fervor of the Auburn game was itself a kind of myth, fed by sportswriters preparing themselves for the Golden Age of Sports. Their grand prose would in time nourish America's papers with a swank vocabulary that in both North and South tended to portray players as wearing cleated seven-league boots. The truth about Auburn in 1917 was simply that it was a good football team playing another good team. The game had nothing to do with the ideals of honor and manhood, nor a dispirited country rising in opposition to villainous outside forces.

The game carried national importance because Ohio State brought a 7–0 record with it. The Buckeyes were considered to be the top team in the West, averaging nearly 38 points a game and, even more impressive, no opponent had crossed its goal line all season. (They'd given up only a pair of field goals.) Ohio State's reputation only bestirred the sportswriters. "Auburn did not defeat Ohio State," wrote the *Montgomery Advertiser*, "but the result is a practical victory because of playing against odds." Auburn was described as playing "straight football," the implication being that the Auburn Tigers played more honorably than Ohio State with its duplicitous variety of running plays. The tie was labeled "a shocking upset," particularly when Ohio State had first downs at the Auburn two, and again at the five. Chic Harley also missed two field goals.

Afterward, the sportswriters unveiled more offense than Harley and the newspapers unleashed what Mark Twain called, in his fulmination against Sir Walter Scott for having caused the Civil War, "inflated language and other humbuggeries." Said the *Atlanta Journal*, "The Tigers won this moral victory because they are brave; because when the critical moments came they rose to grand heights and staved off defeat. All honor to them. I say God bless them." The campy prose made it seem that Sherman had just been turned away from Atlanta and hidden himself in the Chattahoochee.

History doesn't tell us what happened to the efforts to cast the entire Auburn team in bronze and mount them on the statehouse lawn. It was clear, though, that football was the new emancipationist vision in which Constitutional equality could be gained on the gridiron. Football, as the SEC would demonstrate in years to come, was a war in which a single loss meant little, for there was always next Saturday. The South could rise, exponentially, forever.

That early intersectional contest between Auburn and Ohio State was a national harbinger. The Midwest, by the mid-teens, had equaled the old Eastern powers, with the South and the West working for their own place in the big picture.

Five days later, on Thanksgiving Day of 1917, Auburn played the team regarded as the best in the South—Georgia Tech. In an era where comparative margins of victory held sway over most college football kingmakers, how each team faired against Auburn would go a long way in determining the final national standings. Tech, coached by the legendary John Heisman, was closing in on an undefeated season. So was Ohio State.

At the apex of his career, he had traveled to Montgomery to watch the Ohio State–Auburn game. The 10,000 fans made up what was said to be the largest event ever staged in the capital, and it was bolstered by a healthy contingent of Ohio State folks who had just launched the school's reputation for frequent follower miles. Heisman, the Clevelander who by virtue of his more than two-decade residence in the South was now virtually a Southerner, echoed the down-home postgame sentiments. "My hat is off to the valiant Auburn team for the noble stand in defense of Southern traditions," he said.

His thoughts on Ohio State have gone unrecorded, but he had to have been gleeful at the outcome, for the more widely recognized Buckeyes—Walter Camp, football's paterfamilias, had deigned to travel to Columbus to see his All-American, Harley, play—had come into the game with an inside track on the national title.

Then when Heisman's boys upended Auburn, 68–7, in which the Tigers were no more than an afterthought, Georgia Tech won it—the South's first national title. Heisman coached until 1926 when he left the profession to become athletic director of the Downtown Athletic Club in New York City. In 1935, when the club decided to award a trophy to the best college football player east of the Mississippi, Heisman objected to having it named after him because he didn't like the idea of an award that singled out one player in what was supposed to be a team game. So it was called the Downtown Athletic Club Award, and when he died in 1936, the club changed the name.

In time, Ohio State players would by 2020 win the award seven times. Perhaps—if you believe in that kind of thing—it was John Heisman's way of rewarding the school that not only gave him his first win but his national title, as well.

THERE WAS THE FALLOW SEASON OF 1918 WHEN MOST OF OHIO STATE'S PLAYERS WENT OFF TO WWI (on the day Chic departed for his service physical, the *Columbus Dispatch* requested that its readers have a drink in his honor). Then in 1919, Wilce's boys back in the fold, Ohio State beat Michigan in Ann Arbor—the first time—before heading into its finale undefeated, playing a one-loss Illinois team on soggy Ohio Field.

There, a crowd nearly twice its normal capacity crushed into the North High Street neighborhood, climbing trees and clambering onto rooftops to watch an injured Harley lose the only game of his college career, 9–7. (*The New York Times* called the Illinois–Ohio State game "the Yale–Harvard game of the West," and many thought it was the best—and most dramatic—one of the year. An OSU win would likely have given it the mythical national title. As it was, in a muddle of contenders, four teams claimed the title, Illinois among them.)

Advocates for the building of a new stadium saw the numbers—varying estimates of the crowd went impossibly to up 40,000—and not the defeat. They saw that in his brief time Harley had tripled the original crowds at Ohio Field, which dated back to 1898 (officially christened with a flask of spring water in 1908 during the burgeoning temperance movement).

Harley had emboldened them in their thinking, which only a few years before would have seemed preposterous: a new stadium whose predicted attendance numbers were so large the school didn't do much to publicize them. Now, however, Wilce's teams had legitimized the preposterous.

If one disregarded the 1918 wartime season, Wilce had turned in five teams that had lost only three games, two on the cusp of national titles, with yet another stellar season ahead. In 1920 Ohio State was unbeaten in the regular season, then headed west for its first New Year's game in the Rose Bowl, playing a ridiculously unheralded California.

Ohio State was now, oddly, an *Eastern* team, about to play in what is still considered one of the most historically important college games. Insult to the eventual injury, Big Ten champion Ohio State wasn't even Pasadena's first choice: Princeton had already turned down an invitation, which, as it turned out, was a prescient move for the Ivy League.

The oddsmakers put Cal down as an 8-5 underdog, demonstrating that the prejudice for "Eastern" teams had reached even the bookies. At the time, Western schools were thought to lack Eastern proficiencies, and the Rose Bowl crowds of 1916 and 1917 made up not much more than a good crowd at old Ohio Field. Nobody in January of 1921 seemed to know the Golden Bears, and even some of the West Coast papers had provided better coverage of Eastern teams, although California had torn through its schedule and outscored its foes 510–14. (A prophet, it seems, is always jonesed in his own country.)

The Bears, though, beat a good Ohio State team, 28–0, and they didn't lose another game for five years. "Ohio did not have a Chinaman's chance," wrote the politically incorrect Oregonian sportswriter Harry Grayson, "and don't let anyone tell you that the long trip or the bright sunny afternoon had anything to do with the result." The Buckeyes had practiced in the Ohio snow and they surely weren't conditioned for the California heat, but Grayson and his fellow Westerners were having none of the old transcontinental-train-ride alibi.

Grayson took particular glee in relating All-American halfback Pete Stinchcomb's failure to intercept a long second-quarter pass thrown by California's Brick Muller, describing the Ohio State star standing "dumbfounded as the oblong pigskin sailed over his head, whirling after the fashion of a highly charged torpedo."

Stinchcomb was in coverage, but he stopped after 30 yards or so because, he said later, "Frankly, I didn't think anyone could throw the ball that far." ("Where do you think you're going?" he'd yelled at end Brodie Stephens, off on a 53-yard jaunt.) It was one of the most famous plays in Rose Bowl history and, as the sports historian Raymond Schmidt wrote, "caught the imagination of football fans around the country."

It was something of an odd turn for Wilce, for he was an early advocate for throwing the football. He was, after all, a student of the game. (The year before he took the Buckeyes to the Rose Bowl, he had traveled to the West Coast to see Oregon play Harvard "at his own expense simply to learn what he could.") He thought the pass was the most spectacular play in football and loved what he called "its elements of uncertainty which give it great zest and interest." After Ohio State had beaten Michigan in 1920 to remain undefeated, the *Ann Arbor News* wrote, "His methods involve a merger of the new and old football; his teams buck the line with proficiency and play the overhead game up to the hilt." Ohio State beat Wisconsin and Illinois that year—and won the conference title—by throwing the ball.

While the conventional coaching wisdom used passing largely in an emergency, unconnected to the broader game plan, Wilce saw it as "an integral part of a unified attack." Even more radical, he saw that the pass could loosen the secondary defense and therefore set up the run. Heterodox at the time, this would become the concept that defined the modern game.

At the time, though—and for some time to come—football was a *running* game. Quarterbacks held a custodial position, simply making sure the ball got back on the team bus. Coaches were not yet ready to head out into the hinterlands to measure the hands of schoolboys. The good ones tended to be set apart by having big, strong hands, like George Roudebush, just up the road at Denison University, a baseball-playing farm boy who'd learned accuracy by chucking corncobs at chickens. Roudebush didn't try to palm the ball and shot-put it, as others did; he gripped it near the end and threw it with a modified pitching motion. He was, in fact, among the very first—if not the first—to run a passing offense that was not only fully integrated into his team's offensive scheme, it *became* the offensive scheme.

Wilce, of course, knew about Denison and Roudebush. The question occurs: why didn't he have a Roudebush in Columbus? A guy who could single-handedly influence almost any outcome was just up the road. But Wilce didn't because he didn't have to. (His three Chic Harley teams lost one game, for instance.) Even after the Rose Bowl loss, Wilce watched as another great throwing quarterback—Cleveland's Benny Friedman—left Ohio for Michigan where he became America's premier college passer.

Benny's hands grasped the fat ball perfectly, then he'd cock it behind his ear and let fly. His favorite moment came in 1926 when he beat Ohio State in a come-from-behind win in Columbus, 17–16, ruining a perfect season for the Buckeyes.

Benny's dad, a Russian immigrant and a tailor, saw that one, too, the first time he'd seen his son play. He was astounded by the size of the Ohio Stadium crowd, and he asked, "Who gets all this money?" Someone explained that the schools split the receipts. At about that time, two Ohio State linemen whacked Benny as he was throwing and knocked him dizzy.

There was a timeout, the trainer came over and stuck smelling salts in Benny's face, and Benny got unsteadily up.

"The players, they get nothing?" Mr. Friedman asked.

"Nothing," he was told.

Mr. Friedman sighed at the unfairness of it. "For this my Benny went to college?" he said.

THE MIRACULOUS SEASON WAS STILL 1919, HOWEVER, FOR OHIO STATE HAD BEATEN MICHIGAN, and the Illinois defeat was leavened by the astounding crowd and its aftermath—the surge of enthusiasm for a new stadium. In another year, most of the money had been pledged. The stadium had begun as far back as 1908, in the minds of a couple of fellows in the school's engineering department. One of them was Thomas French, a minister's son from Mansfield who had worked his way through Ohio State as a draftsman. French saw football at Ohio State being played on a grand scale and a new stadium, he thought, would accomplish this. The precedent had been set in the East where the great powers drew huge numbers of spectators—capacities only dreamed of by Midwestern colleges.

French's ardor provided the ultimate picture of Ohio State's ambitions, which was put in place for the rest of the century and beyond: Ohio Stadium. It was, in one sense, a simulacrum for the peoples' ambitions, how they saw themselves. Ohioans were people who made things and the stadium was one more grand made thing. It was unique, it was excellent, and the contests therein would be as well. It was also communally built, and the people saw it as *theirs*, whether they'd attended the university or not.

The most visible piece of Ohio State's design was about to be unveiled, and even the subpar 1921 season did nothing to forestall it. The year had begun in January with the Rose Bowl loss, then the Buckeyes suffered an early-season 7–6 loss to Oberlin and a late season one to Illinois. It was the last time in the century Ohio State lost to another state team, and the Illinois loss signaled the end of what one commentator called Ohio State's first era of football greatness. The stadium advocates already understood their new paradigm: they would need better competition and better players.

And so one era ended and another began. Ohio State was not yet one of football's aristocrats, but the aristocrats had been put on notice. That notice would be served by Francis Schmidt, but first came the tangible moment which demonstrated Ohio State's aspirations. That, of course, was the building of Ohio Stadium.

> "The Horseshoe should be like Alcatraz. Nobody wants to go there.
> —Kirk Barton, tackle, 2007

A cathedral for football

Build it and they will come

THE BUILDING OF OHIO STADIUM REMAINS ONE OF THE GREAT OHIO STORIES, EQUAL PARTS AMBITION, FORESIGHT, and imagination. The conventional wisdom says Chic Harley built it, and while Chic did more than his share, he was only the most visible part of the story. It began in the minds of a couple of fellows in the school's engineering drawing department, as far back as 1908.

One of them, Thomas French, a minister's son from Mansfield who had worked his way through Ohio State as a draftsman, envisioned a spectacular horseshoe-shaped stadium that would hold something like a fourth of the Columbus population. The in-house numbers predicting future attendance seemed so impossibly large that some feared the athletic department might be placed under the aegis of the psychology department.

In 1919, though, when Ohio State met Illinois on old Ohio Field for the Western Conference title, there were 20,000 people in the bleachers and along the perimeter of the field, and thousands more standing farther out. While French's numbers still seemed preposterous, *something* had to be done. And here was the astounding moment: an unusual accord among the university minds, all of which bought into the radical notion. This, in its own way, was more unusual than their plans for 63,000 spectators in a new stadium (which, at its inauguration *was* more than a fourth of the Columbus population). Such a stadium existed only on the East Coast, and even there, only Yale's had a larger capacity. Closer to home, Wisconsin's new Camp Randall Stadium had opened in 1917 and held fewer than 11,000; Michigan's old Ferry Field had been upgraded to 21,000, and part of its seating was still wooden.

Cultural factors coalesced, as well. Ohio had improved its highway system—all roads now led to Columbus—and the aftereffects of the war presaged the end of a lingering Victorian earnestness; there were new appetites for amusement and spectacle, even in Ohio. The stars were aligned—and not just on the field, which had been recently vacated by the resplendent Chic Harley and his lesser known but equally valuable teammate, Pete Stinchcomb, an All-American in his own right.

The university's stadium enthusiasts were surely aware of the larger factors, and as they had gone East for players, coaches, and knowledge, they were now about to go East for a stadium. But even in the trend-setting East, there were not many places to look. There was the University of Pennsylvania's Franklin Field, the oldest, dating from 1895, but it was wooden. The Yale Bowl, around since 1914, held over 70,000, and there was Harvard. The ambitious locals were, no doubt, looking at Harvard. Open in 1903, Harvard Stadium was horseshoe-shaped, the first large-scale use of reinforced concrete, and could hold 40,000. (It was called "the biggest single chunk of concrete in the world," and to answer critics who feared it wouldn't stand up under the weight of a crowd that large, the construction superintendent walked under the stands as spectators filed in on opening day.)

The horseshoe surely caught the eye of the Ohio State brain trust. It was open on one end with curved side seating offering good lines of sight, as well as putting spectators closer to the field.

Then the Ohioans went Harvard one better: Ohio Stadium's revolutionary engineering would be the first stadium to have an upper deck. It had sophisticated crowd movement, and it was elegant, or as one critic said, "It was a good engineering structure possessing architecture."

The timing of Ohio Stadium was exquisite. The 1920s brought about an unprecedented amount of stadium construction. In 1913, there had been fewer than half a dozen stadia in the country. By 1920, there were twenty, either built or underway, and by the middle of the decade that number would double. "Blame the Greeks for the horseshoe-styled stadium and the Romans for all those high-rising cheap seats," *Sports Illustrated* would comment, nearly a hundred years in the future.

The media loved comparisons with the Roman Empire. The metaphor of sports being fueled by testosterone, ours were bigger, of course. And we had more than double the number found in the Roman Empire. Historian Lewis Mumford drew another parallel with antiquity; he saw Rome's violence and decadence manifest on the gridiron. "The barbarian has already captured the American city from within," he wrote, alluding, one supposes, to the kind of defensive linemen a good university team needed. *The New York Times* struck closer to home: "He who thrills at reading of a gladiatorial contest can get the same thrill, experience the same 'mob psychology' by attending a football game…in the new stadium at Ohio State University," it wrote, in an article entitled, "Rome's Colosseum Outdone by Our Football Bowls."

While it may not have been obvious to the spectators—or even some of those upstairs in the athletic department—the sport was being remade. The mammoth new stadiums were now a business. To fill them required intersectional games, national competitive parity, and excitement. Football was becoming part of the entertainment business, and Ohio Stadium was a large concrete icon that implied its audience—soon to be wider than all of Ohio—must be entertained. (Before the decade was out, two magnificent new theaters were built in the downtown, the Ohio and the Palace, and between them they held more than

5,000 spectators— a third of old Ohio Field's capacity in Chic Harley's time. Columbusites were thus bracketed between the evolving forms—sports and film—which would dominate the rest of the century.) The stadium was also the first nod to the semi-professionalism that would emerge among the top-tier schools in the second half of the century.

The various executives justified the stadium and its attendant facilities as a visible symbol of progress, an elemental aspect of the student's physical life, and a totem for alumni. Ohio State was one of the first schools to tie its new stadium to its geographic region, and the fund-raising float banners read, "Columbus discovered America. The stadium will help America discover Columbus."

JOHN WILCE, THE OSU COACH, SAID THE STADIUM WASN'T A MONUMENT, but rather "a living stimulation toward the maintenance of strong, virile, clean, active elements in the broad field of education." (In a few years, though, he'd leave to practice medicine. He'd helped put Ohio State on the map, but he wanted a smaller map. He wanted to fill up the stadium and beat Michigan, yet he saw it all as being a little too much. "Football," he said, "was becoming too much of a business. The game was being taken away from the boys. I was a faculty-type coach who believed educational aspects were more important than winning games.")

All the missionary work aside, the stadium also created a big-time atmosphere. Which created "the graveyard of coaches." It would provoke a conflict with the academic side of the campus that became a crisis before the very size and excellence of the university permitted each—athletics and academics—their own secure orbit. What was certain, though, was that there was no turning back from the looming commercialism. "The transformation of college football into the world of big business was irreversible and would remain as one of the most significant legacies of the golden era of the 1920s," said the sports historian Raymond Schmidt.

There was at least one detractor at the time, and an important one. He was Dr. T.C. Mendenhall, the first professor hired by the university back in 1873 (he was a professor of physics) and an influential trustee. He was a formidable-looking man with a walrus mustache and strong opinions, which included an insistence that a stadium capacity of 35,000 would be more than enough, as well as his preference for brickwork over concrete. No one else agreed, however. (No one listened to his advocacy for adopting the metric system, either, but he was probably right about *that* one.)

Ground was broken in the late summer of 1921 in a pasture adjacent to the campus. A deal had been brokered with the Animal Husbandry Department, which surrendered its pasture in return for future amenities, and the ground was turned over with a horse-drawn plow. There was unprecedented hoopla, and in the spring of 1922, the university had to ask both students and the citizenry to stay off the site because they were wandering around and displacing the reinforcing cables put down in the stadium concrete.

When it was finished, it was the largest stadium west of the Appalachian Mountains, and it highly influenced the stadia yet to come. It was, as *Saturday Review* pointed out, about twice the size of an average city block in Manhattan, and its outside wall was the height of a ten-story building. Given the nature of geologic time, it hadn't been that long since the OSU Athletic Stock Company had issued certificates and built a grandstand in Dr. Detmer's cow pasture where games were played in the early 1890s.

As one more example of the radical nature of the stadium, its capacity was so large that it could hold every Ohio State graduate, his or her spouse, their three kids, as well as the entire student body and faculty, with several thousand seats left for the visiting side.

The day before the stadium was dedicated, the university president and his staff spent the day helping sweep up because construction had not been completely finished. *The New York Times* called the October 21 dedication game "the largest crowd in football history," said the crowd was more than 75,000, and that "additional thousands clamored for admission."

OSU's opponent was none other than Michigan; no homecoming patsy for the Buckeyes' big day. Michigan, unimpressed, won 19–0. Michigan coach Fielding Yost gave the best quote of the day: "We put the dead in dedication," he said. A scribe for the Cleveland *Plain Dealer* noted Columbus took the dedication calmly. "Prohibition then was young in the land and bootleggers had hardly begun to flourish," he said. "So it was unnecessary for innkeepers to clear the lobbies of furniture and destructible objects. The wild High Street nights were to come later."

And so they would. It was the notion that French and the other decision-makers had understood when most others had not: *build it and they will come*. It was a magnificent gesture that put the national football establishment on notice. It said Ohio State would be a permanent challenger, a fixture; it announced to everyone "the seriousness of its efforts." French had a prescient reading of his audience for, in time, Ohio Stadium became a secular pilgrimage. Spectators came from all over, hoping to see a miracle, which happened almost casually there. And for a time, no matter how brief, they were relieved of their ordinary lives.

It would take a while, though. The stadium's first decade was memorable largely for the architecture. Jack Wilce had put the team on the cusp of greatness but greatness itself was proving elusive. Wilce had three straight losing seasons, most of his winning seasons were marginal ones, and he lost to Michigan six times. Sam Willaman came on in relief and produced five winning seasons, but still beat Michigan only once.

By the mid-1930s and the arrival of Francis Schmidt, the architecture of both stadium and team finally aligned. Then after a flirtation with greatness, Schmidt's prodigal creativity was no longer able to function well without more fundamental stability. When he lost his touch with Michigan—and a sizable contingent of the boosters—he resigned.

The board's choice this time was as unorthodox as its decision to hire Schmidt: it chose a high school coach. Massillon, though, was a high school in name only.

Section Two
Transition to the big time

By the 1930s, the history is not so dim, the names more familiar. Looking back, it all seems like a long-term master plan perfectly executed: first, shed your local roots and go regional. Bring in the best player in college football—who happened to be in your own backyard. Build the most magnificent stadium in the country. Then hire—back-to-back—two of the most innovative football minds in the business.

The first of them was that odd fellow Francis Schmidt, who popularized the term "razzle-dazzle" and frightened traditionalists everywhere with an offense no one had ever seen before, and only a second-half miscue vs. Notre Dame kept him from a national title. The other was that frosty football wonk, Paul Brown, who *did* win a national title.

Their startling proficiency seemed to be a bit much for Columbus. Schmidt lost his touch, then his job; Brown moved up to the nascent pro game, which he imprinted with his parenting skills. Columbus, meanwhile, made do. There was Carroll Widdoes's undefeated team in 1944 and Wes Fesler's Rose Bowl win over California in 1950—a rematch of 1921 when California won—which was also the first time the Buckeyes played before 100,000 people.

Columbus wasn't a factory town, but it still preferred its football to be blue collar and working class. It would take a while to get back to Schmidt's offense and Paul Brown's methodical innovation, which wouldn't be seen again until the next century.

But between Schmidt and Brown, Ohio State was transitioned into the wholly big time.

"If I'd hired me at the time, I'd have done it then gotten far away.
—Paul Brown

Brown's Town

That championship season

PAUL BROWN'S HIGH SCHOOL TEAM ONCE BEAT KENT STATE IN A SCRIMMAGE and only the Buckeyes themselves topped his home attendance crowds, provoking a Cleveland sportswriter to say there were but two big-time amateur football teams in Ohio—Ohio State and Massillon. The high school coaches lobbied heavily for Brown's Ohio State candidacy and he said, perhaps not in jest, that they were just trying to get rid of him.

He'd made Massillon into such an institution that moving on to Ohio State wasn't much of a change. He had sized the place up some time before, when he attended summer school, and in the evenings he'd walk around in the stadium and imagine what it'd be like to coach there. And it was everything he imagined, certainly during his first two years.

In 1941, Brown took Francis Schmidt's 4–4 team and lost only one game. (That loss was to an Otto Graham-led Northwestern, and neither man knew that Graham, who passed for two scores, was in a sense auditioning for the man who'd be his professional coach.) Brown's Buckeyes, ranked No. 14, also tied No. 5 Michigan, but after Francis's 40–0 Michigan loss of the previous year, even a tie seemed like a win.

"In the pluckiest and most heroic showing in the fifty years' history of Ohio State football, a magnificent band of Buckeyes, classed as underdogs, fought mighty Michigan to a 20–20 tie," said the Cleveland *Plain Dealer*. The governor, John Bricker, was so happy he made Brown a license plate that said, "PB-20," which stayed on his car until he moved to California after Art Modell fired him as coach of the Cleveland Browns.

He was now The Great God Brown, having converted all of Columbus. Even the convicts in the old State Penitentiary on West Spring Street were rabid fans, and Brown turned up there to show films and talk about his team's prospects (even if their own weren't nearly as promising).

Yet even among the faithful, there were misgivings about the Buckeye prospects for 1942. The season would be played against the backdrop of World War II, although the war wouldn't immediately affect the football program. Tobruk and Stalingrad had not quite yet supplanted Fort Knox Army and Iowa Pre-Flight, two of the Buckeyes' own offensive campaigns that fall. Ohio State was rebuilding, and only three starters were among the forty-three who showed up. It was the smallest, most undersized Buckeye squad long-time observers could remember. But that sophomore-laden group was ripe with possibility. Among them were kids who in an extraordinarily brief time would be professional players (almost a team of them, including two perennial All-Pros), a rookie coach who won the Super Bowl, Ohio State's first Heisman Trophy winner, and several war heroes (including a Bronze Medal winner at the Battle of the Bulge). And they were fast, almost all of them.

Whatever Brown was selling, his guys bought it. "You could give him a job selling toothbrushes at Broad and High and he'd make a fortune," said his fullback, Gene Fekete, who led the conference in rushing in 1942. Still and all, the Buckeyes were expected to finish far behind Minnesota, which was picked to repeat as Big Ten champions, having won the previous two titles—as well as the last two national championships.

But Minnesota was knocked off early, as was that other preseason pick of the litter, Notre Dame. When the first AP poll came out, an unlikely Ohio State was sitting on top of it, where it would stay until October 31, when the Buckeyes went off to play No. 6 Wisconsin in Camp Randall Stadium.

Here, Ohio State became a wartime casualty. The best passenger cars were taken by the military, leaving the team only ramshackle carriages that, as Brown himself said, "looked as if they hadn't been used for years." Worse, the cars' water tanks hadn't been flushed in God knows how long, and half the players came down with dysentery. A record crowd of 45,000 showed up in Madison, and more than two hundred radio stations broadcast the game across the nation. Even the BBC got into the act, using a short wave broadcast that beamed the game to servicemen in Europe.

Unfortunately, the weakened Buckeyes spent more time sprinting for the locker room than for the goalposts, and what followed was a dispiriting 17–7 loss. Wisconsin was aided mightily by Elroy "Crazylegs" Hirsch, a triple-threat halfback who, along with running mate Pat Harder, accounted for 212 yards. Brown was classy in his post-game comments. "We met a good team—easily the best we've played so far—but we might have shown a little more life if we hadn't been physically weak," he said. (Brown, as usual, brought something away from that game other than a queasy stomach: his teams wouldn't travel on a train again unless they brought their own water.)

The Bucks dropped to No. 6, and, peculiarly, a 59–19 win over Pittsburgh the next week saw them drop four more places. The game was also Dad's Day, and Brown's fullback, Fekete, played for eight minutes and ran for 140 yards on just three attempts. One was for 89 yards—a record that stood for sixty-eight years before being tied in 2010. "I broke it to the side, where the dads were all lined up," he said, "and you know, when I took off to the sideline I could have reached out and touched my dad as I went by." Fekete said his running style—knees up—had been perfected in Findlay by learning to run in freshly plowed farm fields.

When Michigan—No. 4—came to town on November 21, Ohio State was back up to No. 5 (a solid win over No. 13 Illinois had helped). It was a cold, rainy day in Columbus, but it didn't stop Ohio State from throwing the ball: all three of its scores were by air. Brown's flexible attack stymied the favored Wolverines, and it also presented observers with the canny kind of offense they'd soon come to expect from any Brown team—wherever it might be.

Halfback Paul Sarringhaus, who wore contact lenses—one of the first football players to use them—and would be discharged from the quartermaster corps for poor vision, accounted for all three scores, in one way or another. He caught a pass for the first score, then threw for two more, ending up four-of-five for the afternoon, with 121 yards. The game was typical for the rivalry, complete with a fourth quarter escapade by a fan who rushed onto the field and threatened to take his pants off in the end zone. Then he ran up the field, smacked himself into a Michigan player, and passed out.

THE WIN SECURED THE BIG TEN TITLE FOR OHIO STATE—THE FIRST GAME BETWEEN THE TWO that would determine the conference champion. The weekend for the home folks was also enlivened by news that No. 1 Georgia had lost to Auburn. Title hopes, all but dead in the middle of November when the Buckeyes fell to No. 10, stirred again. Now, the last week in November, the corpse looked ready to sit up and take nourishment. And there was one game left, the Iowa Seahawks, a late addition to the schedule. The Seahawks, called "the Green Bay Packers in Navy Blue," represented the U.S. Navy pre-flight school at the University of Iowa, a formidable team of both college and professional players—including Dick Fisher, a standout halfback from Brown's 1941 team—playing what some called the toughest schedule in the country: The Bucks won handily, though, 41–12, their quickness and speed more than overcoming the Seahawk weight advantage. It was but one of three losses for the Seahawks that season—and the worst.

The win didn't hurt Ohio State's rating, and neither did a loss by the new No. 1, Boston College, who was overwhelmed by its archrival Holy Cross, 55–12. It was also good news for Boston, ironically, because the team called off its post-game celebration at the Cocoanut Grove nightclub where the deadliest nightclub fire in history occurred that night, killing nearly five hundred people.

There were pretenders to the throne, notably Georgia (and even Wisconsin), but that was always so in the days when four and five teams sometimes shared—unhappily—the title. But the Associated Press, considered the king maker, said it was Ohio State. No team had ever come back from such a late-season deficit to take the national title, and now one had. Still, history put an asterisk on the title, although it wasn't visible in Columbus. (The analytics liked Georgia, because the Dawgs—11–1—had beaten No. 3 Alabama, then ended their season by blanking No. 2 Georgia Tech, 34–0, and toppling No. 13 UCLA in the Rose Bowl.) Ohio Staters tended to look at their title as simply the intervention of fate for that "bad water game" at Wisconsin.

There was a moment at the annual football appreciation dinner when Brown wondered, if just for a moment, whether he'd actually won the title or not. He arrived at the door, only to discover he'd lost his ticket. And as the coach was still new to Columbus, the doorman didn't recognize him. So Brown forked over the requisite $1.50 in order to go inside and hear himself praised. Perhaps in time, the coach might have recognized the irony of it—a man with a reputation for being tight with a dollar had just lost one.

His good time at Ohio State was now on the wane, though, for the realities of the war were about to intrude into the season, so much so that there almost wasn't one. Most schools had military affiliations by this time; the difference was that many of Ohio State's rivals were affiliated with the navy—which allowed their enrollees to play football—and OSU had chosen the army ROTC, which did not.

His good freshmen team of 1942 was all but gone, and when fall rolled around, the larder was bare. The Big Ten ruled incoming freshmen eligible and allowed summer practice, as if that could make up for the lost players. Brown wet-nursed forty-seven 17-year-olds that summer, and there was a run on undersized football pants. His "Baby Bucks" were game but unready, and they struggled to a 3–6 mark that went into the record books without an asterisk explaining why.

Brown was gone then, off to Great Lakes Naval Training Center and a lieutenant's commission. There was much talk of him returning to Ohio State after the war, but Brown was through with college ball, and it seemed that his last season in Columbus caused it. The Baby Bucks were war victims, he said, and he was incensed that neither the school nor its supporters had even given the kids a year-end banquet. He had made some enemies in Columbus, and he needed an environment he could control. College football was, as Brown had learned, a bear garden: control it one year, lose it the next.

The professional game was open to autocracy, and Brown lost no time in imposing himself on it. He once scolded a player for yawning during halftime and he cut rookies for the sin of slovenly attire. His quarterback Milt Plum remembered him calling a player out of a dorm card game to fine him for "abusive language." He was determined to reinvent—and dignify—that backyard brawl of a game that professional football was at the time.

And so he did. He was always making things bigger than when he found them. He'd done it at Massillon, he'd done it at Ohio State, and the sporting world watched as he did it in Cleveland. Still and all, there were Buckeye fans who never got over the notion of what he might ultimately have done in Columbus.

If only he'd stayed.

> When you win, say nothing. When you lose, say less.
>
> —Paul Brown

The lost dynasty

Brown's departure was more costly than it seemed

The event that set the course for modern Ohio State football wasn't the Snow Bowl but World War II. Without the intervention of the war, Paul Brown may well have remained the school's head coach for decades. It is a near certainty that the Buckeye dynasty beginning in the mid-1950s, absent the war, would have begun a decade earlier—only it would have been Paul Brown's, not Woody Hayes's. And if Paul Brown had stayed in Columbus, Woody Hayes may never have torn up a single yard-marker on national television. Hard to imagine, but perhaps Ohio Stadium would have become a place where the lion and the lamb amicably shared the sidelines, with Woody's normal animosity channeled into Brown's more cerebral approach.

So what would a Paul Brown dynasty at Ohio State have looked like? Winning seasons and championships, no doubt. He is the only coach to have won national championships on the high school, college, and professional levels. At Massillon, between 1935 and 1940, he won six state titles and four national ones (during this time he lost but one game, when half his team came down with the flu). He won a national title at Ohio State in 1942, then added seven championships in his pro years. After a brief respite from his firing in Cleveland, he brought the start-up Bengals into Cincinnati and took them to the playoffs in only his third season. Judging coaching at all levels, Paul Brown is the most successful coach in football history.

He coached almost as long as Woody, until 1975, and should he have remained at Ohio State for that entire time, he would have coached the Buckeyes for thirty-five years—around 350 college football games. If he won 76 percent of those games (as Woody did), he would have had 258 college victories (Woody had 205). Up the percentage to 80 percent—like Bo Schembechler—and his total would have been 275. Move it up to that of Mount Union's Larry Kehres's 92 percent, and Brown could have had 315 college wins.

Brown's career suggests that at least some would have resulted in national titles. After all, he didn't just win games; he won titles. A long Brown tenure at Ohio State, however, would have given the program a different look and feel. The tradition of winning would still have been there but a different ghost would hover over the Horseshoe.

One autocrat would be exchanged for another, and Brown was an entirely different one than the hot-tempered, window-rattling Hayes. (It was reported they roomed together, taking summer classes at Ohio State, but Mike Brown said they merely had adjoining rooms where his father was amused at the noises of Woody shadow-boxing next door.)

There were similarities, though. They had both been small-college players, Hayes at Denison and Brown at Miami. Brown had aspired to the larger stage—Ohio State—but he was dismissed. "They told me I was too small for that caliber of football," he would say later. "It was a mortal blow to my pride." And his pride was perhaps the largest thing about him. He'd been a Massillon quarterback whose brassiness amused his coach, Dave Stewart, who said he was "a banty rooster, full of authority and confidence," and insisted that he, Brown, make all the game substitutions. He was not yet seventeen and already out to run his own show.

Both were absolutists although each in his own way. Woody was loud and volatile, a near-fanatical adherent to an offense that would soon be seeking its own museum. "Convinced that holding his tongue would give him an ulcer, Hayes said just what he thought about officials, opponents, reporters, administrators, peers, freaks, gays, commies, and anyone else he was of a mind to reprove," said Alan Natali in *Woody's Boys*. "He called everything by its right name, or at least the name by which he knew it."

At one moment, he was superintending his players with a whip and a chair; the next, making sure they got cookies and milk the night before games. His great All-American lineman Jim Parker said, "If he told me, 'Go out there and move that stadium two inches to the right or four inches forward,' I would do it." And, said linebacker Ken Kuhn, "You loved him. You hated him."

WOODY WORE HIS EMOTIONS ON *YOUR* SLEEVE. PAUL BROWN DIDN'T APPEAR TO HAVE EMOTIONS, as if they might interfere with his decision-making. "A figure of icy resolve," he was called. The columnist Jim Murray said he was spare and fussy and, as a pro coach, "treated his players as if he had bought them at auction." The appreciation players had for Woody usually came in hindsight, and because he was such an irascible eccentric their affection for him arose over time. Brown, whose inordinate dignity came with just a touch of malice, would never have become beloved in the manner Woody did. "We are all useful," Brown would say, "but no one is necessary." Not words to inspire great affection.

The two shared a distrust of the media, but again their expressions differed. Woody was confrontational, once shoving a scribe out the door, while PB might eviscerate the ink-stained wretch—his term—with his tongue. "Someone in the media would come up to Brown and say, 'You don't remember me, but…' And Brown would say, 'No, I don't,' and walk away," recalled the Browns quarterback Otto Graham. "He didn't give a shit about it, and it hurt him in the end."

They were a pair of staid guys, too. When the Buckeyes' pregame movies contained sex or profanity, Woody threw a tantrum. In Champaign, Illinois, the assistant coach had taken the team to see *Slap Shot,* a sports movie starring Paul Newman. It was colorfully profane, however, and filled with sexual references. Woody stood up in the theater and yelled, "This is TRASH!" He went out, found the manager, and told him, "You're fired!" Then, by himself, he walked back to where the team was staying.

Brown wanted to regulate his players' sex lives. "No sex after Wednesday," he told us," said Otto Graham. "'Save yourself for the game.' It was right there in our notebooks. We had to write it down. Cliff Lewis and I were neighbors out there in Bay Village, so our wives traveled together. Two nights before the game, we went out and had dinner. We escorted the girls back to the lobby of their hotel. We went back to the cab, and the driver said, 'What's the matter, couldn't you make out?'

"We said, 'No, those are our wives.'

"He said, 'Your *what*!'

"He couldn't understand what was going on."

Brown, finally, would have brought something to Ohio State that Woody didn't—innovation. He would have revolutionized college coaching, just as he did the evolving pro game. The role of college head coach as CEO would have come much earlier, because other colleges would have followed Brown's businesslike approach—from recruiting to game management. When he first arrived at Ohio State, he analyzed Francis Schmidt's methodology and found it wanting. Brown said that Schmidt had so many plays that his practices might run two and a half hours, and still the players didn't always know what they were doing. To Brown, who was even then creating the *business* of football, it simply wasn't efficient. "Francis Schmidt certainly wasn't as detail conscious as I was, or as demanding," Brown said, "nor had he put the same emphasis on teaching or execution."

Brown is often overlooked for his role in the development of the modern passing game, while Sid Gillman—through Francis Schmidt—is seen as its chief architect. There are those, though, who think it was Brown who gave Gillman's offense its most valuable component: precision. Before Brown, pass offenses weren't complex, and quarterbacks typically waited for a receiver to get open. Brown thought that wasn't very efficient. His response was: why wait?

Brown's biographer, Jack Clary, says it was Brown who developed intricately-timed pass routes, with the ball thrown *before* the receiver was open. The exact route, and the precision between receiver and quarterback with its emphasis on time and space, created a more formidable offense. Pass routes then were run as drawn; if the play sent the receiver into an area occupied by a defender, that's what he ran. Brown, however, said "read and react"—if the receiver is going right and a defender is there, then go left.

Brown finished his tenure at Ohio State a year before Gillman became head coach at Miami, but it's obvious that Gillman—through observation as well as clinics—followed Brown closely and knew what he was doing. And it's highly likely that Gillman took the creativity he'd learned as Schmidt's assistant and married it to PB's precision. (Clary said that many coaches looked askance at claims bestowing the title of "pioneer" on Gillman. "Check Gillman's files," one of them said, "and see if he still has that old Browns' playbook.") While the record isn't clear as to exactly who did what and when, one should remember that in the incestuous world of football, it never is.

The point is that while Brown was in Cleveland, he contributed a list of innovations to the pro game, and there's nothing to suggest that his fertile mind wouldn't have brought the same flourishes—from game management and statistical analysis to film study—to Columbus. The flanker had appeared here and there on the football landscape, but many observers think it was Brown who systematized it into the offense. Imagine what Brown would have done with Paul Warfield, who caught 39 passes and 525 yards for Woody in his three Ohio State years (1961–1963), then morphed into a Hall of Fame receiver in Cleveland. Even the facemask and the draw play might now be recognized as having originated at Ohio State.

There was another arena in which Brown's enterprise came to the forefront: integration. A handful of African-Americans had played pro football, but from 1934 to 1946, there'd been a tacit—read *racist*—old boys' agreement to keep Blacks out. Then when the newly relocated Cleveland Rams negotiated with Los Angeles in 1946 to play in city-owned Memorial Coliseum, the city pressured the Rams into signing Kenny Washington, a former UCLA running back who was the first consensus All-American in school history (but only second team, given his status as second-class citizen).

That happened in March of 1946. PB signed Bill Willis and Marion Motley in August, and the difference was this: the Rams were more or less coerced into being nondiscriminatory; PB *wanted* his players. Therefore, a case can be made for the postwar Civil Rights Movement beginning on a practice field in Bowling Green, Ohio. Black players had always been a part of Brown's teams, even in high school.

The popular version of the integration of major league sports begins in 1947 with Jackie Robinson and baseball. It's the predominant image in the minds of most Americans because football did not then have the hold on the public that it does now—and baseball did. So that other transcendent Ohioan, Branch Rickey—the Dodgers' general manager—gets the credit for integrating sports. Yet Rickey followed PB, and he said if he hadn't seen Willis and Motley playing for Brown without incident, he may never have had the courage to bring Jackie Robinson into the majors.

Willis immediately dominated the Browns' defensive line and Marion Motley, a steelworker who'd played some semi-pro football, came in and—bigger and almost as quick as Willis—dominated *both* sides of the ball. Brown brought them in quietly, without fanfare. "If you can't get along with your teammates, you won't be here," Brown said, and without mentioning race, the players knew what he meant. (It wasn't easy for either player, but as Motley would say, "They found out that while they were calling us niggers and alligator bait, I was running for touchdowns and Willis was knocking the shit out of them.")

PB had simply moved far past most of his contemporaries, and his stance wasn't about elevating civil rights, it was simply about personnel. "I take colored boys because I think they can win for me," he said, after signing Willis. It was no social experiment, Mike Brown said, and his father did not see himself in "socio-political terms." The Black press, though, saw it differently, and *Ebony* magazine called the Browns "the most democratic team in football."

Once again, though, PB was at the forefront of the sport, and his foresight—and courage—strongly suggest he would have pushed the process at Ohio State, where Woody Hayes admitted to Jim Parker in the mid-1950s that he couldn't put more than three African-Americans on the field at the same time. It wasn't because of Woody's thinking; it was the antiquated pressure of the time, and Woody recognized that he did not, at the moment, have the necessary wherewithal to challenge it. PB, with a national title under his belt, had an early credibility that Woody did not. Therefore it's difficult to see him waiting for the native mindset to catch up. It's therefore easy to picture Ohio State at the vanguard of integration, and much sooner than even Michigan State where Duffy Daugherty's championship team of 1966 featured a starting Black quarterback among its twenty African-Americans.

The final analysis is that Paul Brown would have irrevocably altered Ohio State football. He would have recruited versatile quarterbacks, developed trend-setting offenses, and changed how college football was played. He'd have won more championships, too. But even though he said his first two years at Ohio State were the happiest of his life, it's difficult to imagine him as a permanent college fixture. The college program was more difficult to control, and his methods seemed best suited for the professional game.

And so Paul Brown's impact in Columbus remained minimal. The dislocations of war—and his own fierce ambition—sent him to Cleveland where his quick and orderly mind made him football's most influential modern coach. A temperamental decade passed before a new coach began his own dynasty in Columbus.

It would be an historic three decades, and the new man would prove to be more exceptional—in ways both good *and* bad—than even his record.

> We give place to no man in our ardor for the game as it is played at Ohio State.
> —James Thurber

James Thurber, devotee and scourge

Forgive him his trespasses, for he was always a fan

WE PAUSE IN THE MIDST OF THAT REMARKABLE DECADE, THE 1940S, TO COMMENT ON SOMETHING LITTLE-REMEMBERED IN COLUMBUS, which was the rise of native son James Thurber, who was one of Ohio State's biggest fans, that is, except when he wasn't. An odd duck, he was very much bred in his hometown but also not of it. This fact accounted for a wonderful tension in his work, whereby the temperament of a Midwestern foozle lay beside a fellow reading Henry James, someone equally at home in Paris or Parma but not really from either.

Thurber once explained Ohio as "a region steeped in the traditions of Coxey's Army, the Anti-Saloon League, and William Howard Taft." When he went off to Ohio State in 1913, the university's primary function was still vocational training and most of its 4,000 students were solidly grain-fed Ohioans. It was the kind of place, Thurber observed, where it was dangerous to be found with a copy of Shelley in your pocket. A German teacher of Thurber's time contended that "any stirring of the mind" on campus was considered high-brow and undemocratic. Still, there was a good English department and a small, lively band of students, and Thurber always acknowledged both.

Midwestern to the core, Thurber could never quite make up his mind about football. On one of his typing hands, he wrote that Ohio State was a college "for football players, Boost Ohioers, and stock-judging teams." On the other, he wrote, "We give place to no man in our ardor for the game as it is played at Ohio State." And he said football "has more beauty in it than any other competitive game in the world, when played by college athletes."

So he vacillated, scheduling trips back from New York to coincide with Ohio State's home games and illustrating the cover of the official program for the Ohio State–University of Michigan homecoming game in 1936, but also fretting over the emerging big-time nature of the football program, which, he thought, was diametrically opposed to any equal fealty to the arts. (He was fond of quoting his old professor, Joseph Denney, who'd said of the university, "Millions for manure, but not one cent for literature.")

BECAUSE OF HIS NATIONAL PLATFORM, HE HELPED GIVE RISE TO THE NOTION THAT OHIO STATE WAS A "FOOTBALL FACTORY." By the 1940s, Thurber had established himself as a literary lion, first at *The New Yorker*, where he'd written "The Secret Life of Walter Mitty," his most famous short story, and several books, including the autobiographical *My Life and Hard Times*, which cataloged the deeds—and misdeeds—of his Columbus relatives. It's generally regarded as his masterpiece, a portrait of a particular Ohio world soon to be overrun by modernity: his grandfather, who wasn't sure the Civil War had concluded, his Aunt Sarah who lived in nightly fear of a burglar blowing chloroform under her door, and a grandmother who thought electricity leaked out of the empty light sockets.

Biographer Charles Holmes characterized the events of the book as representing "What ought to have happened, if only the world were a little more artistically organized."

It was Thurber's essay, "University Days," in *My Life and Hard Times* that gave America an enduring picture of the dim bulb football lineman, personified by the Ohio State tackle Bolenciecwcz, whom Thurber described as "while he was not dumber than an ox he was not any smarter." When the economics professor asks Bolenciecwcz to name any means of transportation, the ensuing colloquy among Bolenciecwcz, his classmates, and Professor Bassum is classic Thurber:

"You may choose among steam, horse-drawn, or electrically propelled vehicles," said the instructor. "I might suggest the one which we commonly take in making long journeys across land. " There was a profound silence in which everybody stirred uneasily, including Bolenciecwcz and Mr. Bassum.

Mr. Bassum abruptly broke this silence in an amazing manner. "Choo-choo-choo," he said, in a low voice, and turned instantly scarlet. He glanced appealingly around the room. All of us, of course, shared Mr. Bassum's desire that Bolenciecwcz should stay abreast of the class in economics. For the Illinois game, one of the hardest and most important of the season, was only a week off.

"Toot, toot, too-tooooooot!" some student with a deep voice moaned, and we all looked encouragingly at Bolenciecwcz. Somebody else gave a fine imitation of a locomotive letting off steam. Mr. Bassum himself rounded off the little show. "Ding, dong, ding, dong," he said, hopefully.

Bolenciecwcz was staring at the floor now, trying to think, his great brow furrowed, his huge hands rubbing together, his face red.

"How did you come to college this year, Mr. Bolenciecwcz?" asked the professor. "Chuffa chuffa, chuffa chuffa."

"M'father sent me," said the football player.

"What on?" asked Bassum.

"I git an 'lowance," said the tackle, in a low, husky voice, obviously embarrassed.

"No, no," said Bassum. "Name a means of transportation. What did you ride here on?"

"Train," said Bolenciecwcz.

"Quite right," said the professor.

“The little wheels of his invention are set in motion by the damp hand of melancholy. —The Clocks of Columbus

Did Thurber really create the vacant-minded Bolenciecwcz with his boyhood friend Chic Harley in mind? Hard to believe, but his college chum Elliott Nugent says he did. Thurber also wrote an epic poem about Harley that went, in part:

There's a thousand other stories of the games of other years,
But one from out the thousand like a flash of light appears,
And there's nothing half so thrilling from the first year to today,
Like the glory of the going when Chic Harley got away.

Easier, of course, for the world to remember Thurber's portrait of poor, laboring Bolenciecwcz over Chic Harley's iambic pentameter, and therein the Thurber dichotomy in which he was at once university devotee and scourge. In 1940, he had added more parody to Ohio State football, this time in the play he'd written with his old classmate Elliott Nugent, *The Male Animal.* (Nugent, a man-about-campus and future actor-playwright of note, had taken the fledgling Thurber under his wing, made him get a haircut and a new suit, and got him into Phi Kappa Psi. The two men would remain lifelong friends.)

By the mid-century, *The Male Animal* was regarded as "a small classic of the American theatre." It was in a Midwestern college town (read: Columbus) on the eve of The Big Game (Michigan, of course), and the play involved a professor; his winsome wife, Ellen; and a returning jock who in his own spangled university days had been Ellen's boyfriend. The dominant theme is the romantic triangle and its resolution, with a backstory of whether or not Professor Turner—who plans a classroom reading of a letter by the executed anarchist Niccolo Vanzetti—will buckle under the pressures of censorship.

Another of Thurber's several biographers, Burton Bernstein, said the play was "like a tipsy midget at a teamsters' outing, its academic-freedom theme bravely, absurdly, asserting itself in an otherwise conventional Broadway romantic comedy." Reviewers generally agreed it was "a palatable way for the theatregoer to take his dose of social conscience." Thurber blanketed Ohio with tickets, admonishing visiting firemen from Columbus that the play's setting could be *any* Midwestern campus town, but no one was having any of it. (Thurber and Nugent wouldn't publicly admit the setting was Ohio State until years later, "to avoid libel and mayhem," as Nugent put it.)

In 1942, the play moved from Broadway to Hollywood. The local references in the film rendered "Midwestern University" even more clearly as OSU, to wit: the Neil Avenue gate, the scarlet-and-gray school colors, and, of course, the team fight song—"*We Don't Give a Darn for the Whole State of Michigan.*" Speculation was that the relatively innocent audiences of the 1940s were not yet accustomed to such immodesty as "damn," even though Clark Gable had famously used it a couple of years before when he walked away from a tearful Vivien Leigh at the end of *Gone with the Wind.* Ohioans, though, had no such reservations. It was, first of all, *Michigan* they were talking about, and they'd been not giving a damn about Michigan since the 1920s.

According to local lore, it was sometime in the 1920s when an inebriated fan wandering through the old Deshler-Wallick Hotel lobby had yelled, "We don't give a damn for the whole state of Michigan." That was followed by a wonderful impromptu moment in which a musical combo in the lobby—and several dozen well-lubricated OSU fans—spontaneously set the phrase to the music of "The Old Gray Mare." And thus a legend was born.

The Male Animal, with its serious underlying note of an unpalatable censorship, made Thurber seem terribly prescient in the 1950s when Joseph McCarthy burst onto the national scene, infecting the country with the specter of a communist under every bed. Thurber wasn't happy with McCarthyism, of course, but he was also unhappy with Ohio State because the university in 1951, after a "faintly socialistic Columbia University professor" gave a talk on campus, instituted a gag rule for speakers.

Thurber's position was that no communist could sway an Ohio State audience and not allowing them to speak forewent a splendid occasion "to heckle and confound such speakers." A few months after the gag order, the university decided to award Thurber an honorary degree. Both the timing and the manner of it—the university hinted Thurber didn't actually have to be present—was insulting, and he declined, rather graciously but pointedly.

The gag rule eventually went away (as, thankfully, did McCarthy), but it left a dent in both the university and Thurber, further provoking his contradictory feelings about Columbus and Ohio State. As usual, though, his Buckeye DNA held sway, bringing him back home in 1959 to receive the Distinguished Service Award of the Press Club of Ohio. In 1960 he made the dedicatory speech for a new OSU Arts and Sciences Building named after his old professor Joseph Denney. Thus his affections swung back and forth, for he was at heart an artist with an artist's concomitant aesthetic liberality, and he was also bedrock

Columbus, bound by the same conservative fetters as his mid-century Ohioans. The truth was, he never really got far from home. Once, traveling through Carcassonne in the south of France, he was delighted when he spotted an automobile with a Cleveland license plate. "You just can't outrun Ohioans," he said proudly.

WHAT OHIO STATE FANS SHOULD REMEMBER ABOUT THURBER WAS THAT, FIRST AND FOREMOST, HE WAS AN OHIOAN and, in his own way, one of them. His early life was suffused with sports, particularly baseball, because Columbus in those days was a baseball town and Thurber, as a 12-year-old kid, saved his nickels to go to Neil Park and watch the Columbus Senators. Ohio State, having lost to Michigan 86–0 when Thurber was eight years old, was still a work-in-progress. That would be changed, in part, by the ministrations of a young man named Chic Harley—one of Thurber's classmates at East High who'd played baseball on a team captained by Thurber's brother.

Thurber was a couple of years ahead of Harley; he looked on while Chic helped establish Ohio State's national presence. He would later write the quintessential description of Harley on the football field, for the New York newspaper *PM*, and it went like this: "If you never saw him run with a football, we can't describe it to you. It wasn't like Red Grange or Tom Harmon or anybody else. It was kind of a cross between music and cannon fire, and it brought your heart up under your ears."

It isn't difficult to see why Columbus—and Ohio State—figured so prominently in Thurber's writing. One, he was born into a family so inventively moonstruck they begged to be herded onto the printed page where they could be consumed at leisure. (Personal favorites: Aunt Mary, who survived until the age of 93 on what seemed to be copious amounts of chewing tobacco, and Thurber's mother, Mamie, an inveterate showoff who once appeared on the stairs in her dressing gown, her hair awry, and announced to guests she was being kept in the attic against her will because of her hapless love for Mr. Briscoe the postman.) Two, at Ohio State, he was known for cramming four years into five and still getting away without a degree. He managed to noodle through most of his course work but biology (where his faltering eyesight kept him off the microscope) and military drill, which he hated unreservedly and complaining that the uniform made him look like a streetcar conductor. ("You're the main trouble with this university," the ROTC commandant told him. "Either you're a foot ahead or a foot behind the company.")

Thurber lived at home and ferried himself back and forth on the streetcar, a somewhat spectral figure floating about the campus, awkward and dreamy. His was the frequent picture of the artistically-inclined loner who combats isolation with a rich imaginative life (the salon of the mind holds many a lively event where the bashful introvert is the life of the party).

In the 1920s, Thurber landed a reporting job at the *Columbus Dispatch*, where he stymied the old hands with his approach to the news. "He was a scribbler, a *writer*," sniffed one of them, with the superiority in which the profession held the suspiciously literate among themselves. Thurber, who was addressed as "Author" by his city editor, bemoaned what he said was the paper's perfect lead for every story: "John Holtsapple, 63, prominent Columbus galosh manufacturer, died of complications last night at his home, 396 N. Persimmon Blvd." The city editor, a man named Kuehner, who'd trained on the police beat, hated departures from journalistic rigor, especially flowery introductions, and whenever he spied one, he shouted, "This story is in *bloom*!"

Thurber's experiences with the city desk lent him a recurring anxiety dream in which the editor races over to his desk carrying a shoe and barks out, "We've got just ten minutes to get this shoe in the paper!" His basic job was covering city hall, but his fertile imagination overrode the beat's minimal qualifications. It sometimes caused him to ignore important numbers, such as his story on the municipal debt, in which he overstated it by $6 million. That incident was followed by a bulletin board directive at the *Dispatch* forbidding Thurber to write any story that dealt with sums above five figures.

He was not inspired by the prosaic dramas of city hall, his interests gravitating naturally to the collection of oddballs wandering in and out of the mayor's office. (They included a man who could receive a local radio station on the rims of his spectacles and a woman who predicted earthquakes by a twinge in her left side.) Thurber's working day was a brief office appearance after which he took off, "a sheaf of folded copy paper in my pocket and a look of enterprise in my eye," heading for Marzetti's, a restaurant whose main population seemed to be newspapermen who sat around drinking coffee and doodling on the tablecloth.

In 1922, he covered the dedication of Ohio Stadium, and he wrote his college chum Nugent about the event. "Too bad you can't be here to whiff the football air and to see the stadium dedicated," he said. "It is nearly completed now, a wonderful structure, set down in the pastoral back eighty of the OSU like a modernized Greek temple or a Roman coliseum born of mirage. Michigan plays here October 21, dedication day…"

THERE HE WAS AGAIN, A *FAN*. HE REMAINED ONE, TOO. Even as an adult he could recite Columbus batting averages, and at *The New Yorker*, when the vaunted proofreaders spelled Chic Harley's first name as "Chick," he threw a fit. Biographer Bernstein called it "an error no Ohio State man could ever live down."

When Thurber died in 1961, E. B. White, one of his closest friends, wrote, "There were at least two, probably six Thurbers. His thoughts have always been a tangle of baseball scores, Civil War tactical problems, Henry James, personal maladjustments, terrier puppies, literary rip tides, ancient myths, and modern apprehensions. Through this jungle stalk the unpredictable ghosts of his relatives in Columbus, Ohio."

And his Columbus always featured Ohio State at its center. Because he hadn't concluded his university stay with a proper graduation, it was as though he'd hang around in perpetuity, awaiting resolution to some vague and unfinished hometown business. Even with his typical ambivalence, there's little doubt he'd have been pleased when in 2016, as Ohio State played

Nebraska, the Buckeyes unveiled replica uniforms from the famous undefeated 1916 Chic Harley team. They featured red jerseys with gray vertical stripes and the look was called "music and cannon fire," after Thurber's famous description of Harley running.

The fans may have only dimly recognized Thurber's name, but they surely knew Harley's. It's unlikely many would have recognized the commonality of the two men, though. They were classmates when Chic almost single-footedly ushered in its first golden age. They were present at the creation, you might say. Thurber's depiction of Harley running is still the single quote everyone uses when Harley's name comes up. From a relatively young age, they both suffered physical debilities; Harley began a descent into dementia, Thurber into blindness.

Thurber, of course, was no athlete—he once said his most notable accomplishment was "hitting empty ginger ale bottles with small rocks at a distance of thirty paces." He was the afflicted American male, slight of build, awkward, so nonathletic that he passed gym only by enlisting another student to masquerade as him and swim across the pool in his place. Harley, of course, *owned* the gym. Yet even such disparity bound them together, for Thurber envied Harley's easy grace and converted the idea of it into his writing. Even today, Thurber's mid-twentieth century essays are the epitome of grace. They appear to be effortlessly tossed off when they're nothing of the kind—deceptively simple declarative sentences that in their quiet rhythms blend both humor and, to use Thurber's own phrase, "the damp hand of melancholy."

Thurber's athleticism was an *inner* one, given voice in a story like "The Secret Life of Walter Mitty" where Mitty's alter ego—as with Thurber's own—*became* the athlete. No one understood better than Thurber that life was an obstacle course. Like his boyhood hero on the football field, Thurber slipped past many of the obstacles with Harley's own dexterity. Only the expression differed. Then one day, there they were, both Ohio State immortals. Chic Harley and James Thurber: two peas in an Ohio pod.

Passing fancy

The so-called West Coast offense, or: The Ohio/Cincinnati/Banks-of-the-Ohio-River offense that didn't stay home and the OSU guys responsible for it

THE DECADE OF THE 1940S WAS, OF COURSE, OVERSHADOWED BY THE WAR. IN ADDITION to the innumerable local sacrifices, there was Paul Brown's 3-6 "Baby Bucks" team of 1943, composed largely of freshmen, none of whom weighed two hundred pounds. It opened with the Iowa Pre-Flight Seahawks, who came to Columbus loaded with former professionals and beat OSU 28–13, the margin merely a courtesy extended by the Iowa coach, and it closed with a 45–7 loss to Michigan.

There were bright moments in the decade—there was the university's first Heisman (Les Horvath), Carroll Widdoes's unbeaten team in 1944, and the Buckeyes' first Rose Bowl win (1950). The longer, historical view was more interesting, for it was one that presaged monumental changes, both locally and within the sport at large. One, it trained Lieutenant Commander Wayne Woodrow Hayes, soon to be Ohio State's coach. It was, no doubt, the commander's formative experience, helping nurture his already militaristic point of view, as well as the notion that football itself was merely war with closer formations. And, two, by the time Paul Brown left Columbus, Ohio State had already produced a small cadre of men who had an outsized and ongoing impact on the game, if not in Columbus, then certainly elsewhere.

To those who chronicle history, the relationships between these men—and those who followed—are often presented with Old Testament reverence as one coach or system begat another. Francis Schmidt and Paul Brown begat Sid Gillman just as Paul Brown and Sid Gillman begat Tiger Ellison. For it was in Schmidt's offensive mind of the 1930s and early 1940s, coupled with Paul Brown's organization and precision, that the modern collegiate passing game came about. And given their creative ferment and ultimate influence—Ohio State men all—it seems safe to say that even in spite of the bland and bare-knuckled years that lay ahead, OSU's place in the firmament of passing was secure.

Football's modernity has a broad ancestry, but virtually all of it goes back to Ohio State (with a side bit of Cincinnati DNA). Francis Schmidt was not only a great creative mind, but he had an assistant coach who was one of football's great understudies—Sid Gillman. Gillman was team captain and All-Big Ten in 1933, had a cup of coffee with the old Cleveland Rams, then got down to business with Schmidt. He loved Schmidt's wide-open game, which laid the foundation for everything that was to come. After Schmidt, Gillman never saw the field the same way again. And before long, no one else would, either.

The second influence on Gillman was another Ohio State guy, Paul Brown, who followed Schmidt to Columbus. Gillman was a natural for Brown's new staff, only he wasn't. No one knows exactly why the two shared a personal dislike of each other—but they did share a mutual football respect. "I always felt before Paul Brown," Gillman said, more than once, "coaches just rolled the ball out onto the field." But Brown didn't offer Gillman a job, and Gillman didn't ask for one. Instead, he got an assistant's job at Denison, then went to Miami. They kept in marginal touch at Brown's coaching clinics where Gillman, no doubt, took careful notes. We do know that if Gillman's influences began with Francis Schmidt, they—more or less—finished with Brown. Schmidt showed Gillman passion and innovation; Brown showed him precision and discipline.

The other thing Gillman and Brown shared was their love of film. Both are credited with being first to use film as a coaching aide. We don't have a specific date for Brown using film—he may have been using it as far back as Massillon High—but Gillman started looking at film while his family was operating Milwaukee movie theaters. There, Gillman had his brother inveigle a projectionist into clipping the football parts off newsreels. Then he took them home and watched them repeatedly on a bedsheet tacked to a wall.

Even here, though, there were differences in their methods: Gillman used film to develop ideas; Brown used film to organize and evaluate. What seems clear is that Gillman kept a close eye on Brown's developments. Gillman was always tinkering, improving, adding, and quite a bit of what he was improving had been shown to him by Brown. Brown was football's first CEO. He applied corporate practices to a game not fully defined, and he made it over in his own image: terse, pragmatic, efficient. Gillman was football's first artist-in-residence. He was also, as one writer said, "football's Jefferson and Adams, a revolutionary. If the game had a harbor, Gillman would have dumped tea into it."

For most of the decade between 1944 and 1954, Gillman was head coach at Miami then at the University of Cincinnati where the creative expression of his teams showed up in wins (81-19-2, three bowl games), fans, and converts. Particularly if you didn't know him personally. If you *did* know him personally, you might *not* have been a fan. When he took the UC job, he took Miami players and coaches—including head coach George Blackburn—with him, angering the people at Miami, particularly Woody Hayes, who came in as the new Miami coach and found the cupboard bare. People there also complained that Gillman's free-spending habits left the school saddled with debt.

Gillman was unapologetic on all accounts. "I'm a big spender," he would say. He said you had to spend to win, and the profits came with winning. He wasn't known for his subtlety; subtlety was reserved for his offenses. At practice, one of his players got hurt and Gillman said, "Move the ball over and let's get on with practice."

According to Cincinnati sportswriter Earl Lawson, the players pulled off their helmets and headed off the field. Gillman later apologized. "He antagonized many people in his own school, and others through his tactless statements, his extravagant demand on the athletic budget, his high-pressure recruiting tactics," Lawson wrote.

No one questioned his burgeoning mastery of the game, though, and his spring clinics at Cincinnati might draw a thousand high school coaches. There's little doubt that among them was a young Middletown High coach named Tiger Ellison. He might have even been on one of Gillman's programs. For Ellison was also making a name for himself, and by the mid-1950s, his prep teams were terrorizing opponents with a wide-open, pass-happy offense featuring four receivers in something he called the "Run-and-Shoot." Surely he remembered what Gillman himself was doing.

AND SO: THE TWO PARAMOUNT AGENTS OF THE MODERN PASSING GAME WERE WORKING ABOUT THIRTY MILES FROM ONE ANOTHER. Gillman had the stage, though, and in 1955, he was head coach of the Los Angeles Rams, where his high-flying offense really took off. Tiger went off to Ohio State, the home of the massive ground assault, and the only way he kept his Run-and-Shoot offense alive was by writing a book. A decade passed before another prescient high school coach read the book—in the Pacific Northwest, of all places—and brought Tiger's offense alive again. This time, it found a home, first with a guy named Mouse Davis, then into various maverick football leagues, making it into the sport's mainstream about a quarter of a century after Ellison had come up with it.

So who gained what from whom? Probably neither Ellison nor Gillman learned much from one another. For one thing, Gillman didn't like the Run-and-Shoot because it didn't have a tight end.

But Ellison and Gillman were otherwise kindred spirits, and they were after the same thing—using the entire field. Ellison was more improvisational; Gillman liked precision routes and timing.

By the time Gillman got to the Chargers in 1960, he'd synthesized everything. "Spread the field, put your wideouts at the extremities to force the defense to cover more ground, fill all five passing lanes, pre-read the defense, and hit the receiver on the break," he said.

Given how Gillman looked at a football field, it was no strange idea that he liked jazz. Once, when he was asked who his idol was, he said, "Art Tatum." He could even play some barrelhouse piano, and he'd played in a dance band when he was a teenager. Dizzie Gillespie called him "the jazz coach." And why not? Gillman's brand of offense was *like* jazz, in that an unusual kind of order was made out of chaos.

MEANWHILE, BILL WALSH, A FORMER QUARTERBACK, STARTED OUT IN 1966 WITH THE OAKLAND RAIDERS and absorbed Gillman's offense—by way of Al Davis—before ending up in Cincinnati with Paul Brown's start-up Bengals. When a shoulder injury forced his sensational rookie quarterback, Greg Cook, into retirement, Walsh ended up with Virgil Carter, described as "small, active, and very heady." (Carter taught a statistics course at Xavier University.) To overcome Carter's physical deficiencies, Walsh took Gillman's offense and emphasized the horizontal, ball-control aspects of it. The next year, the canny Carter led the NFL in pass completion percentage.

When Paul Brown made what might have been the worst personnel decision of his life and let Walsh leave Cincinnati, the name of Walsh's offense—in reality, the second generation of Sid Gillman's offense, maybe the third—went with him. In San Francisco, it became mistakenly known as "the West Coast Offense." It got the name in 1993 when Bernie Kosar, then a Dallas backup quarterback, was asked what the Cowboy offense was like. "Oh, you know," he said, "the West Coast Offense. Turner and Zampese and Don Coryell and Sid Gillman. *That* thing."

Kosar had just compressed two or three generations into one, crediting Norv Turner (offensive coordinator when the Cowboys won back-to-back Super Bowls) and Ernie Zampese and Don Coryell (with the Chargers when they led the league in passing a record six consecutive years from 1978 to 1983). And all of them were Gillman acolytes, whether they'd have said so or not.

Kosar's quote was attached to Walsh's passing game at San Francisco, which Walsh disparaged. "Call it the Walsh Offense or the Cincinnati Offense but not the West Coast offense," he said. "That's something completely different."

Walsh saw the West Coast offenses as a *vertical* game, while his was the *horizontal* one he'd brought from Cincinnati. It was all a matter of emphasis: the West Coast guys used Gillman's vertical game; he, Walsh, used Sid's horizontal one. (Walsh intuitively understood, as one writer said, "that the surest way to hit those deep passes is to consistently hit the underneath ones." Gillman even kidded Walsh about his short game. "Bill," he said once, "you going to lengthen out your passes to 10 yards this year?") Four Super Bowl wins later, it was the ball-control game that had become "the West Coast Offense."

Walsh always credited Gillman with whatever he, Walsh, had done, and he said that if Greg Cook—the best quarterback he ever saw—had remained healthy, he may never have become as smart as people said he was. With Cook's arm, he said, there would have been no necessity for a new, ball-control offense.

Finally, back in Oxford in 1991, they'd forgiven Gillman enough to put him in Miami's hall of fame. It'd taken only forty-four years. By this time, he was at last off the field, keeping up by watching film, a lifelong preoccupation. He'd probably seen more film than the National Society of Film Critics. At his La Costa house (where he had a football-shaped pool), he also had something like five hundred cans of film (gray ones for passing, blue for running). His football descendants had, by one accounting, won twenty-six Super Bowls. Most of them, like Walsh, acknowledged the debt. "Until Gillman got his mitts on it," wrote one writer, summing up the consensus, "a football was basically something to be tucked away for safekeeping. Gillman put feathers on it."

Finally, Gillman's offense morphed off into so many variations that it became all things to all men. Bill Walsh's offense was born in Cincinnati, became West Coast in name only, and its DNA was Sid Gillman by way of Ohio State and Francis Schmidt. Gillman even got his bow tie from Francis. By the end of the century, it was a grand exercise in football socialism—what *Sports Illustrated* writer Tim Layden meant when he said, "Everything belongs to everyone."

The irony was that it might have all remained in Ohio.

The day weather changed history

How a blizzard made Woody Hayes a Buckeye

THE THANKSGIVING SNOW BOWL OF 1950 HAS GONE INTO LEGEND, FUELED BY EYEWITNESSES—and players—who couldn't even see the goalposts. Thousands of others, in that wholly understandable way in which we acquire ownership of the grand and improbable events around us, soon dreamed themselves present. Sometime afterward, Chuck Ortmann, who won the game for Michigan, said that from his travels he estimated at least 300,000 people had been present that day. Everyone had a story, for the weather was the essential event, and everyone in Ohio had seen *that*.

The holiday on Thursday was rainy, with temperatures in the 40s. But that evening the rain changed to sleet and snow, and during the night a storm moving up the Carolina coast hurled ocean moisture westward into a frigid blast coming up from the south. These turbulent systems collided over Ohio and Pennsylvania, unleashing heavy snow, near-zero temperatures, and gale-force winds. There were six-foot drifts in northern

Ohio, and travel across most of the state was near impossible. It was five degrees Saturday morning and the snow was unceasing, although a few trains managed to get through to Columbus from Toledo, bringing the Michigan team and its fans. Several hundred automobiles were already stranded in the downtown, even as the Ohio Stadium crew—under conditions never before seen in the Horseshoe—was pretending business as usual.

The first business—and controversy—was deciding whether the game would be played. Neither coach wanted to play, and OSU coach Wes Fesler objected strongly. Michigan had already lost three games, and its odds of going to the Rose Bowl were smaller than the crowd that would remain in the stadium that afternoon. The Michigan AD, Fritz Crisler, didn't want to reschedule, and a cancellation would have given the Big Ten title to Ohio State. Cancellation wasn't a great option because of the chaos of refunds—and the lost revenue.

There was another thought, and it seems likely it would have occurred to Crisler: the Bucks, averaging 35 points a game, were six-point favorites, but it was axiomatic among coaches that inclement weather evened teams up. The great sportswriter, Arthur Daley, who covered the game for *The New York Times*, wrote afterward, "From time immemorial, mud has been football's Great Equalizer, and snow, sleet, and cold are lesser known members of the same family." And so the game went on, with OSU's offensive advantage lost in the storm.

In spite of the blizzard conditions, thousands of spectators made their way into the stadium, demonstrating a devotion bordering on the monomaniacal. There would surely be stories for the grandchildren, if one survived to have any grandchildren. The fans were described as looking like "well-to-do refugees from a war-torn region," while another observer saw in them the spirit of the great Arctic explorers, planting their flapping Buckeye flags in the end zone snowdrifts.

The most intrepid fan was surely a service station owner from Marion, Ohio, who won the honor hands down—in a manner of speaking. On the morning of the game, Harold Henry fell over a car jack in his shop and broke both his arms. Not to be deterred, he chewed aspirin and headed off to Columbus where he sat in the blizzard with his broken arms and watched what passed for a game.

Official attendance was 50,503, but few close observers believed it. OSU's quarterback, Tony Curcillo, said maybe 20,000, while others said half that. The officials didn't bother with taking tickets, so anyone could simply walk into the stadium. The field was ringed by snow banks, the yard markers were obliterated, and all the toilets at the top of the stadium were frozen. The fans huddled monk-like, some of them sitting with their heads in cardboard boxes through which peepholes had been cut. Others used Halloween masks to ward off the wind and snow, and the Ohio State marching band members used antifreeze in their horn valves. At some point, Ortmann, the Michigan halfback, looked into the stands and saw small bonfires scattered here and there.

WHEN THE GAME FINALLY GOT UNDERWAY, IT REVERTED TO ITS ANTIQUATED TURN-OF-THE-CENTURY ORIGINS when everything was about field position. "Wise coaches always play the breaks under execrable weather conditions," wrote the *Times* man Daley in his November 27 column. "They punt early and often." On Michigan's first two plays from scrimmage, the Wolverines punted on first down. The strategy was to give the slippery ball to Ohio State on the other side of the field. "Both teams treated the ball as if it were a bouquet of poison ivy," said *The New Yorker*.

The Buckeyes scored first after blocking an Ortmann punt and recovering the ball on the Michigan 8-yard line. After three running plays netted minus yardage, Vic Janowicz kicked a 38-yard field goal for a 3–0 Ohio State lead. The kick was into the wind, with the goalposts barely visible, and a panel of sportswriters would later call it "one of the Greatest Feats in American Sports."

Unfortunately, it was two other Janowicz kicks that sealed the Buckeyes' doom. The first came in the second quarter when a Janowicz punt from deep in his own territory was blocked, and the ball rolled out of the back of the end zone for a safety. The Bucks hung by their frozen fingernails to a 3–2 lead, which evaporated at the end of the half when, in a similar circumstance, another Janowicz punt was blocked. Michigan's Tony Momsen—scurrying after it and nearly upending a broom-wielding volunteer—fell on it in an end zone snowdrift. The score (and the point after) made it Michigan, 9–3, where it would remain.

The game then simply turned into a punting exhibition. Janowicz punted 21 times for 685 yards. Michigan's Ortmann 24 times for 723 yards. Janowicz had four punts blocked; Ortmann one. Ortmann, though, who wore a pair of freshly-cut deerskin gloves, seemed to be playing with glycol in his veins. His punts dropped where he wanted them—14 either rolled dead or went out of bounds inside the OSU 20.

In the manner in which good men are sometimes undone by a frivolous fate, Janowicz's spectacular field goal was largely forgotten while his blocked punt became legendary. It was helped along by an anecdote from Earle Bruce, then a redshirt halfback (before a career-ending injury sent him into coaching) who was watching the game as a spectator. Bruce was in the west stands, on the 40-yard line, behind a little old lady swaddled in an enormous snow-covered blanket. With forty-six seconds left, third and nine, she spotted OSU's blocking wingback, Bob Demmel, come into the game, and she knew what was about to happen.

"She threw off her blanket," said Bruce, "jumped to her feet with snow flying everywhere, and yelled as loud as any woman I've ever heard. 'Don't punt the ball, Fesler!' she yelled into the blizzard. 'Please don't punt the ball!'

"She knew disaster when she saw it," Bruce said. He'd win 81 games as the OSU coach, but he couldn't help second-guessing Fesler. Fesler, though, was a victim of the elements as much as anything else. He said there was too much time left to run out the clock, and, besides, teams don't punt to be blocked; they punt to execute. Janowicz agreed with him. "So it was a 50-50 deal," he said, "The bad part was that, at that point you just couldn't see. So

I could only drop back five yards." It was a day when Fesler's triple-threat tailback had been edited by nature down to a single threat, and many coaches would likely have made the same call.

The Bucks switched to tennis shoes for the second half but to no avail. Conditions worsened, with visibility near zero, and neither team got close to either goal line. The game, the entirety of it resembling some bizarre playground scrimmage, slogged to a close, even if the storm didn't. Michigan had won without making a single first down.

Most of the cars in the parking lots were buried, as those hardy remnants learned when they staggered out of the stadium. The stadium crew traversed the Horseshoe, making sure everyone was out and, sure enough, there found a handful of fans passed out from the stimulants necessary to stay through such a game. By Sunday morning, the blizzard had dumped nine inches of snow on the city. And while *The Plain Dealer* was describing Cleveland in the last great storm—the Big Blow of 1913—it may as well have been portraying Columbus, writing that it was "mute and deaf to the outside world, a city of lonesome snowiness, storm-swept from end to end."

Most of the faithful stood no chance of making it home and found themselves in various stages of distress along the highways out of Columbus. Some of those headed north made it as far as Marysville, then a thousand people were stranded, taken in by residents, sleeping in strange homes, the city building, even hay lofts. The hospitality record was thought to have been set by a farmer in Mount Sterling who packed his eight-room farmhouse with ninety-two people, most of them trying to get home to Wilmington. Hospitals in the city of Warren reported twenty-seven new mothers over the weekend, seventeen of them arriving by fire truck, snow plow, and army ambulance. In Cleveland, bulldozers plowed streets and army tanks delivered milk.

Fifty-five Ohioans died in the storm, half of them heart attacks from shoveling snow or pushing cars, the other half, it was surmised, from apoplexy at the game results. Michigan had beaten the odds, Mother Nature, and Ohio State. On the same afternoon, a three-loss Northwestern team upset No. 6 Illinois, sending Michigan to the Rose Bowl where—utilizing warmth and sunshine they thought they might never see again—beat undefeated California, 14–6. It was all highly improbable.

Janowicz acquired some redemption by winning the Heisman, but Fesler, the three-time All-American who'd now lost to Michigan four straight times—and had been suffering migraines all season—was done. He resigned, somewhat unexpectedly, and left for a career in business.

Now here's the rest of the story, which took place that same weekend, in the same blizzard, 120 miles to the southwest. There, another even older rivalry was being played—one between the University of Cincinnati and Miami. They'd begun theirs in 1888, two years before the Buckeyes even had a team and nearly a decade before they played Michigan for the first time.

The UC-Miami rivalry intensified after the Miami coach, Sid Gillman, left in 1947 to become line coach at Army. Gillman, a former Ohio State All-American, had posted a four-year 31-6-1 record in Oxford, and after a year at West Point, he reappeared in 1949 as the head coach of Miami's chief rival, the University of Cincinnati. In addition to showing up in the enemy camp, Gillman also took some of the Miami furniture with him: the head coach, notably, and several players.

That same year, Miami's new coach was Woody Hayes, who'd just coached Denison—his alma mater—to back-to-back undefeated seasons. Woody bristled at the loss of his players although, in truth, he probably ran some of them off with his heavy-handed methods. "We all loved Sid," said Miami's junior tackle, Bo Schembechler, "and here was this grim-looking guy taking his place." Wherever Woody went, the first year was no honeymoon. Gillman was no diplomat either; swapping one rival for another—especially ones that were practically in each other's backyard—was something like the Montagues sleeping with the Capulets. And everyone knows how *that* turned out. Suffice it to say, it surprised no one when the two met under Nippert Stadium at one of their games and threw a few punches before one of the UC basketball players broke them up. (Nothing seemed to have been bruised but egos.)

Miami was a step up for Hayes, and he had some trouble making it. First of all, there was the little matter of coaching styles. Hayes liked power; Gillman preferred speed. Hayes was a drill sergeant with a voice that broke windows; Gillman was management with the threat of demotion. (Said one of Gillman's players, "If Sid stopped talking to you, then you were better off joining the soccer team.") Hayes was Presbyterian; Gillman Jewish. Hayes believed that the coach, like God, was sovereign, that there was no free will (particularly among his linemen), that imperfection tainted us all, and only through endless repetition could one be delivered. Gillman saw himself as a kind of latter-day prophet, a righteous football person, and he thought, as the Torah did, that actions were more important than belief, particularly in, say, the matter of his linemen's splits. As the writer John Lombardo pointed out, "Woody's football field was a battleground; Sid's was a laboratory."

Given such disparity, it was natural for Hayes's players to think their program had just taken a backward step, and he struggled to a 5–4 season, ending it with a 27–6 loss to UC. When they met in 1950, Hayes had regained his footing: Miami had lost only one game when it met Gillman's Bearcats in Nippert Stadium on Thanksgiving weekend. Miami was still a two-touchdown underdog, and Hayes was worried, because he had to stop UC's vaunted speed—and its passing.

Not to worry, Woods. For there was another Snow Bowl that November day in 1950, and while it was overshadowed by what happened in Columbus, the Cincinnati Snow Bowl was the important one, with much more significance for Columbus—and the rest of Ohio. It would just take a few weeks to play itself out.

When the weather struck, Hayes knew he had caught a break. Gillman's passing game—as happened in Columbus with Ohio State's superior offense—was thwarted by the conditions. And Hayes had exactly the weapon such a day called for—a big, fast fullback from nearby Hamilton named Boxcar Bailey, who ran the hundred under ten seconds and was averaging 8.9 yards a carry.

To add more flavor to this meeting between two guys who didn't much care for each other, it seems that both teams had been considered for the Sun Bowl, although a bowl representative told one of the sportswriters that Miami wouldn't be considered "because the Redskins have a colored player, Jim Bailey." They didn't exactly object to having him in the game, they said, but they weren't prepared for "the housing and entertainment of a colored boy" in El Paso.

Of Woody's various sins, prejudice was never one of them, and Miami declined. Then it beat UC 28–0 behind Boxcar's 7.5 yards per carry. ("Take little steps," Woody had instructed.) It was the first shutout given to a Gillman team and one writer said of Bailey, "He seemed to be wearing snowshoes on his size 15 feet."

Gillman accused Hayes of sharpening his players' cleats, but Hayes, magnanimous in victory, ignored him. His guys then accepted an invitation to the Salad Bowl, practicing in a Quonset hut on the Miami campus over the holidays where two big potbellied stoves filled the place with heat enough to imitate the conditions they expected in Phoenix.

There Western Civilization presumably maintained itself even while housing and entertaining "a colored boy," who responded by scoring twice and helping Miami beat a good Arizona State team, 34–21. A demonstration of Woody at his best occurred on Miami's return flight home. Because of the weather, the flight made an unscheduled stop in Nashville—the old, segregated South—and Woody took his players to an airport restaurant. The manager, pointing out Bailey, said, "We don't serve his kind."

"If that guy doesn't eat here, then none of us will eat here," Woody said.

The manager said Boxcar could eat upstairs.

"Fine," said Woody. "Then we'll *all* eat upstairs."

The manager said the upstairs wasn't big enough for the team.

"Then Boxcar and I will eat upstairs together, and the rest of the team will eat downstairs," Woody said.

The story was told by Bo Schembechler, a tackle on that team, who finished it by saying, "Woody won us all over that night."

When Wes Fesler unexpectedly resigned from the Ohio State job, the winnowing process began. (On Thursday, November 25, Fesler was guest of honor as the Columbus Quarterback Club held its final meeting of the season, where he was presented a set of traveling luggage. "Now don't you or anyone go reading any hidden meaning into this gift, just because they are traveling bags," the chairman said. But after the strangest loss in Ohio State history, the gift of luggage proved to be a prophecy.)

On the list of potential candidates, Woody's name appeared in agate. Paul Brown seemed to be everybody's candidate, but from where Brown stood, Ohio State might have been a demotion. Missouri coach Don Faurot was offered the job, accepted it, then changed his mind. Sid Gillman's family said he'd been offered the job, accepted it, then lost it because he was Jewish. In a *Columbus Citizen* readers' poll, Woody finished behind Lassie, the actress Lana Turner, President Harry Truman—and an unnamed inmate in the Ohio Penitentiary.

Here's what Hayes had done to advance his candidacy, though: he defeated a favored opponent in a rivalry game, in an opponent's stadium, in a blizzard that the Ohio State team couldn't handle. Then he beat a favored Arizona State team in the Salad Bowl. The committee also knew about the recruiting coup when Woody had pulled twelve kids off the 1949 North-South Ohio All-Star Game. (Ohio State got two; Gillman got two.) That was no small consideration.

When all was said and done, Hayes was the last man standing. He'd made the leap from the Cradle of Coaches to the Graveyard of Coaches, and he'd gotten there by determination, an act of God, and a big fullback named Boxcar Bailey. Given that determination, he was already convinced *he* wouldn't be buried there. Interment in Ohio Stadium, as he understood it, was for *visitors*.

> Put your hats on the bastards.
> —Woody Hayes

Section Three
The legend incarnate

Woody Hayes arrived in Columbus as if he'd been prompted by history. The early promise of the 1940s had been left unfulfilled, and Michigan usurped the decade with a series of its best teams, constantly near the top of the national rankings. After Ohio State's undefeated team in 1944, Michigan wouldn't lose to the Buckeyes for another seven woebegotton years, claiming two national titles along the way.

The postwar Ohio State coach was Wes Fesler, a matinee-idol of a guy who'd been a two-sport OSU All-American, but he soon learned that Buckeye laurels had a short shelf life. He was a decent coach—his 1949 team beat California in the Rose Bowl—but he disagreed with the subliminal master plan that said Ohio State must perennially occupy college football's happy place, which was atop the national polls.

Like his old coach, Jack Wilce, he, too, thought education was the university's first order of business. He said he wanted the program to become "strictly an intramural effort," which was something like George Washington crossing the Delaware and inviting the Hessians to tea and biscuits. "I'll say it as long as I have a voice," he said, "that no boy will come to Ohio State with the primary thought of playing football."

It was the kind of sacrilege that might lead to being bound and chucked into the Olentangy. ("Olentangy," *Sports Illustrated* would say, was an old Indian word that meant "first down.") As it was, Fesler developed something like an early form of PTSD, the definition of which is a disorder that occurs after the experience of "a shocking, scary, or dangerous event," i.e., coaching at Ohio State. He was left sleepless, with staggering headaches, and finally he resigned.

There was a small, final irony in this good man's passage: unable to satisfactorily manage the hundred yards of real estate that was Ohio Stadium, Fesler eventually left coaching and headed to California where he became very successful in—yes—real estate.

By this time, it was understood that the coach of Ohio State football must not only manage the game but also the rabid expectations of its fan base. There was only one thing Woody Hayes couldn't manage and that was his own temperament. He was a permanently agitated man, the very symbol of aggrievement, at odds even with nature (hence the wearing of short-sleeve shirts at cold weather games). If the modern world was too much with him, he'd stave it off by dint of his fearsome personality.

For a while, he actually did. He was so good at building teams that he almost singlehandedly established the reputation of Big Ten football as being brutally unambiguous and straightforward, just like he was. He was aided by a confluence of events: the slow evolution of the game, as well as the wealth of his Ohio recruiting base—and how good he was at talking to the young players who'd never seen anything like him before, especially sitting on their living room couches.

In the decade beginning with 1954, he laid claim to three national titles. With his formidable 1968 team—historically one of college football's greatest—he added a fourth. He was now, officially, "Woody Hayes, Legend." The downside of becoming a legend is that one must remain legendary. If we disregard the aberrant 1971 season, then from 1968 through 1975 he had seven seasons with a total of just three regular season losses. Depending upon one's evaluation, however, Woody may have left as many as four national titles on the field. He was, in other words, chasing his own legend.

He'd set expectations that couldn't possibly be met, even by himself. It was his legacy to Ohio State's most fervent fans. By this time the game, no longer "brutally unambiguous and straightforward," was passing him by. He should have retired with his 1975 team, unbeaten and No. 1, and heavily favored to beat UCLA, which Ohio State had already done earlier in the season. But erratic play-calling doomed the Buckeyes, and Woody stayed on until that other erratic moment, this one in the 1978 Gator Bowl when, sick and weary, he punched a Clemson nose guard. It cost him two fifteen-yard penalties and his sporting life.

So he didn't leave the game on his own terms. But he'd done everything else that way. Nearly half a century onward, his place in the Ohio State firmament is still secure. You can dent a legend, but you don't retire one. A legend *abides*.

Feafully and wonderfully made

Wayne Woodrow Hayes and his culture

We can only imagine what contemporary currents swirled about—and possibly invigorated—the young pup that Woodrow Hayes was in the 1920s, growing up in Newcomerstown, Ohio. He was all of eleven years old when Grantland Rice wrote about the Four Horsemen of Notre Dame, thereby creating the most ballyhooed piece of sportswriting in the history of the profession. Woody would surely have read about The Horsemen even in Newcomerstown, for The Golden Age of Sports had reached even that most unassuming of Midwestern outposts.

The period, in fact, was a kind of prototype for the Digital Age; here, though, the streaming device was the radio, and it made the 1920s as novel and almost as unruly as our own. Through the radio receiver, a panoply of sports figures romped into living rooms everywhere. Conversation around the water coolers of America was forever altered and a public fascination with sports figures would grow throughout the century until these figures occupied—

along with entertainers and the very wealthy—what passed for royalty in a country otherwise without one. The revolution of the twenties wasn't immediately recognized, but it was one in which sports merged with entertainment and big business. The old school concept of "the gentleman athlete" was dismissed as being hopelessly out of date.

But what Newcomerstown kid could see all that? What he *did* see, however, was the athlete himself, who had been elevated into that airy realm previously occupied by business titans, presidents, and generals. The name "Babe Ruth," for instance, was likely known in Newcomerstown's most isolated domicile. The Babe was an unabashed sybarite and thereby a grand representative of the emerging consumer society. He consumed everything, most notably baseball pitchers but also beer, hot dogs, and women. The sportswriter Paul Gallico called him "an American Porthos, a swashbuckler built on gigantic and heroic lines, a great athlete, a Golem-like monster, a huge, vital, vulgar fellow in whose bosom surge all the well-known elementary emotions..."

Gallico's prose came right out of the Gee Whiz School of Sportswriting which was the dominant form for sports over several decades and described by Stanley Frank—who was not always an adherent—as "when breathless adjectives were laid on with a trowel." Gallico himself ultimately repented by leaving sportswriting for the more empyreal enclaves of fiction, saying in departure, "We sing of their muscles, their courage, their gameness and skill because it seems to amuse readers and sells papers..."

Woody would have liked this kind of uncritical prose—sentimental, forgiving, effusive—and his admitted propensity for hero-worship may well have begun here, for he would have read about Notre Dame (whose Horsemen were, in reality, an undersized backfield of guys who probably wouldn't have made any of Woody's Ohio State teams), and being himself a baseball player, he would have followed the exploits of The Babe.

The radio had brought home—in often spectacular ornamentation—the exploits of this new species of humanity, the media-embraced athlete. The twenties were filled with other unsettling ideas, even in Ohio where, to counter the nefarious influences of bathtub gin and late-night automobile rides, the state legislature took on women's fashion and proposed a décolletage limit of two inches. In the Midwest, anyway, the female breast was still considered a utilitarian instrument, and most of a half century would pass before it would be, in a manner of speaking, liberated.

Even so, the larger universe had come to even pastoral Newcomerstown. It was amplified by the magazines of the day, such as *Collier's* and the *Saturday Evening Post*, which featured college football on its covers and diatribes by Jock Sutherland, the great Pitt coach of the twenties and thirties. Sutherland said Pitt was "a sock-it-to-'em school" that had little use for passing, which he said was "an attempt to sissify a man's game." Power football built character, he said, which Woody would echo two decades later, as though he'd been personally instructed by Sutherland, which, courtesy of the *Saturday Evening Post*, he might have been.

Sports fiction had become a distinct pulp genre, too, and the football pulps were given to coaching stereotypes: the authoritarian whiplash who belonged to the Piss-and-Vinegar School of Coaching, and the kindly father figure (often called "Pop") who saw the players as his extended family. The kid from Newcomerstown certainly read some of these, and if he was influenced by them, it happened in equal measure: Woody absorbed *both* types, thus accomplishing in real life what fiction couldn't.

HE WAS ALWAYS A READER, A TOUGH GUY WITH AN EGGHEAD STREAK, AND HIS OLDER SISTER remembered him carrying around a small pocket dictionary. It was a quirk that followed him to Ohio State where he required his freshmen to read a little book called *Word Power Made Easy*, then to their amusement—and dismay—quizzed them. Once, bathing after practice, he said, "This shower is innervating!" Then he demanded that defensive back Bruce Smith define it. (He couldn't, of course.)

Hard to say what literature came within Woody's purview. He could have come across *The Great Gatsby* but a book about

Long Island swells wasn't his kind of story and, given his age, he was not yet "privy to the secret griefs of wild, unknown men." (It was the kind of phrase that, given time, would sound suspiciously like a lineman's longing to be a running back.) Both T.S. Eliot and William Faulkner were unfathomable, and Sinclair Lewis too cynical. Woody would have agreed with the opening sentence of *Main Street* when Lewis wrote, "Main Street is the climax of civilization." But desolate Gopher Prairie wasn't the small town Woody knew. He probably read some Zane Grey, for Grey grew up not far from Newcomerstown, and like Woody he was both irascible (see: *Word Power Made Easy*) and a brawler. If Woody didn't read Thomas Wolfe, he would have admired the protean spirit of Wolfe, which Pat Conroy called "the kiss-my-ass school of American writing," and he would certainly have bought into Wolfe's notion of making "the rude and painful substance of his own experience" into what Wolfe called "the essential pattern."

Woody's essential pattern was set early, his personal makeup part of the DNA of Newcomerstown itself. In the thirties, with the national economy devastated, the world of Newcomerstown was relatively untouched, its people cautious, conservative, and self-sufficient as any. It was the decade of military strongmen whom Woody was, no doubt, already studying. And through sports, he already had a perception of his own strength, physical and otherwise. He had his own notion of order, too, and how he might apply himself to a disorderly world. (It seems fair to add that Roosevelt's New Deal held little appeal for him. Roosevelt played polo, for goodness sakes. And lawn tennis. And he *sailed*.)

There were other convulsions in the old order during Woody's formative years. There was the Great Depression, but he was sheltered away at Denison. The perceptive Michael Oriard, a former football player turned English professor, saw this time as the critical juncture between a farm and village society moving into "the modern commercialized, consumerist, and mechanized mass society of the metropolis." The older America—Woody's America—would soon be gone forever.

Denison, though, was something like Newcomerstown, in that both were at remove from the outside world—and located in a small town so iconic it still seems caught in a nineteenth-century time warp. At Denison, boys played for the scenery, and even today its stadium is one of the grand Saturday afternoon venues for watching college football. But outside such sanctuaries, the forces of industrialism and urbanism were building. They wouldn't erase Woody's own experiences, but they would make the inward-turning values of the small town less applicable to the world he'd inherit.

The older idea of the sporting universe was changing, too. Early in the century, progressives saw organized physical activity as the basis for a unified national culture. They thought this culture could, as they said, "produce good citizens and able leaders, inculcate liberal tenets, and convert immigrants into 'Americans.'" It was an optimistic vision of America with sports as a kind of secular religion in which the dehumanizing fractures of rapid mechanization would be checked, outlets for community enlarged, and a wholesome democracy enhanced.

IT IS DOUBTFUL THAT WOODY, AT SUCH AN EARLY AGE, PARTICIPATED IN SUCH ACADEMIC FORMULATIONS. He would, though, have sided with the progressives on the issue of sports creating "good citizens and able leaders." It was something he was fervent about. For he believed that his players were going out to be exactly that. He, like that other great sportsman, Teddy Roosevelt, believed in "the doctrine of the strenuous life."

Only late in his life, some years removed from coaching, did he question the direction collegiate football was taking. John Lombardo, in his good book, *A Fire to Win*, said Woody's obsession with football had by this time faded. "I worry about the game getting out of hand," he said. "I do. I really do. The money involved, the over-commercialization…"

The old theme of purity that ran through the sports biographies of Woody's adolescence posited an athlete who triumphed by inspiration, hard work, and clean living. It was the kind of athlete Woody was—and the kind he wanted to coach. The notion of sports as a progressive force, though, was already headed in another direction. Its high-minded, reformist tenets were being shanghaied by the emerging sophistication of Madison Avenue, and big business had a sharp and possessive eye on how sports could be monetized. Ohio State, in fact, was at its forefront, having built one of the largest stadiums in America, and this alone announced the university's intentions of running a big-business football program.

Even in the 1920s, with Woody still in high school, the influential Carnegie Report said intercollegiate sports had become unmoored from what it called "principled amateurism." The report criticized aggressive recruiting, alumni subsidies to players, and an overall commercialism that fostered "a negligent attitude toward the educational opportunities for which the college exists."

The Carnegie influence didn't appear to reach Ohio State where, in the twenties, it built new tennis courts, baseball fields, tracks, and added nearly two million dollars of improvements to the stadium. By the start of the 1930s, few public universities had athletic incomes larger than Ohio State's.

At first, it appeared as though the Depression wouldn't impact Ohio State, but even as Woody sojourned at Denison, Ohio State was forced into belt-tightening. By mid-decade, students were protesting the cancellation of subscriptions to academic periodicals and the closing of the library cloakroom. This resulted in students tossing their hats and jackets on the floor, which gave the place "the appearance of an ill-kept warehouse." Over two hundred positions were abolished, most of them from the teaching staff. "The bitter medicine stage has been supplanted by amputation," said one commentator.

Ohio State president George Rightmire threatened the state legislature with canceling the 1936 football season if the university didn't receive more funding. The governor, Martin Davey, wouldn't have any of it, though, and by the end of the decade—Woody was coaching at New Philadelphia High—Ohio State's financial condition had improved. The university no longer had to lease the golf course land for the grazing of livestock.

Finally, there was the war, the ultimate molder of Woody's personality. He had always been a fighter, and now he was looking for a different kind of opponent than merely another schoolyard brawler. He was not exactly like his hero General Patton who believed that in previous lives he had been, among other things, a Roman legionary and a Napoleonic warrior. But like Patton, he had a martial spirit. With his wartime experiences as commander of a destroyer escort, his love of military history was made manifest. And there would be no more militant coach, for Woody saw the gridiron almost literally as a field of fire. To him, even the vocabularies of war and football became interchangeable.

Woody fought the culture, too, in a losing battle to restore the order of that older America into which he'd been born. Unlike his encounters on the football field, though, he'd lose this fight. For he believed in a world that no longer existed, if it ever had. His was the ultimate romance of a pragmatic man who was not otherwise romantic.

> Woody could take a guy with a wooden leg and make him run a hundred-yard dash. —Jim Parker, tackle

The dynasty begins

General Sherman in La-La Land

A FREEZING DRIZZLE OF COMMENTARY FELL OVER OHIO STADIUM AT THE END OF 1953 AND PERSISTED WELL INTO 1954. There was instability in the Columbus atmosphere all winter, and by early spring the entire city was supersaturated with theory, all squalls and blowing spray. Disturbances were the order of the day, and there were wind advisories in every High Street bar.

The critics felt Woody was trifling with their affection, and his undistinguished 6–3 record in 1953 was no way to keep it. In his three years in Columbus, he'd never finished better than third in the Big Ten, he'd been blanked by Michigan twice, and OSU hadn't won in Ann Arbor since 1937. The last Michigan game had been, as the Cleveland *Plain Dealer* reported, "painfully inept." There were five interceptions and a fumble. Fumbling was particularly galling to Woody; he understood that throwing the ball might result in an interception, but fumbling was a character flaw; he said it was "antisocial."

Woody was no more pleased with his slow start than anyone else, but such starts were habitual with him—witness his tenure at Denison and Miami. He was so unhappy with his first three games in 1951—win, loss, tie—that he forbade his players to sing in the shower. Now, two years later, on a pleasant summer evening, Woody was on his porch in Upper Arlington while one of his neighbors was having a gathering, and he heard someone say, "This is the year we get rid of Woody."

It was a nice little grievance for Woody, or as he would say, "It always helps to have a chip on your shoulder." Although by this time, he was probably believing some of the things he was hearing about himself. His staff was unhappy, too; Woody's niggling attempt to control everything was driving them batty. Perhaps all this unhappiness made him receptive to athletic director Dick Larkins's suggestion that he hire Lyal Clark to run the defense. The inside accounts implied it was more than a suggestion. It was something like the memorable exchange between father and son in the Ring Lardner story that went: "'Shut up,' he explained."

To his credit, Woody understood some of what had been happening. He'd never worked under a big-time coach and he was used to doing everything himself. "I supervised more than I coached," he said, "and I managed to get into everyone's way."

THERE WERE TWO CONSPICUOUS MOMENTS IN THE 1954 SEASON: (1) THE ARRIVAL OF CLARK, one of the country's best defensive coaches, who had come to work for a guy who hadn't actually chosen him, and (2) Clark's defense, which—flash forward—held Michigan at the six-inch line and preserved a perfect season. It took the latter moment, though, to validate the former one, and who could have seen it coming? That latter moment was off in the future at a time when the faithful weren't even sure there'd *be* a future.

One thing, there didn't seem to be a quarterback—John Borton had been injured and was an uncertain commodity—and the pundits picked OSU to finish fifth in the Big Ten. The players sensed otherwise; they could see the talent, both extant and emerging. It was, all in all, a remarkable confluence of boys about to be men, and they emerged in the presence of each other.

There was the gifted junior halfback, Howard "Hopalong" Cassady, a hometown boy who'd come out of the poor west side Columbus neighborhood known as The Bottoms and in another year would win the Heisman. There was the understudy quarterback, Dave Leggett, who'd taken over after Borton was hurt and played his new position like the fullback he once was. He was a big rugged guy and the *Washington Post*, watching him call his own number, said, with admiration, "There's no sneak at all in his quarterback sneaks..."

Leggett was one more moment of serendipity in a season of them: who better to run Woody's ground-based offense than an old fullback? It was a notion made in Woody's particular heaven, that place where the angels wore cleats, had a quick first step, and considered wings an affectation.

Then there were the two sophomores, an unusually big African-American named Jim Parker who would turn out to be one of the greatest linemen ever at Ohio State. (In time, he would be one of the greatest linemen *anywhere*—the first fulltime offensive lineman in the Pro Football Hall of Fame.) Woody found him working in a Toledo parking garage and persuaded him to come to Columbus.

The other was Hubert Bobo, a small-town kid from Chauncey, Ohio, described by *Sports Illustrated* as "a handsome, Atlas-type fullback." Bobo, it was reported, had promised to "put Chauncey on the map," and indeed, after more than half a century, Bobo still held three Ohio prep scoring records, including most career points—890—and most career touchdowns—123. Bobo's diligence seemed to apply largely to the football field and, by his own admission, he remained eligible largely by the diligence of four tutors, which Bobo called "a modern indoor record."

So there was more to this 1954 crew than met the jaundiced eye of either critics or the fan base (who were often one and the same); both groups had the Buckeyes unranked when they opened the season. Five weeks later, everyone had been silenced but Woody; his boys were ranked No. 4, and they were playing Wisconsin in Ohio Stadium. The Badgers were bringing along a No. 1 ranking and a thoroughbred fullback, Alan "The Horse" Ameche, who in a couple of months would be the new Heisman winner.

Were Woody's boys impressed?

Not that anyone could tell.

They were behind at halftime, 7–3, then late in the third quarter, Cassady made all the sportswriters—most of whom came to see Ameche—sit up and take notice. He intercepted Wisconsin quarterback Jim Miller at the OSU 12 and took it to the house. He made an incredible cut (you can see it on YouTube), after which Cassady's teammate Dick Brubaker, commenting on the defensive player, would say, "His jock strap is still on the field somewhere."

The play was voted "The No. 1 Football Thrill" by an AP panel and went immediately into the Ohio State image bank of great plays. Better yet, it cemented Cassady's bid as All-American and, given his audience, put him at the forefront of the Heisman hunt for the next season. OSU scored three more times in the fourth quarter and the Buckeyes won 31–14. The Horse got an un-Horse-like 42 yards and, as good as he was, never scored a TD against OSU.

The play was emblematic of the season, during which one player or another arose at exactly the right moment and changed the course of the game. The Bucks were now the top team in the country, and their rise from nowhere to No. 1 would be an AP record for sixty years.

Ohio State slipped by stubborn Northwestern (the 14–7 squeaker momentarily cost the Bucks their No. 1 ranking), had easy afternoons with Purdue and Pittsburgh, and were once again No. 1—and poised for the all-important homestand with 6–2 Michigan. There were more than 82,000 in the Horseshoe, with an estimated eighty million viewers in ABC's television audience, and scalpers were selling the few tickets they had for $30 (the equivalent of about $700 today).

Michigan scored on its first possession and, as *Sports Illustrated* would report, "Things looked bright for the forces of evil." The game was tied, 7–7, early in the fourth when Michigan drove to OSU's goal line, only to be met with a ferocious defense led by the sophomore Parker. There, fourth-and-goal, the Buckeyes stopped Michigan's fullback at the six-inch line. Buckeye historians rank it as one of the monumental defensive plays, right there with the 2003 Fiesta Bowl's fourth-and-one, double-overtime stonewall against Miami for the national title.

What came next was even better for the home folks: Leggett, standing in his own end zone, calmly took over. Said the writer John Lombardo, commenting on Leggett's precarious position: "It was still better than having to stand next to Hayes on the sideline." Leggett kept the ball three times for a first down on the 11 (technically, the 10- and-a-half), faked to Bobo and handed off to Cassady, who slipped outside and went 52 yards down the sideline before being forced out at the Michigan 37.

The ensuing score—with this group, surely—was preordained: 14–7. When Michigan came back late, Cassady intercepted on the 38 and with seconds left, he scored OSU's final TD to make the score 21–7. Cassady's running balance, said the *Washington Post*, "is almost superhuman." Up in the press box, as the final minutes ticked off, ticket director George Staten sprayed rose-scented perfume into the air-conditioning system, annoying several sportswriters who now had to explain the perfume to their wives.

THE TEAM HAD ONE OPPONENT LEFT, BUT WOODY HAD SEVERAL. On the way in from the Los Angeles airport, his first opponent was the scenery. Depending upon whose account you believed, it was either the palm trees or the bronzed California women pointed out by his quarterback, Leggett. "Goddamn it, Dick," Woody said, "we're not here for the sights." Next up were the West Coast writers—the beginning of a longstanding feud—and finally, he managed to insult his host team, USC.

His boys, though, having proved their resourcefulness through a tough schedule that featured five nationally-ranked opponents, weren't about to be stymied by the old man. Somehow they managed to elude both bedcheck and Woody's wider scrutiny. They sneaked off to Tijuana, and once Leggett himself stayed out all night, returning just as practice started. He was saved only by quick-thinking trainers who stuffed him in a large footlocker until they could get him safely on the field.

His profligate nights out only seemed to bolster his performance. He ran for 67 yards and completed six passes, keeping USC constantly off balance with his option running. In a season when most things had gone right for OSU, even the vaunted California sunshine disappeared. The game was played in a downpour, conditions that favored the inlanders: Leggett took eighty snaps and never fumbled, and his offense rolled up 370 yards. USC, meanwhile, acted as though it had never seen inclement weather, and the OSU defense, led by Parker, who was finally healthy, forced seven fumbles.

Woody praised his team by climbing on a locker and saying, "See, boys. That's what clean-living will do for you." The boys, particularly Leggett, who was the game's MVP, looked knowingly at each other and laughed.

Woody told the writers that there were about five teams in the Big Ten that could have beaten USC, and USC's coach, Jess Hill, said, "A winning coach can make that statement. I'd still say I'd like to meet 'em on a dry field." There was another minor controversy because the undefeated UCLA Bruins—ranked at the end of the season as No. 1 by UPI—had been locked out of the Rose Bowl, due to their conference's no-repeat rule. The Bruins had smothered USC, 34–0, and some said an OSU-UCLA game, featuring for the first time in Rose Bowl history two undefeated, untied teams, would surely have been the greatest Rose Bowl ever.

That game was never played, though, and so the beef came largely from the West Coast. (The *Los Angeles Times* had reported in November, when one of the Columbus papers ran a story on UPI ranking the Bruins No. 1, that pitchfork-wielding locals had turned out in protest. Whatever the protest, it was seen back home as merely a patriotic display.) The kingmaker, AP, put Ohio State as its No. 1, and the coaches' association threw a sop to UCLA by naming the Bruins' Red Sanders as their coach of the year, with Woody second.

It didn't seem to bother him. No matter how one looked at it, Woody was at the apogee of his profession. There wouldn't be many moments this good. There would be better teams at the university, but there might not be another one with better chemistry. There was a saying back in Columbus: good teams have talent; great teams have talent and luck—and Hopalong Cassady.

Cassady would be back in 1955, along with Jim Parker. Lyal Clark, whose defense forced thirty-five turnovers and allowed only 7.5 points a game, would be back and he'd stay for a dozen years. Most important of all, though, Woody was back, filled with new resolve—and impetuosity.

But there was fresh trouble in paradise.

The end of innocence

Woody and the great divide

PICTURE CHARLES DICKENS WRITING ABOUT THE 1961 SEASON IN COLUMBUS: "IT WAS THE BEST OF TIMES," HE MIGHT HAVE SAID, "it was the worst of times, we had everything before us, we had nothing before us, we were all going direct to Pasadena, and we were all going direct the other way." Woody was undefeated that year, his record marred only by an unsightly opening game tie with lowly Texas Christian University, but by November the Bucks were back with a vengeance, witness the Thanksgiving game in Ann Arbor when they devastated Michigan 50–20. Next up: the Rose Bowl, and because of a longstanding confluence of events—in both Columbus and elsewhere—it would be the only time Woody lost a Rose Bowl without actually being in it.

Because of the close and competitive national scene, that early tie with TCU had cost OSU another title. (Said a Texas writer after the tie, "We don't know where Hayes went to college, but he must have majored in monotony.") Before the TCU game, the Bucks had been ahead of Alabama, but afterward the Crimson Tide never faltered, winning the first of Bear Bryant's six national titles. Still, all was well in America's football capital as OSU finished No. 2—with roses in the offing. Then the unthinkable: OSU's faculty council voted against going. "Buckeyes finally lose, 28–25, in bowl debate," read a *Toledo Blade* headline and, added the venerable *Saturday Review*, "The scent of roses vanished from the air of Columbus, and over the city and the campus settled the acrid odor of ashes."

There was an outpouring of rampant unhappiness in which the university president Novice G. Fawcett was hanged in effigy, along with alumni secretary Jack Fullen, a longtime Rose Bowl critic. In two days of protests, several thousand students marched on the statehouse, smashed the glass door to the faculty club, tossed firecrackers, rocked cars, and lit a bonfire. (At some point, it was reported that students also commandeered a streetcar, among them an upstart basketball player named Bobby Knight.) The faculty was branded as a nest of Communists, and one letter writer asked plaintively, "Cannot something be done to see to it these little people not hinder the football team in the future?"

The two sides were thus drawn, although it was a moment that had been several years in the making. Football's rising fortunes had created nervousness among many academics. They complained of funding shortfalls, the migration of top faculty members, and a decline in academic rankings. Matters were not helped when the campus was visited by Leverett Saltonstall, a Massachusetts senator, who said, "All I knew before coming here was that the university has a great football team."

As far back as June of 1955, the faculty—already termed "restive"—set up the Fullington Committee, headed by English prof James Fullington, to report on intercollegiate athletics at Ohio State. Its work was surely colored by the happenstance of what came next. That fall, Woody Hayes told a *Sports Illustrated* writer about how he helped his players if they were "in need." No one who had any real understanding of the coach believed that his help was anything other than humanitarian, whether it was money for a new pair of shoes or a few dollars to help out one of his players. But even such "humanitarian" aid violated Big Ten rules.

The careful reader will recall that this was the era before the NCAA had codified athletic grants; prior to the mid-1950s assistance might be anything from tuition to new siding on the house of a player's parents. Then, aid for athletes—*legitimate* aid—was the same as it was for any other student: be in the top third of your high school class or, once in college, get yourself a 2.5 grade point average. Woody's All-American tackle, Jim Parker, talked about being so hungry at Ohio State that he and his roommate followed the milk truck around, waiting for a chance to swipe a carton of milk. Surely it would have been better for Woody to have *bought* him milk. The Big Ten said otherwise.

Unfortunately, the story—"The Ohio State Story: Win or Else"—created something of a national scandal. It alerted the NCAA and the Big Ten (who could no longer look the other way, which both had obviously been doing), and early in 1956 the Big Ten came in and immediately stumbled into the athletic department's "jobs-for-jocks" program. (It was a *Casablanca* moment, as when corrupt Captain Renault feigned outrage at finding gambling in Rick's Café Américain. "I'm shocked, *shocked*, to find gambling is going on in here," he says, while making off with his winnings.)

The jobs-for-jocks was how the school aided its athletes—by finding them work, both on campus and around town. The jobs—the legitimate ones—were part of an old practice; Jesse Owens had one as elevator operator in the 1930s before graduating to a better one as a page in the state legislature, and Governor Martin Davey in 1936, under pressure to secure more funding for the university, pushed back by saying the legislature had done its part, "because we have most of the football squad on the state payroll." In the 1950s, Jim Parker cleaned the coaches' offices (which was probably an *illegitimate* job).

The local chamber of commerce administered about eighty jobs, each of which supposedly required some fifteen hours a week, paying $100 a month for ten months (the cost for a year at Ohio State in 1956 was about $1,300). The best jobs, of course, came from wealthy alumni. The problem at OSU, investigators found, was that some of the jobs didn't exist or, if they did, no one worked them. Upwards of half were called into question. And it was a loose institutional practice that led to other likely infringements. (Robert Vare, in his book *Buckeye*, reported, for instance, a story of an athletic committeeman who sold his two-year-old Cadillac to an OSU quarterback for five dollars.)

There were three immediate results to the investigation: (1) Ohio State went on probation; (2) the ire of faculty members was raised even higher; and (3) there would also be no *Sports Illustrated* writers in the house anytime in the near future—the episode permanently cemented in place Woody's adversarial relationship with the media.

The Fullington Committee finished its report in early 1957 and it was adopted in November, its major import being that control of athletics was placed with a faculty council. This occurred a month after the stunning news that Russia had launched Sputnik I, the world's first artificial satellite. While Sputnik was not much bigger than a volleyball, its impact on the world was outsized; it ushered in the space age—and an unprecedented technological race between the U.S. and the U.S.S.R.

America had been upstaged, and the resulting national clamor wouldn't have been louder if Sputnik itself had dropped into Ohio Stadium at halftime. (When the Soviet premier, Nikita Khrushchev, came to America in 1959, folks in Ohio said he needed to see the Buckeyes play. That way, they said, he'd understand "the real spirit of America.") This news of Sputnik likely gave a final nudge to the Fullington Commission's adoption. Academics, at least for the moment, had upstaged athletics. The new engagement between the Americans and the Soviets was seen as exemplifying two things: (1) the need for a new academic seriousness, and/or (2) the need for a new physical toughness.

It was also a time when sports metaphors took on high purpose and were flung all about the landscape. One of the university's language professors, perhaps looking askance at the new athletic scholarships—and maybe Woody himself—was paraphrased as saying, "Give me eighty Spanish scholarships and in four years I'll beat the ass off the University of Madrid." Others pointed out the disappointing induction rates during WWII: of the first two million men chosen, 45 percent were rejected as unfit. Thus football was seen as a restorative tonic. Even the evangelist Billy Graham got into the metaphorical act, calling Christ "the prototypical linebacker" and saying that He would have been the star of any team (even if His only recorded sport was fishing).

Woody in 1957 was not distracted by any of the national discourse. His Buckeyes went 9–1, beat Michigan in Ann Arbor; edged Oregon in the Rose Bowl; then were named No. 1 by the UPI Coaches Poll (they shared the title with AP's No. 1, Auburn, which went undefeated). With the aforementioned as background, the Rose Bowl vote of 1961 occurred and while it shouldn't have surprised anyone, it did.

"The frustrations and anxieties over the crises, scandals, and confrontations of the previous six years poured forth in a rhetorical bloodletting that took a mere ninety minutes," said the sports historian Kurt Kemper about the brief faculty vote. And in all the ensuing hubbub, the most astounding moment was proffered by that exemplar of restraint, Woody himself, who took no role in the agitations, showing instead a remarkable calm he surely did not feel.

"I don't agree with those twenty-eight 'no' votes," he said, "but I respect the integrity of the men who cast them, if not their intelligence. I would not want football to draw a line of cleavage in our university. Football is not worth that." It was perhaps his finest university hour.

Given the historically amiable nature of Columbus students—as opposed to, say, the woollier denizens of Ann Arbor—it all seemed less of a riot and more of an excuse to misbehave a little and get some fresh air. The pro Rose Bowl faction displayed elevated testosterone levels, while the anti-faction unleashed its long-standing vexation at what it saw as the heightened powers of campus philistinism. "We have a tailor-made opportunity to destroy the image of being the football capital," sniffed a professor of philosophy, evoking howls of outrage from the other side of the campus.

There were few neutral observers in Columbus during the late fall and winter of 1961, and never had the barbershops of Columbus been besieged by the presentation of so much evidence, although most of it was anecdotal rather than evidentiary. The pro-Rose Bowl fans, while boisterously loud, saw football as completing the university experience; the anti-Rose Bowl contingent disliked the glorification of intercollegiate football. Many of the latter, particularly with the advent of a new technological challenge from the Soviet Union, had legitimate questions about academic life.

Others were imbued with disaffection, it seemed, for having found themselves in Columbus. They were a counterpoint for the outrage of Rose Bowl fans, and their expression was wonderfully put forth by one of their own, a liberal arts professor named Harry Jaffe who, in the repose of both time and distance, wrote about his campus confederates in the fall of 1961. "Most of those professors were not Ohioans and had earned their doctorates at Ivy League universities," he said. "They regarded Columbus, Ohio, as a kind of frontier outpost where they were temporarily exiled. Woody and his Saturday circus, they regarded as a Neanderthal ritual of the natives, from which they shudderingly held aloof.

"What they resented most of all was what happened when they went abroad, anxious to tell the world of culture and light about the success of their fastidious efforts to preserve the purity of their souls amidst the bourgeois barbarism of Columbus. But the world of culture and light, alas, was often more interested in hearing about Woody and the team. Pity the plight of the poor literary scholar, who has labored years to produce a monograph on *The Use of the Circumflex in the Early Provençal Chanson*. He arrives at the meeting of the PMLA, burning with the fire of anticipated recognition, only to discover that his professional colleagues, once having done their professional duty, turn the talk once again in the direction of Woody…"

The banner of the fans was carried by the *Columbus Dispatch*, which erupted in a spate of boosterism hidden under the rubric of the public's right to know and printed the names and addresses of the faculty members who'd voted "no." In the process, it got some wrong and subjected all of them to obscene phone calls.

The *Dispatch* asked rhetorically if Ohio State would be better off not going to the Rose Bowl, then answered itself by saying, "Only in the minds of a few narrow, overly sensitive minds, perhaps." This prompted the outspoken alumni secretary Jack Fullen to suggest more scholarships for journalism students, which, he said, "would produce editorial writers who were less gullible."

(Interestingly, when Hayes asked the team to vote—he wanted them on record as wishing to go—some of them *didn't* want to go. "I think guys were sort of fed up with the way we worked out and practiced all the time," said quarterback John Mummey. Halfback Paul Warfield wouldn't say how he voted, but he was less than enthusiastic. "I was a little homesick," he said. "I'd gone through my first year on the varsity. It was Christmas time…the Rose Bowl was a great post-season event, but I'd describe my feelings as ambivalent.")

Fullen was no stranger to controversy. He was an early and hearty supporter of Woody when the coach had few of them. He'd created a prosperous development fund for the university, and he himself was an old jock who'd won an intercollegiate boxing title as an OSU student (which perhaps explained his own pugnacious nature). He was also a football fan and seldom missed a game. Over time, though, he'd become aggrieved by what he saw as the rising commercial entanglements of football, which to his mind created an imbalance with the school's academic mission. At one point, he suggested the university simply hire professional players who'd work under something he called "a bureau of football." His famous quote was "the football tail is wagging the college dog."

He was a longtime critic of the Rose Bowl, too, which he saw as a large economic sop to Pasadena businessmen. He pointed out how fans reserving hotel rooms had to buy five nights when they needed only three. "Pawns for the enterprise," he said. What Fullen failed to see, though, was that inveterate urge of Ohio State fans to follow their team—and they saw the Rose Bowl as the grandest of pilgrimages.

Fullen and Woody were the recognizable and opposing figures throughout what was called by one observer, "the fall ferment of 1961." Yet they were also complementary, although neither of them had the proper distance to see how they were. For one thing, they both considered themselves educators. Woody liked many of the academics, and he was pleased to count himself among them. Beneath the fearsome rhetoric—on both sides—was the overlooked notion of Woody's own peculiar sense of democracy. He was an autocrat on the field, yet he thought a university could have standards and *still* let everyone in. They just had to measure up, and he would see to it. He was an elitist of the windsprint and the blocking sled, and while those were not talents possessed by all, neither were those required by Post-Kantian German Idealism, Linguistic Analysis, or—God forbid—Opera Chorus.

Woody was firmly in the original tradition of the land-grant universities such as Ohio State, whose vaulting ambition was to educate *everybody*. His best case-in-point was the great athlete—and impoverished student—Jim Parker. Raised in a Georgia shack, Parker was not prepared for high school, much less college, but Woody's stance was that he'd not only whip Parker into shape, he'd educate him, too. There was an academic point of view—based on scholastic aptitude not race—which would have left Parker perpetually cleaning offices, because it could not see him as an upward bound student. Forgive those who saw a hint of elitism in the academic rationale.

Woody, to his credit (and the university's), was shanghaiing players with unsatisfactory grades into his house and making them live with him and Anne—egad!—until their GPA moved up. He harangued players until they got a degree. (Even if it took nearly fifty years, as it did with tackle Dick Schafrath who left Ohio State without a degree in 1958 and finally got it in 2006, demonstrating that Woody's influence persisted even from the beyond.)

The coach lost a small battle in 1961—his Bucks didn't go to the Rose Bowl—but he won the larger war: there was quick politicking that made sure the Faculty Council would never cancel another Rose Bowl trip. There were those who thought Woody's naïve remarks to *Sports Illustrated* back in 1955 were the cause of the lost bowl, but they can be excused for not seeing more important results. One, the 1961 council vote represented, as the *Journal of Sport History* wrote, "the last gasp of significant faculty influence over athletic policy. For proponents of big-time football, the Rose Bowl rejection had been only a tiny bump on the pathway to complete domination of policy-making at most major American Universities." And, second, there was the October 1961 Big Ten ruling which established—for the first time—true athletic scholarships.

Jack Fullen didn't like athletic scholarships any more than he liked the Rose Bowl, but the old system was untenable and had been for some time. The Southern colleges had instituted outright football scholarships back in the 1930s. They'd found the Northern "jobs-for-jocks" system both untenable and hypocritical. They said their economically depressed economy left them without jobs and wealthy donors and, moreover, they disliked the moral superiority of the Northerners who used those jobs and donors to subsidize football, all the while commending themselves for their staunch amateurism. Full athletic scholarships were a foregone conclusion; they'd been so since the arrival of Ohio Stadium back in the 1920s, which plainly announced the evolving business of football.

So Woody and Jack remained adversarial, two old boxers warily circling one another. Fullen, though, always professed admiration for his opponent. He said Woody was honest and courageous and a good coach. "I don't think there's ever been a better one," he said. His objection was simply—or not so simply—that the team was what he called "a professional athletic empire with a different set of values from the rest of the school."

Woody wasn't quite as generous. "That old prick," he snorted.

Here again, they shared similarities: they were both principled men but old-fashioned and out of date. Woody couldn't see football's evolving offenses. He'd have several more good teams but only one great one. Fullen couldn't see—or care to see—that he was a man with a bucket trying to thwart the rising tide.

When the *Dispatch's* Paul Hornung complained after that 1961 Rose Bowl vote that "the customers have been wronged," Woody's old public relations man-cum-sports editor was right about one thing. The fans of Ohio State *did* see themselves as customers. They wanted spectacles, of which the Rose Bowl was then the paramount one.

And the customer, as everyone knows, is always right.

Rules of the game

Woody, on the side of angels

LEST ONE PERSISTS IN VIEWING WOODY HAYES IN SOME TROGLODYTE FASHION, leave us review that momentous occasion when the old coach came down on the liberal side of one of mid-century football's most controversial arguments: the debate over limited substitution and one-platoon football. Before WWII, the college game was played by stalwart lads who came off the field only for the final score or Armageddon. (If you came off the field, you couldn't return to the game in the same quarter. That was the rule.) Thus the notion of the all-around athlete was buried deeply in the mythos of the sport and—according to anyone who'd ever pulled on a leather helmet—one-platoon football was how God wanted the game to be played. "Down and dirty football," *Sports Illustrated* called it, "before prissy wide receivers started streaking onto the field as play-carrying messengers and myriad other substitution travesties multiplied."

The travesties began in 1941, a result of wartime manpower scarcities—Ohio State's 1942 national title team, for instance, returned only five of thirty-nine players to Paul Brown, who started four freshmen in his 1943 backfield. (Freshmen playing varsity was another unhallowed wartime measure.) In 1941, football's brain trust relaxed the limited substitution rule, allowing a player to enter the game at any time. "Unlimited"—for the moment, anyway—simply meant that given the shortage of players, coaches could now substitute players of more measured abilities. They looked at their rosters and found, for instance, a player who could throw but couldn't play defense. So he came off the field and his roommate—who wasn't much on offense but played decent defense—went in at safety. The rules now let the coaches play to the various strengths of their players.

The brain trust saw it all as temporary; after the war unlimited substitution would be shelved and *real* football would be played again. What the gate-keepers didn't foresee, though, was how many coaches *liked* unlimited substitution. And among these unregenerate policy liberals was an unlikely adherent: Woody.

One-platoon football was voted back by the NCAA in 1953, its powerful rules committee loaded with die-hard traditionalists, largely older coaches who'd gone over to the dark side and become administrators. Their priorities, now as athletic directors, had shifted and money had become the overriding issue. Ray Eliot, the Illinois coach and proponent of two-platoon football who'd served on the rules committee, once said, "the shortest memory in the history of man is that of a football coach who becomes an athletic director." The rejoinder by the ADs was that the coaches didn't have to balance the books. And in their favor was the number of colleges that had by 1953 dropped football, citing expense as the reason.

So when the pre-war substitution rules came back in 1953 and the huzzahs went up from the game's old warhorses, Woody wasn't among them. The next year, he announced he'd simply field two different units. He thought he had enough depth for two units of equal talent, and—because a player who left the game couldn't return until the *next* quarter—Woody would replace the entire *unit*; he'd just alternate them in and out, splitting the quarters. He was proposing his own version of two-platoon football—*two* alternating units of two-way players. (It wasn't unique to Woody; he got it from that old Notre Dame warhorse Knute Rockne, who had used a two-unit attack back in the 1920s. He'd start his second-stringers, whom he called his Shock Troops, said to be the best second team in the country. After the "softening up," Rockne sent in his regular unit.)

Woody's version didn't really get implemented, though, probably because one of his two best quarterbacks, John Borton (the first quarterback in school history to throw for 1,500 yards in a season), was injured. And when the OSU passing game sputtered in 1954, Woody blamed the substitution ban; he said there wasn't enough coaching time in an ordinary practice session. "We simply cannot train a boy to play both offense and defense in that time," he said, adding that he was "thoroughly disgusted." Ultimately, none of it mattered, for Ohio State who—unranked in its season opener—rolled unimpeded through the season and beat USC decisively in the Rose Bowl to win the national title.

THE LIMITED SUBSTITUTION RULE MATTERED TO THE PROFESSION, THOUGH, and the two factions squared off: the old warhorses and their hardening-of-the-aptitude, versus the mostly younger guys who wanted to coach a more specialized game. What occurred was a bitter fight in the trenches that went on for more than a decade. The old boys even had *The New York Times* in their fold: that preeminent sports classicist Arthur Daley was incensed when the American Football Coaches Association in 1960 voted for unlimited substitution. He saw dollar signs, that is, more of everything: more coaches, more equipment, and more scholarships. ("For more muscular meatballs disguised as scholars," Daley groused.) And more cost. The preservationists on the NCAA's rules committee were still in charge—not the coaches—but the cataclysm had been let out of the bag.

With the advent of the 1960s, the NCAA, hearing footsteps, pretzeled a variety of "weird and overly complicated" substitution rules into being. The rules, said *Sports Illustrated*, had been fooled around with more than three dozen times since 1876, "often in horribly convoluted ways," and the rule-makers were now using convolution as a delaying action against unlimited substitution.

The 1960s also brought a quantum leap in exposure for the game, and this brought more knowledgeable fans who watched the NFL with its unlimited substitution and wished it upon college football. (One of the reasons the NCAA liked one-platoon football was that it was *unlike* the pro game, and it posited its players as amateurs, not professionals. By the end of the century, that would be one more discredited notion; by then, colleges and pros were *both* in the entertainment business.) The attempt to bring back one-platoon football was the last hurrah for what was known as "the classic college sports ideals," although who knew exactly what *that* meant?

In 1963, the rules committee passed a substitution rule that attempted to be as liberal as possible and *still* prohibit platoon football. Like most rules with restrictions and exceptions, this one specified that if you weren't confused, then you hadn't read it. Woody was disappointed again. After the season opened, some teams drew offside or delay-of-game penalties to stop the clock on fourth down so they could switch personnel. There were delays as players checked in with officials (critics called it "a cafeteria line"). In the Ohio State-Illinois game in 1963, one consultation over substitutes lasted five minutes.

In one of the later rules meeting, the old ironhead Bob Neyland, Tennessee athletic director and committee chairman, avoided a vote on unlimited substitution by grabbing the hand of the man next to him, thrusting it into the air along with his own while ignoring the votes against him, and saying, "There doesn't seem to be any sentiment to return to that chicken-shit football. Meeting adjourned." Frank Howard, the Clemson coach who'd been calling for a vote, so the story went, chased Neyland down the hall in objection but to no avail.

At one American Football Coaches Association meeting, Woody described the rule changes of the previous two years as "the damndest burlesque I ever saw in my life...the reason we got half-decent rules last year was for one reason, because the rules committee had blotched it up so bad the year before."

This made Frank Howard mad. He'd been working on rule compromises and no one seemed to be happy. He'd had a moment with old General Neyland, and now he was having one with Woody Hayes. (It wasn't as though Howard was an unregenerate liberal himself; after all, one of his most famous moments occurred when he forbid a crew team on Lake Hartwell by protesting, "We ain't never gonna have no sport here at Clemson where you sit on your ass and go backwards to win.")

Howard alluded to Woody's ability to dominate an argument by saying, "I think maybe you fellows lost your cause when you put Woody up there." And: "If he is for something, I am against it." The Clemson coach was still enough of a traditionalist to want his boys to know something about both sides of the ball. In this instance, at least, he remained with the old Tories on the rules committee. Except in very specific and largely antithetical moments, though, *that* game would not be the future.

When substitution was limited, a coach's choices were also limited; he had to give something up, and that something was complexity, i.e., passing. Because coaches could teach defensive play easier, defenses dominated in the 1950s, and the offenses, by and large, were run-based, because passing offenses required more practice time. Woody may have created football dogma out of "three yards and a cloud of dust," but that offense belonged to *everybody*, a natural consequence of limited substitution, and most sports historians look back at the era as dull and unimaginative. The wartime substitution rule, however, had enhanced the sport, and elevated the level of play. A game of specialties, such as evolved passing offenses and kicking units, was on its way.

Woody was not likely thinking of how, under unlimited substitution, he might create the country's most innovative passing offense, but he was surely thinking about a lesser discussed outcome. And that was: who controlled the game? Historically, the game belonged essentially to the players; it was a *student* game. Players, not the coaches, called the game, and during games, coaches had limited communication with their quarterbacks. It was what the old guard called "the educational values" for the players on the field. With unlimited substitution, though, coaches would of necessity have more control. The game would be firmly in their hands—another nail in the coffin that contained the supine body of the all-around athlete. And if there was a rule that gave him more control, then surely an old enforcer like Woody would like it.

The truth was, he was going to win either way. Unlimited substitution *did* provide difficulties for many schools. It would cost more, and not every school had Ohio State's resources. The traditionalists' argument for "educational values," though, was a spurious one. The entire world was becoming specialized. How was *not* becoming specialized a virtue? "Educational value" was the first arrow in the quiver of athletic rectitude, even as the argument worked both ways. (When Georgetown University shocked everyone by dropping football in 1951, its president, Hunter Guthrie, cited "educational reform," saying that funding football "would be like offering P. T. Barnum a chair in educational philosophy.")

In actuality, the traditional arguments were ultimately elitist, for the ideal player had to specialize on *both* sides of the ball. The wartime rule allowed less accomplished players to compete—and more of them, as well, which was something Woody liked—and it changed the very definition of excellence. "Players who might be of use in one phase of the game were now too valuable to be dismissed from the squad because of glaring weaknesses in the other phase," wrote Allison Danzig. A player could now be less accomplished in an all-around sense, although he would soon be required to be more accomplished in a specialized way. Free substitution was thus more democratic, even as it added costs. (It would be, in the future, about having as much democracy as you could afford.)

In 1964, even more leniency was added to the substitution rules, although it was not yet entirely unlimited. ("Virtual unlimited substitution," *The New York Times* called it.) "Just about no one really understood the 1963 law and practically every coach in college football inadvertently violated one of its provisions at some time during the season," said the *Harvard Crimson*, noting that the blighted rules and their complications may have cost Harvard the recent Ivy League Championship. Through all of it, noted Blackie Sherrod of the *Dallas Times Herald*, the rule-makers had been sliding up to unlimited substitution as if it were "a souvenir hand grenade in the attic trunk."

The year of occasion was 1965. The old system was finally gone, archived with other late college traditions such as flagpole sitting and telephone booth stuffing. As one observer pointed out, its return had lasted "about as long as the contents in the hip flask in a fan's pocket." And unlimited substitution was soon everything the traditionalists had feared: bigger squads, more personnel, more equipment, more professionalism—even bigger players, because a 300-pound lineman no longer had to play sixty minutes. Ultimately, the big boy himself would become a specialist, a cog in the defensive line as part of an eight-man rotation with defensive linemen specializing in pass rushing while others were run-stoppers. Even specialties would have specialists, as some teams carried both a kick-off specialist as well as a field goal specialist who was accompanied by his own specialist—the long snapper.

They joked about how with unlimited substitution, two teammates went through four years of college together and didn't meet. And now they never would, according to the logic of the old-timers. The quarterback would seldom call his own plays, either, as he once did. He'd become, as one coach later put it, "a joy stick in a video game." The good thing was that he no longer had to play safety.

The old boys had fought a tenacious rear-guard action but unlimited substitution was too attractive, in too many ways. They knew they would lose, but they fought on to preserve the sanctity of their backward mission, what they saw as the all-around student athlete and the game's proper perspective. And the economies. Given the money, there were points in their favor, for unlimited substitution was the last brick in the edifice of big-business-corporate football. In more ways than one, it would enlarge the game. "Without knowing it," wrote David Nelson, an authority on college football rules, "the committee had legislated a rule that would have as great a fallout and as many side effects as any rule ever enacted." There would soon be teams of over a hundred players and dozens of coaches, trainers, equipment managers, and support people. It would be an American institution, with the same at-large prerogatives to be big and monied. And that, to most observers today, *is* the proper perspective.

Woody's liberal moment is thus an interesting note in the game's evolution, although the return to illiberality in the 1950s—and its run-based offenses—ended with him entrenched in that era even as he opposed it. (So he contradicted himself, but as Whitman might have said of him, he was large; he contained multitudes.) When free substitution came back—and along with it more open offenses—Woody himself had *become* the old guard. In time, the game would push his offenses to become more creative than he wished, and so they would move past him.

His last great two-way player, Paul Warfield, graduated in 1964, which was also the end of the ironman era. There wasn't another two-way athlete of major consequence at Ohio State for nearly forty years, when Chris Gamble had a season of brilliant play on both sides of the ball. It was only a minor historical irony that one of the modern era's few two-way college performers helped win a national title for Ohio State.

> “You chalk it,
> you talk it,
> you walk it.
> —Woody Hayes

Top of the national heap

Woody’s greatest season

THE 1960S, FOR THE MOST PART, HADN’T GONE WELL. THERE WAS 1961 WHEN THE BUCKEYES LOST THE ROSE BOWL without ever seeing it, defeated by their own faculty, which Woody claimed cost him dearly in the recruiting wars. Hard to believe the master recruiter being stymied by one lost trip, but for whatever reason, he wouldn’t see roses for nearly a decade. The luster of Buckeye football in the mid-1960s seemed dimmed, and it was reported that the downtown hotels no longer went to the trouble of taking the furniture out of their lobbies before big-game weekends.

The stadium remained filled, but student interest was lagging. Even the sports information officer, Marv Homan, complained that he could walk through the Oval at noon with the top players, stop a hundred students, and none of them would know who the athletes were. Fielding teams that were merely above average would no longer command the passions.

There was a bit of the Roman arena to Ohio Stadium, in that spectacle and sacrifice were required—local spectacle, visitors’ sacrifice—and in the 1960s, the spectacle had waned a bit. Woody was being questioned again, and the style of his offense was being criticized for boring opponents into submission.

A plane circled the stadium tugging a "Goodbye Woody" banner, with replicas being sold on the Oval during game days. Booster donations dropped by half a million dollars. There'd even been fewer season ticket sales. There'd been a drop-off in talent, too, along with higher academic standards imposed by the conference, as well as stricter enforcement of the recruiting regulations. In the loosening environment of the 1960s, even some of the best Ohio kids were leaving home, striking out for godforsaken places like Michigan and even Nebraska where six members of its 1966 Big Eight championship team came from Ohio (somehow, Nebraska owned Steubenville; four of the six were from there, including the honorable mention All-American halfback, Harry "Light Horse" Wilson, the Cornhuskers' leading rusher in 1965 and 1966).

"We just hadn't been getting enough of those quality boys," he said, understanding, finally, that he had to change his recruiting methods. There was, for instance, Esco Sarkkinen in charge of Cleveland's talent-rich Catholic League. But Sark wasn't Catholic—and he didn't drive. His wife drove him around or he used taxis. Woody needed more African American players, too. There was nothing racist about him—he was an equal opportunity vilifier—and he'd already noted the only problem he had with African Americans was that he didn't have enough of them.

So in that misbegotten middle of the 1960s, the intractable middle-aged coach set out to remake his team, and himself as well. He began by going to his strength—recruiting. He let Lou McCullough change the recruiting methodology, which extended OSU's reach well beyond Ohio. Lou organized Woody's time on the road, too, which multiplied his already formidable presence in a recruit's living room where he was at his best.

The backstory of the autumn of 1967 was the freshman class, and no one had seen anything like it. A week before the home opener with Arizona, Woody wanted to animate the varsity, and so he ordered a scrimmage under game conditions—varsity vs. freshmen. The kids hadn't been on campus long enough to know where the Oval was, they didn't know one another, and they certainly didn't know the schemes they were supposed to be running. An assistant held up cards on which the Arizona plays had been drawn. The varsity led 14–12 at the half, mostly because the kids didn't have a kicker. The upperclassmen pulled the scrimmage out in the second half but the freshman quarterback, Rex Kern, saw the assistant showing Kern's play cards to the varsity so the defense knew what was coming. As David Hyde wrote in *1968: The Year That Saved Ohio State Football*—one of the best books ever written about Ohio State football—"The coaches felt the landscape tilt that day."

The staff could see what was unfolding, even Woody. If they could only make it through the current season. The kids provided another highlight the week before the Purdue game, when Lou McCullough set out to practice his goal line defense. He put the ball on the one for Tiger Ellison's kids and gave them four attempts to score. John Brockington, the big guy from Brooklyn, scored on the first play. McCullough screamed at his defense and moved the ball back to the three. Larry Zelina scored from there. The ball went to the six and Jack Tatum scored. Then Leo Hayden. At the time, of course, none of them knew that Brockington, Hayden, and Tatum would all be first round NFL picks. All they knew was, as Tiger kept reminding the varsity, they couldn't stop his Baby Bucks.

Purdue beat OSU, 41–6, in the third game, and afterward Tiger talked to Woody about changing the offense. Woody threw Tiger out of his office. Then he went into Tiger's office and said, almost contritely, "I think we better get ourselves a few new young coaches in here in the spring and add some dimension to this offense."

It was the most propitious moment of the season. The Old Man was still thinking about his personal makeover, which, given his intractable nature, was a task onerous to both himself and those around him. But he'd listened to Lou McCullough, and now he was listening to Tiger Ellison. Soon, he would be listening to Rex Kern, too, a wonder of another kind, in that Woody generally regarded his quarterbacks as empty vessels to be filled with whatever he, himself, was thinking. (There was a telling moment with Kern as a soph when Woody snorted his way out of the practice huddle then yelled at Kern, "By God, you think you can run the team, run the team!" It was almost as though his feelings were hurt; here was a group of players that might be able to play without him.)

Ohio State went on to finish the 1967 season with four straight wins, including a 24–14 win over Michigan. Tiger, at the winter football banquet, christened his Baby Bucks as "the Super Sophomores," and he called out the varsity. "Fellas," he said, "they are hot to earn your spot." And so they did. (Thirteen of them would be drafted by the NFL—including both quarterbacks.)

There was never a year like 1968, the paramount reason being the sophomores themselves. But there was another reason: Woody set aside some of his old mulishness. It was a monumental stride against his own nature, for instance, that he even contemplated starting a sophomore, for his old thinking was that you lost a game for every sophomore you started. In 1968, he'd start nine. Nine losses? Maybe the banners flying over the stadium had finally gotten to him. (Thirteen sophomores were in the starting lineup at the end of the season.)

There was another less recognizable factor, and that was Woody's staff. (The five who went on to head coaching jobs, after all, won a combined 725 games.) Emboldened by Rex Kern's leadership and his mastery of the offense, the assistants pushed back against Woody's innate conservatism. He even listened—some, anyway—to the rookie coach George Chaump, who wanted to run more from the I-formation.

Woody didn't think much of the I-formation, which featured the halfback upright, six to eight yards back, to better see the defense. It used the fullback primarily as a blocker, which offended Woody, as the fullback was his favored position, the one from which all football wealth derived. In his 1969 book, *Hotline to Victory*, he gave the I-formation a begrudging paragraph before moving on to the split-T and its comeback.

The stars—both heavenly ones and those emerging on the field—were perfectly aligned in 1968. This confluence led the old dictator into having his most democratic year. His staff didn't exactly rise up against him, but there was a unified front consistently pushing against him, suggesting that he do this, do that. He might have seen it as the "broad front" he was always talking about, but the season went so well he saw no reason to rebel. His quarterback, Kern, even waved off Woody's play-calling.

The initial moment happened in the second quarter of the opener, against SMU, fourth-and-10, SMU's 41-yard line. Kern waved off the punter, and on a broken play—the one he'd just called—he scrambled right, leaped over a defensive back, and was finally shoved out of bounds on the 28. The crowd noise power-washed the stadium. Two plays later, Kern threw to Dave Brungard for the score, and it was Ohio State, 26–7, at the half. A sophomore quarterback had just launched one of Ohio State's greatest seasons.

The Buckeyes handily disposed of Oregon, then faced No. 1 Purdue at home, the same Purdue that had humiliated them 41–6 the year before. Woody had taken note of Purdue's big tackles, so he put a no-huddle offense in the game plan, which, for him, was something like sending out his quarterback dressed in ostrich feathers. Woody saw it as his version of the German blitzkrieg, something out of a Panzer general's playbook. The defense turned Jack Tatum into a kind of linebacker/safety, put him on Purdue's sensational All-American running back, Leroy Keyes, and he held Keyes to 19 yards rushing, his all-time low. Tatum seemed to be everywhere, confusing even the wire services: the Associated Press named him defensive back of the week and UPI said he was lineman of the week. The 13–0 win was one of Woody's most satisfying. The Lord, obviously, had heard Lou McCollough's pre-game prayer: "Dee-ah Lawd, puh-leeze let us duh-stroy our en-nuh-mee. Ah-men."

Not that all was sweetness and light, for Woody's habits were deeply imbedded. After a mix-up against Wisconsin (whom Ohio State demolished 43–8) when there was no fullback on the field, Woody fired George Chaump, even though Chaump had nothing to do with the mix-up. (It was believed to be the second time Woody had fired Chaump in what would be, over George's nine years with Woody, an even dozen.) George was also Woody's whipping boy when he watched the practice films. Finally, George got the student manager to edit out fumbles and interceptions, which brought viewings back to a simple PG-rated experience—and less censure of George.

Most of the season passed with only scattered fallout from The Old Man, and the Bucks' tightest win was the 25–20 one over Michigan State, by which time Woody was being acclaimed for his offensive strategies. Ohio State had been No. 2 since its third game, behind USC, and the big Michigan win (50–14) finally reversed their positions. It also set up their match in the Rose Bowl.

Against Michigan, Woody had surprised everyone again: he ran an unbalanced line that put both his offensive tackles on the left side of the ball, and Michigan never adjusted. That offensive flourish was followed by a second half when Kern didn't throw a pass. He didn't have to, of course, but Woody's predilection for the run was a harbinger of troubles to come.

The game ended testily, giving rise to one of the Buckeyes' most controversial moments. The Bucks had scored at the end of the game to make it 50–14, and Woody called for the extra point kick. There was confusion on the field, though, because the regular center for extra points, John Muhlbach, was hurt. The backup long-snapper, Jim Roman, was also the kicker. When the third-string quarterback, Bill Long, reminded him that it would be difficult for him to both snap the ball and kick it, Roman said, "Aw, piss it, let's go for two." Thus a couple of backups made a call that would come to haunt Ohio State. Woody, not a man inclined to aphorism, didn't say that he went for two because he couldn't go for three. But Michigan thought he did.

So Michigan went home nursing a stadium-sized grudge and Ohio State went to the Rose Bowl, facing USC. There, Woody reverted a bit to type. Perhaps it was the West Coast itself, where Woody always seemed to feel a clash of cultures. It was as if the New World was being born out there, and he wasn't sure he liked its direction. Or maybe it was just Woody's big-game nervousness.

Whatever it was, he'd meet that sybaritic West Coast atmosphere with his own sense of good Midwestern purpose: he'd put everybody to work. So as the plane cleared the Rocky Mountains with the players excited about seeing this new world, Woody had the managers tape their ankles. At their first reception, at the Huntington Sheraton Hotel, their dress pants hid—taped ankles.

The practices were hard, there wasn't much free time, and on New Year's Eve, he packed up the team, had them driven up into the foothills, and deposited everyone in the Mater Dolorosa Passionist Center—the place the players called The Monastery. It featured penitential rooms with a small bed, a table, and a lamp. The only other thing in the rooms was a Bible (regarded generally by the players as another lesson plan). The team movie—John Wayne in *Hellfighters*—was shown on a bedsheet hanging on the monastery wall.

The next day, however, Woody's difficult regimen paid off. They were, after all, sophomores. Difficulty was not yet in their mindset. They'd revisit the regimen when they were seniors, with different results. But now, they were undismayed by neither USC's 10–0 lead nor O.J. Simpson, the Heisman winner regarded as the best back in the country. They recovered five USC fumbles and mixed running with a judicious passing game to win, 27–16.

USC underestimated Jack Tatum's speed and how good Rex Kern could be. Simpson was superb, 171 yards and an 80-yard TD run—"80 smog-free yards," reported *Sports Illustrated*—but otherwise, as one of the Ohio papers wrote, "the Buckeyes put the squeeze on The Juice."

The Rose Bowl show gave caution to anyone who happened to be facing Ohio State in 1969. The reign of O.J. Simpson had just ended, said *Sports Illustrated*, and "the reign of Woody Hayes and Rex Kern begins—or continues."

And so it would, all the way to its unpredictable conclusion in—you guessed it—Ann Arbor.

Tiger, Tiger, burning bright

He created "the offense of the future." At the time, though, Ohio State was all geared up for the present

THE ROSE BOWL WIN OF NEW YEAR'S DAY, 1969, OVERRODE A LOSS IN COLUMBUS, which occurred that spring and was regarded as inconsequential. Forgive the locals, for when Tiger Ellison resigned, he was not yet regarded as the prophet of wide-open, gunslinging football. It was an incomparable irony that the visionary Ellison finished his coaching career at that backwater of offensive strategy, Ohio State, where the man Hayes called "the forward-passingest coach in the country" was working for the most non-forward-passingest coach in the country. And by the time his innovation reached the wider coaching world, it was already dead to him.

Just why Hayes hired Ellison—his old roommate at Denison—after thirty years at Middletown High School is open to speculation. Hayes said he wanted Ellison because he possessed "dedication." Conventional wisdom is that Hayes wanted someone to recruit the area. Perhaps he just wanted his old friend around. What was clear, however, was that he *didn't* bring Ellison in to develop the passing game, no matter what he'd done at Middletown.

And what Ellison had done was considerable. In the mid-1950s, on his way to Middletown's first losing season in thirty-eight years, he was morosing his way home from practice when he saw a gaggle of grade-schoolers playing *their* brand of football. "The passer was a slender, willowy young man with a rubbery arm," Ellison said later, describing his moment of epiphany.

"He would scramble around big-eyed and expectant as he studied his receivers cutting downfield right or left or deep or short—according to how the defenders were covering them. Those youngsters were simply doing what comes natural, letting the defense determine their pass cuts…"

The next morning, he unveiled his new offense to his staff; they would stretch the field so that their opponents, in turn, would stretch *themselves*, trying to cover. Red-dogging linebackers, burned by footballs tossed in all directions, would think twice about blitzing. Gang-tackling would be more difficult. To name his new formation, Ellison borrowed a basketball term: "the Run and Shoot." And, over the objections of staff, friends, and even his own qualms, he installed it.

THIS WAS, OF COURSE, AN ERA OF RAMPANT CONSERVATISM. EVEN THE FACEMASK was considered an upstart invention likely to undermine the true intentions of the sport. The best formation was one that functioned like a piece of earthmoving equipment. Its basic configuration revolved around a water buffalo at fullback, a studly halfback, and a crew-cut quarterback in high-tops who knew his middling place in the scheme of things. As Tiger put it, "The ball was only incidental, a necessary evil…"

Tiger, however, had discovered the ball itself. He sent out four-receiver sets—*four!*—who adjusted like the striplings on the vacant lot to whatever the defense did. Even the running back was often motioned out wide. His motto was, "Go reckless, stay loose, enjoy life." Nobody could stop it, he said. "We couldn't stop it ourselves."

In one game, Middletown scored 98 points against Portsmouth and afterward, Tiger's *third-string* quarterback became the top scorer in the league. The Middies scored 70 against Greenhills, 66 points against Hamilton Taft, and 60 against Dayton Fairview. The Middies averaged almost five touchdowns a game, at the rate of one touchdown every ten plays for four years in a row.

What he'd done was enlarge the field. Defenders were no longer watching over a small box in the middle of the field, they suddenly were forced to account for all of it. Tiger's playbook, as someone pointed out, looked as if it had been designed by early-twentieth century Cubists. Some historians contend that it was football's first primary passing system. That is, it was the first time passing actually *became* the offense, rather than merely a few plays that involved throwing. And while it was Ellison's brainchild, it had, as most inventions did, an ancestral debt. Ellison's offensive superiors at the time—Sid Gillman and Paul Brown—were both coaching nearby, and between clinics and recruiting visits, their thinking surely was in Ellison's deep memory. When he watched those Middletown schoolboys running their whimsical patterns on a neighborhood lot, everything he had heard or seen coalesced into the Run-and-Shoot.

Then in the early 1960s, Tiger did something he said he'd never do—he became an assistant coach ("I wouldn't be an assistant for Jesus Christ himself," he had said.) He also thought the Middletown job was the *sine qua non* of football jobs, plus he'd already made plans to die on the fifty-yard line. So he surprised even himself when he said yes to Woody in 1963. Surely he was thinking that finally his Run-and-Shoot might get onto the national stage. Surely he'd be able to influence the old man; why else was he going to Columbus? And soon after Ellison came onboard, he was given time during a coaches meeting to present his Run-and-Shoot offense. When he finished, Hayes took the floor and outlined how the off-tackle play was run. The Run-and-Shoot went straight into Woody's file thirteen.

So Tiger settled in as Woody's freshman coach where, by his own account, he lost one game in six years. To preserve his

Middletown offense, he wrote a book: *Run-and-Shoot Football: Offense of the Future*. The closest Woody got to Tiger's offense was writing the foreword for his book, wherein he said that Ellison "goes further toward opening up the game than any other coach I have known." He said that every coach "regardless of the level on which he works will profit from a study of the revolutionary ideas expressed in this book." Every coach but Woody, that is. *Run-and-Shoot Football* went on to become one of the most influential football coaching books ever written, and while the offense of the future didn't die in Columbus, it simply—like so many things born in Ohio—had to go elsewhere to actually *have* a future.

Tiger thus became largely a footnote at Ohio State. He was the apostate in Woody's Holy Mother Church of the Elemental Offense. He did have two imposing moments in Columbus, though. One of them was coaching that great 1967 freshman class—the one that would win the national title the following year—and they gave Woody's varsity fits all fall. The other moment came in the 1969 Rose Bowl game when OSU soundly beat USC for the national title. OSU's last two touchdown passes were from what Tiger called his Gangster series, right out of the offense he'd invented back at Middletown High.

It was a tribute to Woody simply because the old reactionary allowed it in the game plan, which indicates how different that 1968 season had been. And it was Ellison's finale. At spring practice, he walked into Hayes's office and pointed out that The Buckeyes were ranked No. 1.

"That's the top," he said to Woody. "Above one is zero. I'm going south."

"Damn it, Tiger," Woody is said to have replied. "Don't do this now. You've pushed me to open up the offense for five years, and now that I have, this team is going to be even better next season than this one. This is not the time to walk away."

Hard to imagine Columbus overseeing the collegiate birth of the Run-and-Shoot offense, and so Tiger's name was made elsewhere. He went south; his offense went west. It had to cross the entire country to find a home, which it did in Oregon with another high school coach, Mouse Davis, who stumbled across Tiger's book and became a convert. Davis, who had been a 5' 6", 135-pound quarterback in high school, was looking for ways to utilize his undersized athletes, or what he called "all the little poopers who can really fly."

Ellison's book showed him, and over the next few years, he implemented Ellison's concepts into his own—and won the 1973 Oregon State Championship. The first time he lined up with five wide receivers, the other coach said, "You have an extra man on the field." One time, after Mouse's offense had scored 73 points, the opposing coach ran across the field and thanked him for not running up the score.

By 1975, he was the head coach at Portland State where his quarterback, Neil Lomax, set 90 NCAA records and once threw seven touchdown passes in one quarter. Mouse had taken Ellison's original concept and virtually tossed out the running game; even *Tiger* thought Mouse threw too much.

So it took football's mavericks to bring Ellison's offense into the mainstream. It was, otherwise, too risky, too radical. It needed coaches out for a reputation and nothing much to lose. It hit the college big-time at the University of Houston in 1989 when Andre Ware set more passing records—and won the Heisman. David Klinger followed Ware, throwing for 716 yards in a single game. Over most of a decade, the Run-and-Shoot seemed to belong to Houston: first the university, next the Houston Gamblers of the old WFL that ran it with Jim Kelly, then Warren Moon and the Oilers, who went to the playoffs for seven consecutive years.

It was astounding that Ellison's schoolboy passing scheme had taken a half century to find its expression in the larger world, and it was likely an irony not lost on the old skipper himself (he would have been equally surprised to see copies of *Run-and-Shoot Football* selling for $200 on the internet). It had become, one might say, an offensive sacrament, so widely disseminated that it became part of the fundament: parts of it were used so commonly that only the game's students knew where it came from.

In the 1990s, Rich Rodriguez was using the Run-and-Shoot from a shotgun formation. Then, one day, after a busted play caused his quarterback to "read" the crashing defensive end and scamper outside, he created what became known as the modern "zone read." In essence, it added an option to the spread, and Tiger's old formation had just received a steroid shot.

At about the same time, a former Ohio State assistant by the name of Urban Meyer began to build his own strategy. It was based on conversations with Rodriguez, as well as a veritable Who's Who of other offensive-minded coaches. (This was what was known in football as "the Socialist approach." Or as Mouse Davis said, "You basically steal everything you do and then do what you do and make it your own.")

What Meyer wanted was a sophisticated offense managed by a quarterback who could run. Using what one might say was an amalgam of the offenses his Ohio forefathers ran—all the way back to Francis Schmidt—Meyer won 104 games in a decade and two national championships. In 2012, he was back at Ohio State, and he was something they hadn't seen on the Ohio Stadium sidelines before, certainly not on the Buckeye side of the field. He was one of the first truly post-modern coaches. He'd assimilated all of the game's history, and he knew how to use it in his own scheme. Even more important, he knew how to run the modern football *organization.*

Should that old insurrectionist Ellison have taken in one of Meyer's games, what would he have seen? He'd have seen a spread field, and route-running where the receivers had some room to maneuver. In other words, he'd have recognized *himself.* He would surely have thought: *What I was doing fifty years ago WAS the offense of the future.*

But who in Columbus would have thought the future would be so long in coming?

The sophomores grow up

Looking for love in all the right places

THE 1969 SEASON OPENED WITH GREAT EXPECTATIONS. AS WELL IT SHOULD HAVE. Most of that sophomore championship team was back, and they were bringing with them, in the words of one magazine writer, "the maniacal enthusiasm that only youth can have." The old dog himself, Woody Hayes, had even learned some new tricks. He was running an I-formation, for instance (although never in the red zone, which was reserved for real football, that is, the old reliable 26 and 27, the fullback off-tackle). And his quarterback, the Rose Bowl MVP who'd been described as "a sweet-faced sophomore with a silver bullet for a heart," was back to run the show.

On the first play of the opener with TCU, Rex Kern tossed a 58-yard TD to Bruce Jankowski. It was a first strike in a 62–0 debacle that put the Big Ten—and everybody else—on notice. The Buckeyes scored 54 points against Michigan State and the closest anyone got to them was Minnesota, which was only 27 points down. They outscored the competition by almost 200 points. Kern ran his sprint-out plays and the option to perfection and, moreover, they passed. College football was passing that year—slightly more than 34 percent of the time—and Ohio State wasn't too far behind at 27.8. Steamrolling the opposition, the first units were usually off the field early, giving rise to the joke that Kern might win the Heisman without actually lettering.

By the time the Michigan game rolled around, the Wolverines were almost an afterthought: Ohio State had won 22 straight, and Michigan had already lost twice (one of them to Michigan State, whom the Buckeyes beat by 33 points). But they were playing that old bugbear Michigan, a game that usually ignored the records. And this time, Michigan was being coached by...a former Ohio State guy. Not just any Ohio State guy, but an Ohio guy, Bo Schembechler, who had both played for and coached with Woody.

The 1969 game was played in Michigan Stadium which Bo, driving up from Miami of Ohio just a few months before, had trouble finding. He and his assistants inhabited an old locker room containing some rusty chairs and nails on the wall for their clothes. When the assistants complained, Bo lectured them on Fielding Yost, the patron saint of Michigan titles and championships. "See this chair?" he said, with emphasis. "Fielding Yost sat in this chair. See this spike? Fielding Yost hung his hat on this spike. And you're telling me we had better stuff at Miami? No, men, we didn't. We have tradition here, *Michigan* tradition..."

Most of Woody's young players had never seen Michigan Stadium. It was a hostile bowl-shaped structure once described as looking like "a giant tool shed." Inside was the largest crowd that ever saw a college football game—103,588—and a decibel level that went up to 110 (think heavy equipment or rock band). So there was that, and there was also Michigan's own upsurge: since the Michigan State loss, the Wolverines had tossed off four straight lopsided wins. In addition, Bo had installed Ohio State's defensive scheme so his offense was constantly practicing against it.

Bo's hole card, though, was that he knew Woody. As Kern would say later, "Bo knew Woody so well that he even knew how Woody tied his shoes." Bo's game plan was to give Woody's big fullback, Jim Otis, his yardage but stop Kern, who, he thought, was the real danger. If Michigan could do that, Bo thought, his own offense could run against Ohio State. It didn't hurt Bo's plan that Kern got up that morning with a back so stiff he couldn't get out of bed. "We could see scarlet and gray in our sleep," Bo said. "The mood was electric." And: "My god, I was about to fight my football father."

Ohio State scored on its second series, but Michigan came right back. Then from the 3-yard line, Bo ran an off-tackle play. He called it "Dark 26" but it was Woody's bread-and-butter play. The same play. No irony deficiency in what would become The Big House. It was now Wayward son 7, Football Father 6. By the half, Ohio State was down 24–12 and Kern had thrown two of his four interceptions. Michigan's game was mirroring Ohio State, and Ohio State now knew what it was like to actually play Ohio State. The afternoon went as though Schembechler was standing in Kern's huddle.

Afterward, OSU's middle guard, Jim Stillwagon, talked to Michigan's All-American tackle Dan Dierdorf and asked him what Bo had told his players at halftime. "He said, 'It wasn't what he said at halftime. It was what he said before the game. He said, 'Today's game is only thirty minutes long. If we're ahead at halftime, we'll win the game, because Woody Hayes will be predictable. You only have to play a half-hour today. Be ahead at halftime, and we'll win.'

"We sat back, and they knocked the shit out of us. We had three linemen, me and two tackles. Our ends were in the flats, the linebackers were going back. Jim Mandich had the day of his life, because he was catching 15-yard passes underneath in the no-man zone. At halftime, we said, 'What the hell's going on? We have to go after them.' They didn't score another point. We ran our stunts. We started kicking their ass. But then Woody went right and left, like Bo said. They jammed up the 27 and 26, so we were fucked…"

The Michigan-Ohio State rivalry was already a longstanding classic, but the 1969 game would overlay it with a vendetta between two old-school dinosaurs who hated each other on the field but loved each other off it. The old rivalry was about to be upgraded. For the next decade, it would resemble a sort of family-honor

Albanian blood feud involving two antagonistic clans. Its retaliatory violence would be confined, for the most part, to alternate Thanksgivings in Columbus and Ann Arbor.

A national title was lost that day in Ann Arbor, but something more as well. It was a seminal game for Ohio State in that it set an offensive tone for the rest of Woody's tenure at Ohio State. In one sense, he never got over it. He had never particularly liked the I-formation even though he'd been running the option—and the passing—from it the past two seasons. But now look: six interceptions in the most important game he'd ever coached! It was as if he had been betrayed by giving in to the progressive tendencies shoved on him by his assistants.

He'd gotten to where he was by following his instincts. Now he needed to get back to them.

In 1970, the Buckeyes were off and running again—with the accent on the running. (The Old Man wasn't going to make that mistake again; his fullback was once again relegated to his former princely position.) The wide-open offense was now not so wide. In 1969, Woody passed 27.8 percent of the time—slightly more than 25 times a game. It dropped ten percent in 1970, and thereafter it would frequently dip into the single digits. Passes became so rare in Ohio Stadium that sons asked fathers what those opposing quarterbacks were doing, flinging the ball about like that. Were they trying to get rid of it? (Fathers tried to describe Rex Kern in 1969 and how he had thrown more times in every game than any of Woody's quarterbacks ever.)

"Hayes has adapted to the modern passing game—with some apprehension and regret," The *Los Angeles Times* had written during the winning streak. Now the apprehension had come to the fore, caused by the Michigan loss. The sophomores—all grown up—were winning. but they were no longer playing with their former swagger.

After the 1969 Michigan loss, Kern said, their offense got conservative. "I thought, 'Gee, we had been using an offense that won us every game but one. Woody's trying to find new offenses.'

It's frustrating when you can't do what you know you can do...he was trying to find solutions to why we got beat by Michigan the year before, and he lost sight of what this team was. The irony is that he handed me the controls as a sophomore; then as a junior, I got to call fewer plays, and by my senior year, I got to call fewer yet.

"Getting beat by Michigan made Woody revert back to his old style...our senior year wasn't so much fun. It was confining. At times, we were running new offenses that we had never run before. That didn't make sense to me. Here's a team that has lost one game—and eventually, we lost only two games in three years—and we're trying to fix something that really wasn't broken.

"There was a lot of pressure, and I began to develop ulcers. I internalized it. Physically, I started to deteriorate. I remember playing my senior year at maybe 173 pounds. Woody would say, 'Hey, I'm a carrier. I don't have 'em.'

"'Yeah,' I'd say, 'you get rid of all that stuff.'"

The Buckeyes were still at the top of the ladder but something was missing; they no longer frightened the opposition. Ohio State was Achilles and every other good team was a would-be Paris with a poisoned arrow. At one point Alex Agase, the Northwestern coach, said to Kern, "We were so scared of you guys after what you did in 1969 until we saw Woody come out with the offense. We couldn't believe it, the old man was back to running a Model-T."

The Buckeyes sneaked past Purdue, 10–7, then faced Michigan at home. Both teams were unbeaten and untied—a first for the series. All year, the Buckeyes had gone out to practice by trampling across a rug on which the score of the 1969 Michigan game had been custom-stitched. It had been sent to Woody by a Columbus carpet manufacturer. If hype were AstroTurf, there would have been no grass left in all of Ohio. There was a record stadium crowd of more than 87,000, and the press box was stuffed with at least 600 representatives. Then there was the national television audience, and for most viewers it would be the first time they'd ever seen these two play.

Ohio State forced a fumble on the opening kickoff, setting the tone for the afternoon, and the Buckeyes were up, 10–3, at the half. And they were just getting started. Woody, who'd spent a good part of the season retreating from the offense of 1968 and 1969, surprised everyone—particularly Michigan—by adding a new formation featuring two tight ends. *Sports Illustrated* concluded, speaking directly to The Old Man himself, "Ironically, Woody, in the most monumental game of your crusty old life, you resurrected two of your favorite personal evils to beat Michigan—the pass and the pitch." Nonetheless, it was OSU's defense that won the day—Michigan gained all of 37 yards. It was a 20–9 win for the Buckeyes, although it was costly; following Woody's maxim of leaving it all on the field, they did, and they didn't leave much for the Rose Bowl. "Going to the Rose Bowl wasn't the main thought on their minds," Woody said, prophetically, "it was avenging last year's loss."

Underdog Stanford, who'd lost three games (including one to Purdue), couldn't stop OSU's running game (364 yards), except where it mattered: three times on fourth down, deep inside Stanford territory. Heisman quarterback Jim Plunkett insulted OSU's secondary for 265 yards—and the MVP trophy. That 27–17 game in 1971, though, had been lost off the field, as Woody overworked his players who actually needed a little less of it.

Then he installed a totally new offense, the wishbone. One prescient writer explained it this way: "On the verge of another unbeaten season he wanted to do something, but he didn't want to do too much, and somehow came up with the wishbone. He never fully explained it to his team, but that was the beauty of being the head coach: he didn't have to…It was a risky offense, reliant on timing and coordination, which meant lots of practice…"

On the flight in to Pasadena, he'd again had his players taped on the plane—shades of the last trip—then practiced them hard. The best description came again from Stillwagon. "They start beating the shit out of us, and we were going to leave. We had an agreement that these things weren't going to happen, but they still did. It was just bad management, but it was bad management because Woody didn't understand, he wanted to win so bad.

"We used to spend sixteen fucking days out there. We'd end up doing his lifestyle. We'd wake up and have breakfast. We'd have lunch. We'd go to bed at 10. Nobody did that shit. He beat us down physically, then he beat us down mentally. And then you go out and play somebody who just wants to kick your ass. There's a good opportunity that you ain't going to do too good…when we got beat, nobody even gave a shit. Most people just said, 'I'm glad this is over with.'"

It was an ignominious finish. His 1970 team should have been his greatest team. But it wasn't. And it wasn't because he wouldn't let it be.

"Being young, I thought at the time, 'Maybe I need to go ahead and win that Heisman Trophy again.'
—Archie Griffin

Archie comes running

And Woody goes bowling

THERE WAS THE UNWORTHY INTERLUDE OF 1971 WHEN OHIO STATE LOST FOUR GAMES, and then The Old Man was back on his game. His rightful place in the football hierarchy was indicated by the Buckeyes' No. 3 preseason ranking in 1972, and the happy—and unexpected—appearance of yet another product in the hometown lineage of Chic Harley and Hopalong Cassady. Archie Griffin had attributes of both, and while he wasn't a lot bigger he was both tougher and more powerful. The best description of him came from Alan Natali, who wrote that Griffin was "quick, infinitely courageous, economical in his movements, and ran with bullish persistence, always driving forward, always attacking."

He was mild in manner, pleasant and respectful—of everything but opposing defenses. There, an inner ferociousness gave him the option of running over a tackler as well as ricocheting around him. Tackling him, said one Wisconsin assistant, "is like trying to tackle a falling tree in a windstorm." And—more good news for Columbus—he arrived at Ohio State just as freshmen had become eligible to play on the varsity.

Archie was a surprise. The next big one came on November 11 when Ohio State lost, 19–12, to Michigan State, who came into the game an unimpressive 3-4-1. MSU rolled up 365 yards, though, and won the game on four field goals and an extra point by a player even newer than Archie—one not even listed in the official program. Dirk Krijt was a soccer-playing transfer from the Netherlands who had wandered out to practice and asked if he could kick. Then he asked whether the ball was supposed to go over or under the goalposts.

After the win over Ohio State, he lit up a cigarette and said to his coach, "I'm going out with the girls tonight and have a few beers. Do you want to come along?" Duffy Daugherty begged off, staying behind to explain to the media that Michigan State had new rules "that permitted anyone kicking four field goals in the first half to smoke cigarettes, drink beer, and go out with the girls."

The loss dropped the Bucks to No. 9, which is where they were when Michigan came to town for the annual Thanksgiving slugfest. (It was that old holiday contest where, as one sage put it, "the gravy goes only to the survivors," putting it firmly into the country's historic perspective.)

USC WAS BEATING EVERYONE BY 28 POINTS A GAME, CHASED THROUGH MID-NOVEMBER BY ALABAMA AND MICHIGAN, and because the winner of the Michigan-Ohio State game would play USC in the Rose Bowl, the national title was still a faint Ohio possibility. First, though, there was the demon at hand—unbeaten No. 3 Michigan whose defense had been allowing a meager average of 4.3 points a game. It was cold and wet in Columbus, a day for defense, and spectacularly on hand was linebacker Randy Gradishar, leading a charge that stopped Michigan on eight plays inside the OSU five. (Gradishar was from a little school in the upstate, Champion High, and with such a geography seemed destined to become one of the best linebackers to ever play the game.)

The 1972 game was a perfect embodiment of the personalities of Woody and his former student Bo Schembechler: two old bighorns meeting at the end of each rutting season to settle their territorial ambitions by head-butting one another into submission. Woody's quarterback, Greg Hare, threw for one completion in the game, yet OSU still won, 14–11, even though Michigan marched up and down the field with impunity—everywhere but in the red zone. There, Ohio State played as though Mother's honor was at stake.

The game was a kind of perverse testimony to the old-fashioned football business both coaches loved. Michigan's advantage in yardage—342–192—didn't matter because it was gained in the wrong place on the field. A 30-yard run by Woody's new kid, Griffin, put OSU ahead, then its defense stopped UM twice in the fourth, once on the 20 and four plays on the goal line. Michigan's game—and the Rose Bowl—was thus lost on Schembechler's old-fashioned point of honor: no cheap points—i.e., a field goal—once you're on the five-yard line. It was the sort of pride that rattled the bones of every old leatherhead from the first part of the century and, if you had any sense of history, you had to admire it.

THE ROSE BOWL WAS ONCE AGAIN ANTICLIMACTIC, BUT THIS TIME IT WAS NO FAULT OF THE BUCKEYES, for they were playing one of the great college teams of all times. USC had rampaged through its regular season unimpeded, defeating five Top 20 teams handily. The Trojans answered a 7–7 halftime tie with an offensive explosion, leading one of the postgame reports to say, "Even before the third quarter was over, the Rose Bowl was no longer a football game, only a telecast." Final score: 42–17. Said *Sports Illustrated* insultingly (and not quite true, which the next Rose Bowl proved), "The Trojans were having the kind of fun day against Ohio State that reflects the difference between the currently sad Big Ten and the brash, bruising Pacific Eight."

Still and all, it was a USC team that would eventually send thirty-three players to the NFL. It would be considered one of the best teams of the century. "USC's not the No. 1 team in the country," said Washington State coach Jim Sweeney, whose Cougars had suffered a 44–3 loss against the Trojans. "The Miami Dolphins are better."

But Woody was not one to suffer any defeat easily. He would be back. In the fall of 1973, he'd still have his All-American linebacker Gradishar. And the stellar offensive tackle John Hicks. His star running back, Griffin, would be back—with experience. (They were so good that Hicks was No. 2 in the Heisman voting—the highest finish ever by a pure offensive lineman—while Griffin was No. 5 with Gradishar right behind him.) And there'd be an exciting new quarterback, the kid they called "Flam"—for "flamboyant"—and with good reason. The Old Man had good reason to think he might not lose in 1973.

EVEN SO, HE WASN'T A HAPPY MAN. He was too driven to be constantly happy. Happiness was one of those errant emotions reserved for special occasions, such as beating Michigan, and then not for too long because you had to get ready to play Michigan again the next season. It was 1973 and there was too much change to keep up with. Women were now in the Ohio State Marching Band, and beer in the student rooms. His players wanted to grow beards, for gosh sakes. "These days everybody wants to do their own thing," he said grumpily. Woody wanted them doing *his* own thing. That was how you had a good football team.

Woody said the 1973 team was his most talented. He had a great tailback, he thought John Hicks was his best lineman ever, and newcomer Cornelius Greene was a good running quarterback. Given that lineup, he said, "We are going to run until someone stops us." His big fullback Champ Henson, who'd led the nation in scoring the previous year, described the offense this way: "As many weapons as we had, the whole idea was to pound them with the fullback, then run the option to stretch 'em out, then pound 'em, come back with the counter play, then a couple short passes, then it's like, you know, they don't know what to do..."

The rest of the Big Ten complied by not being very good that year. Other than Michigan, that is. The Buckeyes held the opposition to slightly less than four points a game, and three times they scored over fifty points. By the Michigan game, OSU had spent eight straight weeks as the No. 1 team in the country, and

Michigan, also unbeaten, was No. 4. The Buckeyes headed to Ann Arbor after practicing that week with recorded crowd noise piped in. As if anyone could properly imitate the atmosphere of Ann Arbor when Ohio State came to town.

That 1973 game went much as expected—two unimaginative offenses battering against two of the best defenses in the country. Michigan completed one pass in the first half; OSU didn't throw at all. Cornelius Greene, though, had an injured thumb and he was playing on Michigan's new—and rain-slick—turf. The score was OSU, 10–0, at the half and Woody's assistants were ecstatic to see Michigan stacking its defense. Someone would be open downfield, and all OSU needed was one good pass.

"Downfield!" they said to Woody.

"Bullshit!" Woody explained.

They'd stay where they should, which was between the tackles.

"How about a counter play with the wingback, Coach?" Ralph Staub suggested from the coaches' booth. "How about an option here, Coach?"

Woody yelled at Staub. (His exact words carried all the elegant expediency of his off-tackle play and, according to Robert Vare, were, "Fuck that fucking play!")

In other words, an order of noncompliance from The Old Man, who wouldn't be moved. His offense wouldn't move, either. Archie had gained 99 yards in the first half; Woody would keep running him, even though at one point Michigan had nine defenders on the line. Gaining 174 yards on such a day was the supreme accolade to Archie—and to his line. The day was something like Rex Kern's freshman scrimmage when Kern noticed the assistant coach showing the defense the big card with the offensive play scrawled on it.

The fourth quarter opened with OSU still up by 10. Then Michigan got far enough into OSU territory to kick a 30-yard field goal. One series later, two Ohio boys were responsible for the only Michigan touchdown: quarterback Dennis Franklin from Massillon and his fullback, Easy Ed Shuttlesworth from Cincinnati.

(Shuttlesworth was once described as "a large object amok, bringing to mind aerial photographs of a natural disaster overwhelming a village.")

The score came on fourth-and-one, at the 10, when Franklin scored after faking to Shuttlesworth. Score: 10–10. Michigan had two more chances to win: two field goal attempts went wide. Finally, Woody decided to pass. Greg Hare replaced Greene for the last two series and threw OSU's first pass, an interception. A final series of three incompletions ended the game.

Woody's players and his assistants were poleaxed by the tie. Even the crowd seemed stunned. "We only ran three different plays the whole second half," said an Ohio State lineman. "Shit, they weren't even looking for anything but Archie. We could've scored on them easy if we'd thrown the ball or mixed it up a little…It wounds his pride to pass."

It was an exact mirroring of Bo's own stubbornness in the 1972 game when he refused to kick a field goal that would have sent Michigan to the Rose Bowl. Somewhere, surely, the gods were smiling. Woody and Bo: poster boys for the Midwestern Brotherhood of the Mulishly Headstrong.

Woody told the press that Ohio State's passing was no good "and has not been all season." But one of his offensive linemen had another opinion: "We didn't pass all year because we didn't have to, and when we had to we didn't because we couldn't."

It was a perennial problem with Woody. There was always a reason why the pass didn't work, not the least being that—more times than not—it was neither practiced nor implemented. Thus it was not simply the pass itself but the passing scheme from which it originated.

Rick Telander, a defensive back at Northwestern who played against Ohio State and later became a writer for *Sports Illustrated*, took note of what he called "those season-ending tractor pulls against Michigan," and concluded that Woodyball quite possibly set the Big Ten back a decade. Telander said the run-pass dilemma was perfectly expressed by Woody. "The one form of attack personified the earth, primal struggle, atavism, simplicity, things that could be controlled," he wrote. "The other embodied air, lightness, modernity, freedom, and risk. Hayes was of the earth, an old-fashioned toiler. 'I despise gimmicks!' he often roared. A 250-pound fullback was not a gimmick. A pass was."

In 1973, Woody ran almost 90 percent of the time. (The college average was 73.4 percent.) There, he'd become slightly more creative, which was due to his recognition of Archie's innate ability to ingeniously find running room in impossible spaces. To confine such a runner, even Woody recognized, would be like making him run in rubber boots. No longer did Woody demand that a play be run precisely as it had been drawn up. John Brockington would no longer be threatened with a loss of scholarship for breaking the off-tackle play outside. Jack Tatum, now a Pro Bowler with Oakland, would not be told, after zig-zagging a practice punt 60 yards to score, "Son, at Ohio State we run straight for the goal line."

There was partial redemption, in that the league voted to send Ohio State to the 1974 Rose Bowl. The ostensible reason for choosing OSU over Michigan was that UM quarterback Franklin had broken his collarbone late in the game. Bo was furious, but so were Woody's assistants. Angry at Woody's lumbering play-calling, they'd just voted not to go to the Rose Bowl. The Old Man managed to contain himself and listen. He promised the coaches he'd vary the play-calling, and he promised the players he'd loosen his usual curfew restrictions.

The trip to Pasadena was still not exactly a cruise ship outing, but Woody kept his word. He was positively avuncular, which confused the press. They weren't sure exactly what to do with a benign Woody Hayes. His boys practiced once a day, not two; they stayed out late; they didn't spend New Year's Eve in the monastery. And his game plan was probably the one he should have run against Michigan.

The first Ohio State play was a pass—and an interception. Astoundingly, Woody was not stirred. "We're still going to pass," he told Greene, who'd thrown it, "so be ready." Greene recovered, went 6-for-8, 129 yards, and ended the day as the Rose Bowl MVP. "We thought we could pass on them," Woody said, as unorthodox a statement as he'd ever made.

While it wasn't the same USC team that had handily beaten the Buckeyes the previous year, the Trojans were still leading in the third quarter, 21–14, before Greene's sure-handed passing and execution—and a 56-yard punt return by Neal Colzie—brought about 28 unanswered Buckeye points. The final blow came from Archie himself, on a beautiful 47-yard broken field run. After that, said the *Chicago Tribune*, "the Trojans were as dead as their ancient namesakes."

It was a vindicating accomplishment for Ohio State, but undefeated Notre Dame was named the national champion. The Irish, coached by one of Woody's former players, Ara Parseghian—who'd advised Woody to pass against USC—beat previously unbeaten and No. 1-ranked Alabama, 24–23, to do it.

The Old Man's tie at Michigan, it appeared, had cost him another title.

In the 1974 season, there was the upset by Michigan State when OSU either did or didn't score in the last seconds, a final play so outlandish the Big Ten commissioner was called upon to validate the referees' call. Then a one-point loss to USC in the 1975 Rose Bowl. If the Old Man hadn't already had a heart attack the previous summer, either of these two games could have done it for him.

He did manage to lose some weight, but nothing changed his workload. Even the holidays weren't immune. Alex Agase, who coached at both Northwestern and Purdue, had a favorite recruiting story about Woody. Once, confident that he had sewed up the services of an Ohio kid, he called the kid on Thanksgiving Day to wish him happy holidays only to discover Woody was there and carving the turkey. Woody worked even harder—if that was possible—before the 1975 season.

Archie Griffin was a senior in 1975 and both he and Woody wanted to make the most of it. After all, Archie had played in only two regular season losses. (And what was it with the Michigan State Spartans? Surely Woody had a military analogy about them. Didn't the very name warn him? The Spartans, i.e., history's most notable die-hards, the militaristic regime that used conditioning and terrain against all odds. And who did that sound like?)

The Buckeyes rolled through the season again. They toppled No. 13 UCLA, 41–20 on October 4, moved to No. 1 and stayed there. Then they were upset by none other than UCLA, 23–10, in the 1976 Rose Bowl. Ohio State's game suffered from overconfidence, Archie's broken hand, and a pair of interceptions by Cornelius Greene. Archie had won his second Heisman that fall ("Being young, I thought at the time, maybe I need to go ahead and win that Heisman Trophy again"), but he was one-for-four in the Rose Bowl. Given his innate modesty, he would likely have given up being named the Rose Bowl's All-Century Player for winning just one more of them.

The Big Ten was in something of a Rose Bowl drought. Woody wouldn't make it back, and ended up 4–4 in roses. Bo didn't win one until 1981, and he finished 2–8. The old arch-rivals thought part of the problem was that they played the season for their game, and left it all in Columbus. Or Ann Arbor.

It was the theory of the Rose Bowl as afterthought. Bo, who'd had a heart attack a few hours before his first Rose Bowl, in 1970, was a bit sardonic about his record. "Captain Hook had his crocodile," he said, "and I have January 1."

So Ohio State and Michigan would beat up on the other conference teams, play each other, then head west to play high-powered offenses that passed more than anybody in the Big Ten. And they played on grass before what was, in effect, a home crowd for their opponents.

Some of Woody's players were sure that he would have retired if they'd won the 1976 Rose Bowl, but the defeat kept him in the game, looking for a proper ending that wasn't to come. "The last two games of the season always haunted us," Cornelius Greene would say. He admitted he never understood his coach. "He was difficult to study, difficult to understand. You didn't really know what his antics were for. He was a difficult man on himself. He was very hard-driven. My only disappointment is that we weren't national champions in all those four years. Every year we were right there, but something always happened…"

Ohio State lost to Michigan the next three years, and 1978 ended haplessly in the Gator Bowl where the hit of the game was made by Woody himself, who slugged Charlie Bauman after the Clemson middle guard intercepted an Art Schlichter pass. The rookie quarterback—the most highly touted freshman in OSU history—was brought to Columbus to pass but struggled all season with the offense. Woody had mostly ignored George Chaump's advice and essentially had the best passing prospect in the nation running the option.

With two minutes left, trailing 17–15, Schlichter moved his teammates to a third-and-five on the Clemson 24. He had completed 16-of-20 passes, but all Ohio State needed was a field goal. Woody's third-down play was…a pass.

"We were in four-down running territory, and we should never have been passing in that situation," Chaump said. "But they called a delay pass and, lo and behold, it gets intercepted… here was a guy who never passed when he should have, and when he finally passes the ball, look what happened. …"

Clemson's coach was an even bigger rookie than Schlichter; Danny Ford had just been promoted when Charlie Pell left Clemson at the end of the regular season. "I'm supposed to coach against Woody Hayes, and I ain't never coached a football game," Ford said. "I didn't want to, but they gave me a Jaguar and I changed my mind."

At the end of the game, as Ford remembered it, Charlie Bauman was the nose guard rushing the quarterback. But he got knocked backwards about six yards. "He stands up," said Ford, "and the danged quarterback throws a pass that hits him right in the hands. He ain't never caught a football in his life, but he catches it and he runs to Woody Hayes's sideline and starts jumping up and down—not to embarrass the guy—he just ain't never caught a football. So Coach Hayes kinda tries to knock his head off. He hits him in the head, but he can't hurt him with the face mask at all…"

The Old Man said only three things can happen on a pass and two of them are bad. But there was a fourth thing—you can get fired. Hugh Hindman, the AD, gave him a chance to resign, but Woody couldn't do it. He was fired the morning after the game. Woody's personal public relations man, Paul Hornung of the *Dispatch*, had him resigning. The headline was not quite in the tradition of the *Chicago Tribune's* "Dewey Defeats Truman," but it was close.

Such karma, though. The ex-Northwestern defensive back, Rick Telander, called the punch "Hayes's final rage at the vagaries of the forward pass." The Old Man had become one of the most successful coaches in football history without acceding to the passing game, and now he'd been done in by it—just as he had in certain of his seminal games.

One of the Washington papers said Woody was driven off to his house "and into uncharacteristic obscurity." Like so much written about him, that wasn't true, either. He was a force of nature and thereby never obscure. His last decade found the battered old warrior largely at peace, somewhat professorial, keeping to his modest office in the university's military sciences building, making speeches, fundraising. He even received an honorary degree from Ohio State. There was a report that said The Old Man had called Charlie Bauman at some point and they had talked. Woody, said the report, mostly wanted to know what defense Charlie was in when he'd intercepted that pass. Whether that was true or not, it seemed like him.

There was one final irony: it was Woody's boys that Earle Bruce took to the Rose Bowl after that next season to play for the 1979 national championship…

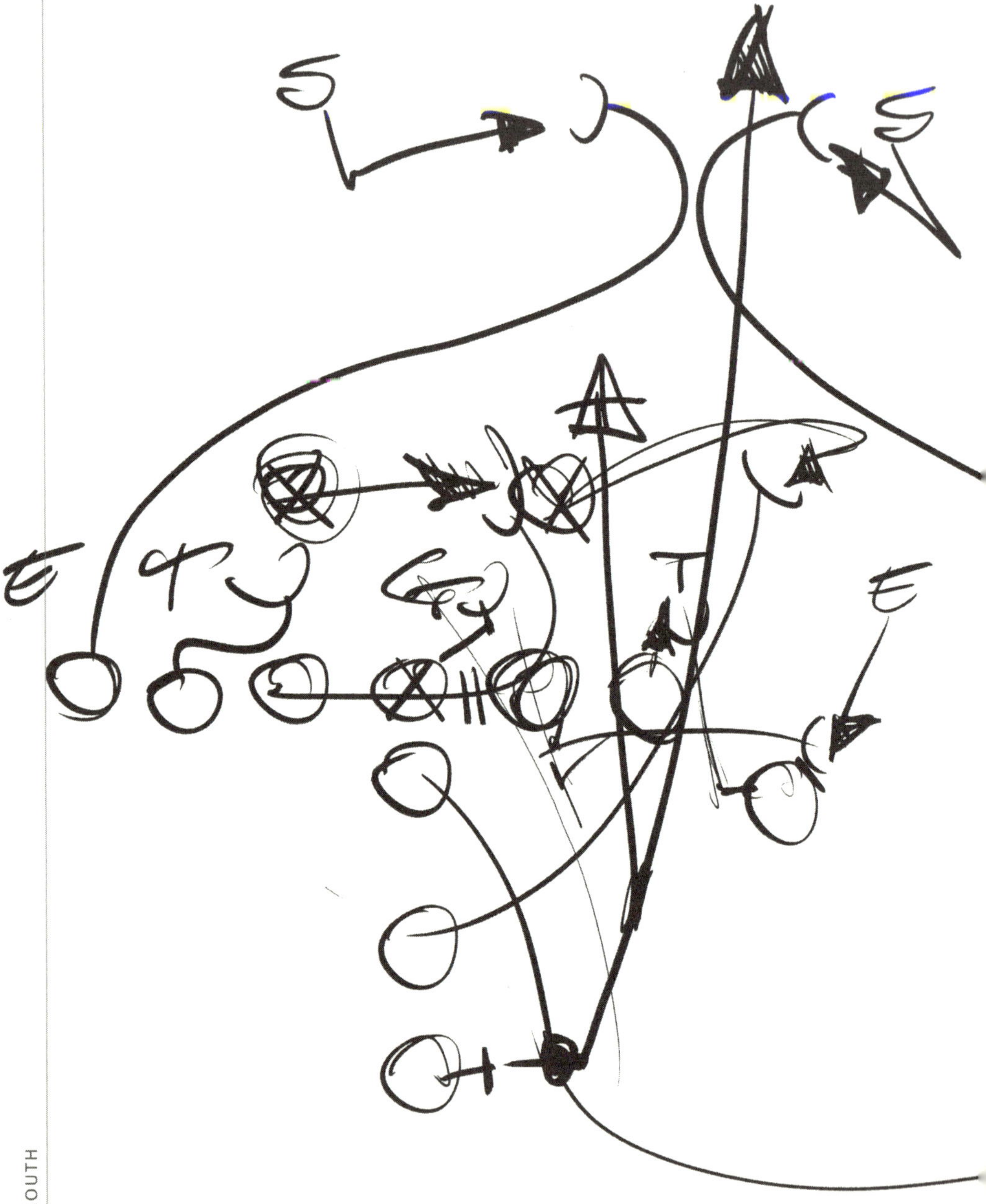
S
S
E
E
T

It is a good, sound football play but in our system, it is vastly overemphasized, said George Chaump. "Bullshit," replied Woody.—David Hyde, 1968: The Year That Saved Ohio State Football

Split decisions

A short history of offense under Woody: Bread and butter, hold the butter

THE ORIGIN OF WOODY'S FAVORITE PLAY—THE FULLBACK OFF-TACKLE—WAS SAID TO HAVE INGRAINED ITSELF INTO WOODY'S SUBCONSCIOUS back in his sixth-grade history class when his teacher related the story of William the Conqueror and the Battle of Hastings. There, William, laden with armor, clambered out of his boat and toppled to the ground. Righting himself, he grabbed two fistfuls of dirt and yelled to his men, "See, my lords, by the splendor of God, I have taken possession of England with both my hands." Woody told writer Robert Vare he often thought of William the Conqueror in those infrequent times when the Buckeyes were actually behind in the score. And in his offense, the conqueror was always the fullback, the man in the dirt claiming the ground.

When Woody first arrived at Ohio State, he brought along the T offense he'd run at Miami. While it was a step up from the single wing the Buckeyes used under Wes Fesler—the offense Vic Janowicz used to win the Heisman in 1950—it was still one of football's oldest formations, dating back to the previous century. It was a complex offense combining power with motion, fakes, and play action passes but in 1951, it was being defended better each week.

With it, Ohio State went 4-3-2 and scored only 109 points (47 of them against Iowa). Janowicz's production was dramatically reduced, for the ball had been taken out of his hands. (His passing yardage, for instance, went from 561 yards to 74.) That season sent Janowicz off to play pro baseball and Woody to Norman, Oklahoma. Woody had promised to upgrade the Ohio State offense, and so far he hadn't.

An old Ohio State hand, Gomer Jones, the Clevelander who'd been an All-American center in 1935, was Oklahoma's line coach, and the Sooners—running the Split-T—were two years away from an unprecedented 47-game win streak (and two national titles) when Woody arrived in Norman in the spring of 1952. (OU's president, looking for money to improve the university, had just told the Oklahoma legislature that he "would like to build a university of which the football team would be proud.") Jones found Hayes a kindred offensive spirit and opened up the Sooner playbook to him.

The Split-T utilized the full house backfield, which Hayes was used to, but it also widened the offensive line splits, and that spread the defense. It was developed by Missouri's Don Faurot, who unveiled it in 1941, for the first time, when Missouri opened the season in Columbus.

As Faurot would explain it, "the option play and split line enabled us to run inside or outside the defensive end without blocking him." Nobody had heard of leaving the defensive end alone, and until defenses had assigned specific duties to the Split-T option, everything the end did was wrong. (Shades of the next century's offense!)

OSU eked out a 12–7 win, but Paul Brown admitted afterward he wasn't prepared for what he'd seen and "we managed to survive only by the sheerest good fortune." (Faurot had been turned down by OSU's selection committee in 1941, who'd hired Brown instead, and he'd come close to avenging himself for the rejection. Nearly a decade later, he was offered the job, and this time, he turned down OSU, which opened the way for Woody.)

So this was the offense Woody brought back to Columbus, although what he learned in Oklahoma didn't take effect immediately. In 1952, gathering the personnel he needed to run the Split-T, the Buckeyes threw the ball 217 times. Throwing the ball was so effective that OSU ended the season ranked fourth in the nation in passing, and quarterback John Borton, a converted linebacker—OSU's first great passer—was fifth in the country.

Borton's 1,555 passing yards was a record that stood for twenty-seven years, but no matter, for the Buckeyes had finished third in the Big Ten (fifteenth nationally), which helped cement Woody's notion of exactly what the passing game could do for you. In his time, the OSU passing game never made it into the national top ten again.

Borton was injured in 1953, and the running game, which accounted for a little more than 70 percent of the plays in Woody's first three years, moved up to nearly 90 percent for the next four. In 1956, the Bucks ran for 2,468 yards and quarterback Frank Ellwood passed for 86 yards, up from 60 in 1955. The only time his hand went up, he was merely asking to go to the bathroom; in two seasons, he completed 16 passes. In 1955 and 1956, the average team passed 23 percent of the time—about two and a half times that of the Buckeyes. "Three yards and a cloud of dust" was now the official Ohio State mantra.

WOODY'S DIE-HARD BELIEF WAS THAT IN ANY GIVEN SERIES, THREE YARDS A PLAY WOULD GIVE YOU A FIRST DOWN. He required consistency and, to him, consistency meant that one of those three plays would yield the extra yard. Woody's math: three plays + three yards = ten yards. If the stars (read: blockers) were imperfectly aligned, and there were only bodies where there should have been space, Woody had an answer for that, too: "Be your own blocker," he said. "Make your own hole." It was why he would always like military-grade fullbacks: Ferguson, Otis, Brockington, Johnson—wide loads who could actually be their own blockers, at least upon occasion.

He was so successful in running the ball that when the rules committee met in 1958 to consider adding a two-point conversion with the ball placed on the three-yard line, Illinois head coach Ray Eliot opposed it. When asked why he said, "Let me tell you, sir, in my conference, the Big Ten, if you put the ball on the three-yard line for a two-point conversion, Woody Hayes will score two points every time he shows up." (Eventually, though, Eliot gave in, and the rule passed unanimously.)

Still and all, reliance on the fullback off-tackle play was—by the early 1960s—beginning to make Ohio State look anachronistic. Woody knew something had to change, but just what it was—and bringing himself to do whatever it might be—would prove nearly impossible. Clinging to his nature, he insisted that a predominant running game worked, and the fullback off-tackle play—which he knew more about than anyone else in the country—would be successful. The team only had to practice harder.

(Richard Hoffer, a Miami of Ohio grad and onetime *Sports Illustrated* regular, summed up the Heartland stance. "Our football lacked imagination, we concede," he said. "But the unspoken agreement among ourselves—that we would offer no undue trickery in our attempts to get ahead—was reassuring. There was an anticipated fairness to it. I always felt this accounted for the unnatural popularity of football in Ohio. We would submerge our skills (at least some of us could throw a pass) in the interests of democracy. Implicit in the three-yards-and-a-cloud-of-dust lifestyle, after all, was the idea that we'd all be there when the game was over, sharing the same modest lives forever, and without complaint.")

Even after bringing in coaches to open up the offense in 1968, Woody would spent three hours lecturing his staff on the precise details of running the play from a full backfield, then return the next day to lecture them on the same play for another three hours.

"Hayes already had spent the previous day sermonizing on every nuance of it," wrote David Hyde in his classic book, *1968: The Year That Saved Ohio State Football.* "How tackles set up a precise twenty-four inches from guards. What foot blockers should lead with. Where helmets were placed. 'Mark this down,' he'd say. 'Underline this,' he'd say. 'Write this,' he'd say. All the assistants would, too. No one said anything. For going on two days! Over this most vanilla of plays!"

Nothing was overlooked. If Woody thought a lineman's splits were off even an inch, he might stomp on his foot. In John Brockington's first scrimmage, the off-tackle hole wasn't open, so he bounced outside for seven yards. The next play was a repeat: six yards. "If you ever run the football like that again," Woody growled at him, "you'll never play a down at Ohio State." That was Woody, pointing out the sacred chalkboard: Run it as it's drawn up. The innovative Split-T might have had football's first option component but Woody, always a purist, didn't like options.

His new offensive strategist, George Chaump, wrote a report in 1968 on the off-tackle play. "It is my opinion that this is a real good, sound football play," wrote Chaump. "However, it is vastly overemphasized in our system, even to the point of monotony…"

"BULLSHIT," Woody wrote on the report, underlining it.

THE YEAR BEFORE, CHAUMP HAD BEEN A HIGH SCHOOL COACH IN PENNSYLVANIA, but many believe he was the point man for the Super Sophs' national title. Woody brought him in to open up the offense and to install the I-formation, but it was Woody at his most contradictory: intellectually, he knew the offense needed to change; emotionally, he was opposed to change. He thought the I-formation made the fullback more of a blocker than a runner, which was true. What Woody didn't see was that the position was on a slow, forty-year decline that would render the fullback nearly extinct.

Conventional gridiron wisdom says that the run sets up the pass, but Woody understood that the passing game, or the threat of passing, set up the run. It was one of the reasons he adopted the

Split-T nearly two decades before. It was also what Chaump was trying to do in 1968: use an I-formation with a wingback in the slot to open up the running game.

The I-formation allowed for more effective passing, but more important, it took a back out of the backfield and placed him on the line where the threat of a pass opened up the running game. The I-formation allowed the threat of the pass to spread the defense and open up more rushing lanes. You didn't have to be a prolific passing team to do this. You just had to be an effective team.

Woody, though, couldn't buy wholly into the changes and would backslide toward his old chalkboard. Even so, the success of 1968 carried over to 1969 and the Buckeyes were passing more and running less than anytime in Woody's tenure—other than his initial years. The Michigan loss broke a two-season win streak, knocked OSU out of a national title—and quelled the passing game. The six interceptions by Michigan surely reinforced Woody's notion about the wickedness that might happen when you passed. In 1970, OSU reverted to running the ball over 80 percent of the time. As for the passing game, OSU threw 25.6 passes a game in 1969; in 1970, a mere 15.2.

THE SUPER SOPHS' TITLE APPEARED TO HAVE BEEN AN ANOMALY. It was a season when Ohio State never faltered—in spite of Woody's fits of playbook passion. Against his own instincts, he'd surrounded himself with a great cast: smart coaches and a quarterback who wasn't afraid to defy him. It was the only year in Woody's long tenure when he wasn't completely in charge. The Michigan loss in 1969 was bizarre and unexpected, and it led directly to Ohio State's loss in the Rose Bowl at the end of the 1970 season. After avenging themselves against Michigan for that 1969 loss, the Buckeyes, worn out by Woody's hardcore practices, were through for the season.

"He took the spirit out of the team," said the All-American middle guard Jim Stillwagon years later.

Woody was constantly at war with himself. He ditched the old single wing offense, which was falling out of favor, and installed the

Split-T. He bowed to the I-formation, which allowed quarterbacks such as Rex Kern more room to operate. He correctly—and creatively—saw that, indeed, passing could set up the run. But deep inside himself, Woody didn't like passing; he liked the threat of passing. If only he could have one without the other!

In another prescient moment, he recruited Art Schlichter and promised him he'd throw eighteen times a game. George Chaump had gone off and studied with Bill Walsh at Stanford, returning with notions of Schlichter taking a quick three-step drop (instead of the customary seven) and throwing quicker to numerous receivers.

But when Ohio State fell behind in the Penn State opener of 1978, Woody benched Walsh's strategy. "We went to a simple passing attack," said Chaump, "and we got killed. There were no fakes, no checkoffs, and no short, little passes. We got blitzed and sacked." And 1978, as every OSU fan knows, was the end of Woody.

While no one would confuse the modern OSU offense with Woody's, there was a similarity or two. Both Hayes and Urban Meyer, separated by more than thirty years on the Buckeye sideline, had a belief in attacking along a broad front. Woody used analogies to military figures like Patton and Sherman (both of whom, unlike Woody, liked radical offensive formations); Meyer demonstrated it with his spread offense. And during Woody's long tenure at Ohio State, his teams rushed the ball about 15.5 percent more than the national average, earning himself a reputation as one of the most conservative coaches in college football. But here's the interesting thing: in Meyer's first three years at Ohio State, he rushed for a higher percentage (16 percent) above the national average than Woody did.

What did that tell you? You could get a good rush from either Hayes or Meyer, but Woody was intently focused on the runner. To Meyer, the runner was one part of the picture. No bias with Meyer. He was not hanging onto the past; he was trying to discern the *future*.

> What have you done to beat Michigan today?—sign on wall where team practices

The oldest rivalry

How hard it is to find good neighbors

OHIO STATE FOOTBALL FANS DON'T REALLY KNOW WHY MICHIGAN IS SUCH A DESPISED ENEMY. THEY JUST KNOW IT IS. The great feuds tend to be territorial, their origins often shrouded by the passing of too much time. Famously, there was the one between Bugs Moran and Al Capone, definitely territorial, and there were the Earps and the Clantons, whose feud was less territorial and more about what the Clantons thought was an unreasonable interference in their frontier right to rustle cattle. (Their noteworthy jam didn't *really* happen at the O.K. Corral, though, which is something like the OSU-Michigan game being played at a neutral site.) There's the Hatfields and the McCoys, of course, whose enmity was territorial (in that two states weren't big enough for them) and may or may not have originated with a stolen pig. Then there is our own Toledo War, which historic-minded Ohioans see as Michigan's original sin—and the origin of the Ohio State-Michigan odium.

It was definitely territorial, although hardly anyone under, say, the age of seventy can tell you what it was all about, only that it was some ancient border dispute that allowed the provenance of Toledo to remain forever ours, thank God. So while this dispute gave our football contests an epic aura, it probably had little to do with the feelings that grew out of them. Over the decades, there were other factors at work.

Starting in the waning days of the Victorian Age, the Michigan-Ohio State games were highlighted—south of the border, anyway—by a notable lack of success. By the time Michigan defiled the opening of Ohio Stadium in 1922, they'd been playing one another since 1897 and Ohio State had won exactly three games. The reason was a decidedly uneven playing field: The University of Michigan had begun in 1817 when Michigan was still a territory, and it had a thousand students before Ohio State got its doors open.

Before the turn of the nineteenth century, Michigan was considered the best football team in the west and, in keeping with its aggressive curriculum and national aspirations, quickly looked east for competition. The Wolverines already had an academic leg up, and the legs wore cleats: when they beat Cornell in 1894, it was the first time The Good Old Boys in the east had lost to a western school.

THE FIRST OHIO STATE-MICHIGAN GAME, IN ANN ARBOR IN 1897, WAS A KIND OF AFTERTHOUGHT. Michigan won 34–0, putting the game away early and converting the rest of it into a practice outing. "The Ohio players made no impression on the University of Michigan line," read one report, and so the interstate dissing began early. If there was a rivalry in those days, it was between Michigan and Minnesota, who for most of the 1890s had been playing each other for the Little Brown Jug, a contest that would become the oldest trophy game in Football Bowl Subdivision football.

For an unconscionable amount of time, Ohio State was little more than another date on the Wolverines' schedule. Which is not to say a rivalry was not a-building, for Ohio State took it seriously from the outset, as evidenced by the *Columbus Dispatch's* apocryphal-sounding report on the 1910 tie game with Michigan. The story began with a taxi driver headed north on High Street as the crowds poured out of the stadium.

"What was the score?" the cabbie is said to have asked.

"3–3, Ohio State," came back the ecstatic reply.

One can only imagine the amount of accumulated chagrin in those first couple of decades. Ohio State had managed to move up, but Michigan had moved on. Michigan was looking east, wishing to be Harvard, and Ohio State was trying to be Michigan. (Wrote John U. Bacon, a close observer, "The Ohio State inferiority complex is as undeniable as it is unjustified. Even more than the Red Sox and the Yankees, the Buckeyes are the ancient Romans to Michigan's ancient Greece—victors valiant, if you will, who superseded the civilization they conquered by imitating it.")

The Wolverines had claimed five national titles before the glorious 1919 season when Chic Harley finally led Ohio State to the school's first Michigan win. That win was followed by two more, then even with a dark interlude during the 1920s, a new rivalry had been definitively born.

THE NEXT STEP IN THE EVOLUTION OF THE CONTEST WAS TO GET THE RIGHT DATE. That occurred in 1935 when the contest was moved to the last game of the regular season. Its place on the schedule assured the meeting a greater significance. Now it would be about more than just bragging rights. It would be about conference championships, Rose Bowl appearances, undefeated seasons—even national championships.

Francis Schmidt marked its importance by downplaying its importance. "They put their pants on one leg at a time, the same way we do," he said, using a prairie colloquialism that apparently hadn't been used this far back east. Before even his first win over Michigan in 1934 (the first of four straight), his expression had become a profundity, and the ensuing pants-shaped charms that gave Ohio State players membership in the Gold Pants Club would be, in time, listed for several thousand dollars on the memorabilia market.

Schmidt's win streak over Michigan was historic, then he lost three straight, which hastened him out of Columbus. There was the brief light that was Paul Brown, then more darkness: in the seven years between 1945 and 1951, a tie in 1949 was the height of

Buckeye success. This run of pestilence paved the way for Woody Hayes, who would frame the game at nearly an existential level.

Ohio State–Michigan was already a good rivalry when Hayes arrived on campus but rather than being cowed by the pressure of the game, he embraced it. For him, victory over Michigan became a year-round focus with success and/or redemption hanging on every contest. Through the 1950s and 1960s, it was the most important regional football rivalry in the Midwest. Then a convergence of factors elevated the game to national prominence and made it the biggest football rivalry in the nation.

Not the least of those factors were the personalities of the two coaches—Hayes and Schembechler. When Bo Schembechler stepped on Michigan's campus in 1969, his pedigree was thoroughly Ohio. He'd played for Woody at Miami, then become his assistant at Ohio State before returning to Miami—Ohio's prep school for big-time coaches. What emerged was an Ohio coach, conservative and competitive, that is to say, a man after Woody's own gruff heart.

He could have stayed a Buckeye assistant, and he appeared to many as Ohio State's coach-in-waiting. Woody said as much when Bo informed him of his intention to go to Miami; Woody said he had only a few more years left and Bo would be there waiting, next in line. "A few more" apparently meant fifteen, and Bo knew if he was going to get one of the jobs he really wanted, he had to be successful as a head coach.

In his six years at Miami, he went 40-17-3, and when the Ann Arbor job opened before the one in Columbus did, Bo went after it. Even if he did have to defect to the north. The Wolverines passed over any Michigan men-in-waiting and tapped an Ohio guy. They weren't proud; they needed their own Woody and that was exactly what they got.

In his first season, 1969, Bo replicated Woody, which meant essentially toughening his team up and running the football. He knew what he was asking of his players, so he plastered a slogan in the dressing room that said, "Those who stay will be champions!" It was meant to hearten the boys who were unused to such punitive conditioning, but not all of them bought into it. At spring practice, one of the players came into the near-darkened locker room and saw one of his less-stalwart teammates, a big lineman from Indiana, packing up his things. Under Bo's sign he had added a postscript: "And those who go will be doctors and lawyers."

Bo was good as his word, though, and at the end of the season he handed Woody the most painful upset of his career. Even now, nearly a half century later, that 1969 Michigan win is still regarded as one of college football's great upsets. It broke the Buckeyes' 22-game winning streak and knocked them out of consecutive national titles. It also began—auspiciously—the greatest ten-year rivalry in the history of college football. That rivalry, "The Ten-Year War," was played out on ABC television at high noon just as the Baby Boomer generation was leaving the stands and piling onto the living room couch, and it turned college football into a ratings giant.

The network wanted to televise more than just a game, though; it wanted to televise an *event*. Or as Roone Arledge said about the viewer, "He must know he is in Columbus, Ohio, where the town is football mad." As for Michigan's part, its prescient AD, Don Canham, had for some time thought television could "sell the game."

To him, that meant network exposure could build the Michigan brand, and he was all for it. If the network wanted it, Canham would try and deliver it. (Said Arledge, plotting camera placement—which would heretofore be mounted everywhere from jeeps and booms to helicopters—"Incidentally, very few men have ever switched channels when a nicely proportioned girl was leaping into the air." To the show would be added show business.)

FOOTBALL WAS, TOO, A DIVERSION FROM THE SCHISMS IN SOCIETY, WHICH WERE DEEPER than any period since the Civil War. Said Ron Powers in *Supertube: The Rise of Television Sports*, "By carefully keeping its cameras trained on the helmeted, disciplined players and the wholesome cheerleaders and snappy, euphemistic, Salute-to-Old-Glory marching bands at halftime, and not on the besieged administration building, the smoldering ROTC headquarters just over the stadium's rim, ABC perpetuated—however passively or unintentionally—a myth of stability, of tranquil disengaged campus life, for those who yearned for such a vision."

It was Woody and Bo, though, who gave the game its larger recognition. They presented to the game two of the most colorful coaches—and programs—in modern college football history, along with a storyline made for telecasting. All in all, The Game made for great television. It featured long-held if dimly conceived prejudices (on both sides), a turf war involving the entire geography of two states, two nationally-ranked teams, and two larger-than-life personalities, one of them who fought with referees, tore up down markers, and occasionally punched a cameraman. (ABC's Mike Freedman, it was said, truly took one for the team, which happened to be his network.) Woody and Bo emerged as football's odd couple, unwittingly thrust into the role of TV performers and exploited as such without ever quite knowing it.

Their natural temperaments couldn't have been better scripted by Hollywood. They were two of college football's last eccentric old-school coaches and fulfilled their roles perfectly. They were pugnacious mirror images, two old tackles, each with a lineman's plugging point of view. Surely Providence smiled when they appeared. They completed one another. They *deserved* one another. They became so iconic, they were known by just their first names—"Woody" and "Bo." Like Cher, Divine, and Leadbelly. Or in a later time: Diddy, Madonna, and Pink.

Without their fiery personalities, it is unlikely Michigan-Ohio State would have emerged from the cluster of regional rivalries and into national prominence.

WOODY WAS FAMOUS FOR STRIKING THE WORD "MICHIGAN" FROM THE DICTIONARY. This, of course, was an old Native American superstition in which pronouncing the name of the deceased was believed to disturb the spirit. Woody's thought, apparently, was that once he had buried Michigan he wanted Michigan to stay buried. Ann Arbor, meanwhile, didn't always say

"Ohio State." Up there, they said "Beat Woody." In the Ten-Year War, Woody had *become* the institution. It was Woody's reign that led the writer Robert Vare to say, felicitously, that "Columbus calendars revolve around the Michigan game the way Western calendars center on the birth of Jesus Christ."

Back when Bo was Woody's graduate assistant, he said he could hear Woody's voice in his sleep. As his fulltime assistant, he said he was fired fifteen times by Woody. Woody, meanwhile, gave Bo the extreme compliment: "He's a hothead, like me." They were both temperamental, single-minded perfectionists ("Put Schembechler in the center of Camelot and he would spot a loose downspout," said *Sports Illustrated*). They were so intently focused they forgot to eat or sleep. They both had heart attacks, which they probably gave to each other.

There was another element of their time, and that was the makeup of the two schools. Ohio State essentially reflected the conservative nature of its many small-town Ohio students while Michigan, on the other hand, was a hotbed of student protest. The Michigan president, Robert Fleming, for instance, came out in opposition to the Vietnam War, which upset Woody. How could these people question America's authority figures, he demanded to know. (Obviously, Fleming was not an authority figure.) Woody, of course, saw *himself* as an authority figure, which meant that this protesting rabble was questioning *him*.

The times emphasized a kind of social conflict between the two, long in place but now dramatically heightened. The writer Robert Vare described it as he heard each fan base describe it, therefore it was "Michigan, forward-looking and academically prestigious, versus Ohio State, hidebound and scholastically unglamorous... salon society vs. the lunch-bucket crowd." He thought that Michigan represented to Ohio State "phony intellectuals" while Ohio State was to Michigan "a preparatory school for farmers."

Michael Rosenberg in *Sports Illustrated* explained it this way: "Michigan and Ohio State are like mafia dons from rival families that wear unfashionable sweaters in different colors. They spend their fall killing the annoying little dudes from Indiana and

Minnesota and Iowa, then turn to each other. Ohio State sees itself as the school of the people, and Michigan sees itself as the school of the smarter people. It's a class war of a different kind."

Michigan's All-American sprinter-turned-broadcaster, Bob Ufer, enjoyed the class struggle and liked to dissect the unruly crowd in Ohio Stadium as "4,000 Michigan fans, 10,000 alumni, and 74,000 truck drivers." (He also liked to antagonize Woody by using Woody's military analogies against him: "Wasn't that Michigan drive just great?" he announced. "That was like riding into Berlin!")

To fully understand the relationship between the two places, one had only to review the tale of Ohio State student Thomas Harrington, arrested in 1970 for public obscenity: his Volkswagen was bearing a bumper sticker proclaiming "Fuck Michigan." In Franklin County Municipal Court, the prosecutor, highly offended, said there was no more obscene word in the English language. The judge, fully understanding the culture around him, disagreed. He said Mr. Harrington's sentiments did *not* offend community standards, rather it upheld them. Said the judge, "Mr. Harrington's bumper sticker accurately expressed the derogatory nature of this mood toward the University of Michigan football team and the state of Michigan as a whole."

Redeeming social value, said the judge—and case dismissed.

A RELATIVELY RECENT COMMERCIAL REVEALS HOW THE GAME HAS BECOME EMBEDDED in the national consciousness. The ESPN commercial shows a closeup of a young couple in a passionate embrace on a couch. As the camera pans out, the viewer sees the man is wearing an Ohio State sweatshirt and the woman is wearing a Michigan one. Then the caption: "Without sports, this wouldn't be disgusting."

Waiting so long for equity can bring about some extraordinary manifestations, such as the fan who claimed to have a Buckeye birthmark on his ass, and the ten-year-old Columbus boy who named his brain tumor "Michigan"—when he went into remission, he said that he had "beat Michigan." And then there was the Block

O member who lived in Michigan and found himself wearing his Ohio State gear to a Michigan mall and getting booed by someone in a wheelchair.

Although the rivalry has been softened a bit, both by the Big Ten splitting into two divisions, as well as Ohio State's dominance in the new century (17–2, through 2020). The Big Ten playoff now means that it's unlikely the Ohio State–Michigan game will ever again decide the league title or national championship. The best that can be hoped for is that it decides who plays for the Big Ten championship, that is, who *might* have a chance to play in the game that *decides* who gets to play for the national championship. Otherwise, until the old bloodlines die out, the game remains intact. Since the opening of Ohio Stadium in 1922, upwards of nine million fans have seen The Game in person.

For at least some of that, and more, you can thank Woody—and Bo.

> Some men wrestle alligators for a living. Others umpire baseball games. Still others munch on razorblades and wash them down with fire. And there are those, the supreme daredevils, who coach football at Ohio State.
> —Look magazine

The last grand eccentric

Wayne Woodrow Hayes, requiescat in pace

Picture him trailed around campus by small cadres of anthropologists who studied him as though he were some missing link between forgotten eras. Perhaps they believed he came from the Pleistocene Epoch when the first archaic human material evolved into the college coaching gene pool. Some might have seen him as a product of the Mesozoic Era when other large predatory creatures roamed the sidelines. The overwhelming surmise, though, was that whatever his origins, no one had ever seen anything like him, nor would they again.

As for the rest of us, we saw him as an isolated figure, fiercely at odds with everything around him: referees, sportswriters, photographers, other coaches, fans, even his own players. The iconic photographs showed him screaming at someone, anyone, really, who came between him and victory. Down by two touchdowns to Alabama at halftime of the 1978 Sugar Bowl, he jogged off the field, despondent, head down—and ran into a goalpost. Then he threw a left hook at it. In Woody Hayes's orbit, even inanimate objects were at risk.

Woody's dilemma was that he had been born in the wrong century; he was a nineteenth century man dropped mistakenly into the twentieth. It was a poor cosmic joke, and he never forgave the universe for misplacing him. His worldview fell somewhere between the Civil War and the turn of the century. He would have been most at home with those other Ohio fellows, Grant and Sherman, for they were totems of offense which he saw as remarkably similar to his own. (In Woody's long reign at Ohio State, he invoked Sherman's strategies so often that some thought Sherman was on his staff.)

He was equal parts stevedore, samurai, and monk, although you were never sure exactly which of them was going to show up. When he commanded the USS Rinehart in WWII, he set up a punching bag outside his quarters and worked on it every afternoon. It was as if the larger war had grown abstract around him, and he wanted to make sure it remained personal. But then everything was personal to him, every encounter. "His nerves were strung together with football laces," *Sports Illustrated* said.

He was the least politically correct person on his entire campus, and he kept no opinion—he had one on everything—to himself. He seemed duty-bound to inform an indecisive world of what it should really think, even as he was continuously upstaged by the forces of modernism. "He called everything by its right name, or at least the name by which he knew it," wrote Alan Natali in *Woody's Boys*. Natali said Woody was certain that holding his tongue would give him an ulcer, and speaking out was thus a kind of fealty.

He was contradictory to the point of perverseness, which was part of his charm. He had a definite intellectual bent, quoting Persian proverbs, Ralph Waldo Emerson, and Vince Lombardi, sometimes all in the same moment. Playing Iowa, he took his team to Herbert Hoover's gravesite only to interrupt the tour guide to lecture them about Hoover himself. He also thought a good punch in the head could set many things right. When Bo Schembechler was on Woody's staff, they threw furniture at each other. He and Iowa coach Forest Evashevski almost came to blows over the grass in Kinnick Stadium, which Woody thought had been purposefully grown long to hamper OSU's running game. (He threatened to get a lawnmower.) Woody had fired most of his coaches at least once (although none of the firings seemed to result in an actual layoff). He even fired a referee he'd hired to officiate at practices because he disagreed with one of his calls. "I try not to be a petty person," he said, "but I am a petty person. And I have a terrible temper."

His rages were unrestrained, even the calculated ones. And they were all so wrathful no one could tell them apart. He hit himself in the face, bit the heel of his hand in fury, ripped his tee-shirts, and destroyed enough wristwatches to lift Timex stock (his players were sure he bought the cheap ones). He shoved a camera into a photographer's face, threatened more than one reporter, and elbowed a heckler in the head. His players were careful not to stand on his right side, for he had an injurious left hook that he might release at any time. He once punched Ron Maciejowski in the stomach so hard the quarterback couldn't get enough breath to call signals. "He had a temper like a toothless cat," said *Sports Illustrated.*

Then there was the other Woody, the doppelgänger who showed up unexpectedly to smile benignly upon the populace, kiss babies, and visit the sick—none of which was calculated. After the 1975 win over Michigan that sent the Buckeyes to the Rose Bowl, someone handed Woody a bouquet of roses when OSU's charter landed at Port Columbus. Woody took the bouquet to Riverside Hospital where he went through the halls, greeting patients and dispensing roses until they were all gone. Another time, a senior member of the Quarterback Club answered his doorbell to discover Woody had come to wish him a happy birthday. He was just a guy Woody occasionally saw at the club meetings, a factory worker. The man's son had called Woody to ask, and there he was. These were not isolated moments but, needless to say, they made no headlines. If they did, they were most often relegated to the back pages where they shared space with the Lithuanian stock quotations.

Woody's best self was reserved for his visits to hospitals, and particularly his visits to recruits. Here, he was superbly at home, and there was more than one report where the worn carpet of some modest house had been converted to marble merely by his footstep. He came as the emissary of a notable power, which was Ohio's state university, and he represented its mission, which was twofold: (1) educational uplift and (2) the making of a manly citizen. He was the best recruiter in the university's sporting history because he believed so fervently in what he was selling, which was first of all himself. And while the athletically gifted offspring had drawn him, that's not who he was visiting; he was visiting them, the parents.

When he went to visit Jack Tatum in New Jersey, Jack came home from school to street reports that his mother had let a vacuum cleaner salesman in the house. What he found, instead, was Woody, sitting at the kitchen table and eating his mother's banana cream pie. "This is the best pie I've ever tasted," Woody said, largely ignoring Jack. "I've got to get this recipe for my wife." Tatum, who was considering Syracuse where the great Jim Brown had recently frolicked his way into legendary status as a multisport star, admitted that Woody recruited his mother. "When he left," Tatum said, "my mom said she liked him because he had little holes in the bottoms of his shoes. She said that a man so famous who had holes in his shoes fit in with us." And he thought, *Oh, Lord, I'm going to Ohio State*...

There was at least one sportswriter who contended that Woody's crusty persona came from all the pie he had eaten. (Each of the piemakers tended to say that her pie had "a special crust.") When Woody told any particular mother that her pie was the best he'd ever tasted, he sincerely meant it, at least until the next pie. "My wife, I love her dearly," he would say, "but she can't make an apple pie like you can." It was one of his few indulgences. His mother had been a pie baker. And, besides, pie was American. Hadn't the GIs fought WWII for pie?

There was a legendary Columbus moment involving pie, which came about when Woody's wife, Anne, found a bedside drawer filled with dozens of cards inscribed with women's handwriting. In a fury, she drove to St. John Arena and steamed into Woody's office, demanding to know what all these women were doing writing him.

He asked her if she'd read the cards.

No, she hadn't. (Hers was a visceral reaction, which mirrored his own.)

"Go back and read them," he said.

That was when she saw they were…pie recipes.

WOODY ATE A BEAN SUPPER WITH TIM ANDERSON AND HIS FAMILY SOMEWHERE IN THE BACKWOODS OF WEST VIRGINIA, and he had his hair cut by Rex Kern's father, a Lancaster barber. In Wilmington, Ohio, just before Thanksgiving, Woody turned up at the local high school to see Gary Williams, another of his recruits. When Williams walked into the coach's office, Woody said, "Are you chewing GUM?" Then he launched into a tirade on Williams's grades. "If you don't get this English grade up," he said, "you'll never set foot in Ohio Stadium without a ticket."

A chastened Williams—who had by this time swallowed the gum—slunk out of the coach's office without any more conversation. The coach, Tony Lamke, learned that Woody ate Thanksgiving dinner that weekend with the Williams family. And Williams went on to a stellar career as Art Schlichter's prime target; only in 2019 was his school record for passes caught in consecutive games—forty-eight—tied by K.J. Hill.

Woody, the recruits recognized—or their parents did—could have talked a blind man across the interstate at rush hour. Or as Jim Parker once said, "Woody could take a guy with a wooden leg and make him run a 100-yard dash."

He possessed an instinctive articulation and was often found at the Faculty Club where he liked to debate the academics, many of whom admired him. (Instruct was the better word here, for Woody seldom debated.) He was both literary and literal—oppositional traits—and he could at any moment be overridden by a remarkable peevishness prompted by almost anything. The 1970s were hard on him: student unrest, Vietnam, gas shortages. Nefarious influences lurked everywhere, the Republic was under siege, and he feared for his players. He hated Japanese cars, mustaches, even platform shoes. "I'm telling you," he said to Tim Fox, his All-American safety, "if you fall off those shoes, your ass is grass."

He coached his boys to stop driving their cars to the practice facilities. "Goddammit, you're wasting gas," he'd say. "People, there's a gas shortage out there. There's no reason for you to be driving. Take a bus. Walk over…" He walked to work from his house on Cardiff Road, which was over two miles. "Goddammit," he'd say, "I'm not going to use any A-rab oil! They're not getting a dime out of me." Fox remembered being on the team bus and Woody yelling at the driver for going over fifty-five miles an hour, telling him how he was wasting gas and "helping the goddamned A-rabs."

Woody was an inveterate missionary for the America he felt was slipping away from him. He was both charismatic and boorish, almost in the same instance. He delivered a long fulmination on women's lib to writer Robert Vare in which he told Vare that the best way to deal with women was to knock them up and take away their shoes. Yet he displayed an Old World courtliness around women and had by every account a good marriage to a strong and resourceful woman.

HIS ARTICULATION WAS BEST ON DISPLAY WITH MATTERS HISTORICAL, PARTICULARLY MILITARY HISTORY, where he was widely read. He said the Battle of Britain was "the greatest goal line stand ever," and that Churchill's famous speech to the House of Commons after Dunkirk was the best locker room speech ever given. Football, too, was warfare, and given his own truculent personality—and the fact that he had actually been to war—it's not difficult to see why he might have confused Ann Arbor with Appomattox.

Football was surely what Woody loved most. And given that he was no longer a player nor a warrior—both avenues now closed to him—then why was his bellicose nature not perfectly understandable? That which was martial had been subsumed into his character. It was how he saw himself: blunt, purposeful, and remedial. He saw football as codified warfare, and its importance was such that he felt he might die in its execution. (It was why he said he wanted to die in Ohio Stadium. And if he were losing, he said, then he wouldn't die.)

It stood to reason that losing felt like death to him, and why he reacted so strongly to it. Football was a grim and foreboding business, and he wanted his players to understand that. It was how he had elevated the sport in his mind, and why when he came on the field, the disinterested fan—should there have been such a person—heard the marching band playing Wagner's *The Ride of the Valkyries*. Football was a quest, and immersed in its rigors one could rise above one's paltry self. It was the ultimate modern test of one's personal quality.

The reward was winning, which was done through sweat and pain. It was what Alan Natali called "the dogma of the willing sufferer." Woody said he might not be smart enough, but industry would carry him through and his boys would be, of all things, by God, industrious. Champ Henson, his fullback of 1972, talked of coming to the practice facility early in the morning and finding Woody had worked all night.

"Woody, man, he'd go in there, watch films, stay in there all night, live in there," Henson said. "Come in the next morning, he'd be asleep, projector just goin' around and around and around. 'Hey, Coach.' 'Oh, I was just resting my eyes. You know, I think I noticed something here,' he'd chuckle. He'd say, 'I know they're asleep right now in their beds, but I'm awake, and I'm working, uh-huh, and I found something…uh-huh.' It was always that uh-huh thing, like he was reassuring himself. 'We're gonna exploit this. They think they're safe in their beds, but they don't know *we're* working…'"

After a while, Woody's grand eccentricity was not even seen as such. His young players had only their high school coaches for comparison, and all the players knew was that these men weren't much like Woody. The truth was that no one was like Woody, but once in his orbit, everything he did seemed of a piece. He'd been known to take players who had failing grades and move them into his house with him and Anne.

Nothing had more effect on a player's grades, as relayed by Moose Machinsky, Woody's All-Big Ten tackle in 1954, who was shanghaied by Woody and became what the British Navy once called "one of the temporarily misplaced" until his grades improved. "He dropped me off at classes, picked me up after classes, made me study constantly, and would review my assignments and quiz me," Machinsky said after his ordeal. "I wasn't permitted to do anything— no dates, no movies, no TV, no beer, nothing but study. Needless to say, I worked my tail off to get out of there…"

Woody gave his freshmen copies of *Word Power Made Easy* and added vocabulary to blocking assignments. A missed word was ten pushups. Once he yelled at his All-American lineman Jim Stillwagon for horsing around in the locker room.

"Goddammit," he said to Stillwagon, "don't you know too much levity will beat you every time?"

And as the coach lumbered out of earshot, Stillwagon asked his teammates: "What the fuck does 'levity' mean?"

On trips, Woody took naps on the artificial turf he had installed in the bed of his pickup, and annoyed his wife by allowing cats to hang around their house (he felt sorry for them). He might call up an assistant at 2 a.m. and recite James Whitcomb Riley poems. And yet his eccentricity defined him simply as a forthright man who said what he thought, a trait others envied. They, too, would like a position where they might say or do anything at all. But they couldn't, so Woody became their stand-in.

The force of his personality was such that he altered the very definition of the city. When one thought of Columbus, it was quite often Woody who came first to mind. Upon his arrival in the 1950s, Columbus was a much smaller place, and the surrounding farmland still seemed to infiltrate a town that had not made up its mind about what it might be. What Woody saw, as Alan Natali pointed out, was Columbus as the potential seat of empire. It was the kind of vision the original stadium-builders had, and now Woody—of all people—would finish it.

There were the early titles, and then the great Archie Griffin teams from 1972–1975, when the Buckeyes filled Ohio Stadium with what *Sports Illustrated* called "the usual Columbus throng of eighty million," went to the Rose Bowl four consecutive years, and lost only two regular season games. An ultimate greatness was precluded only by Woody himself, whose coaching in crucial moments tended to revert to its most conservative expression.

Ohio State football, though, was now a formidable American institution. And Woody was the face of it. Or as Jim Stillwagon so tartly put it, "Woody Hayes would say 'Get fucked,' and you got fucked." Images of Woody were everywhere, so much so that when the New York writer Greg Emmanuel did his book on the Michigan–Ohio State rivalry in 2004, he was taken aback to see how prevalent they still were: in bars, restaurants, and coffeeshops. He thought it made Columbus appear to be, he said, "a strange country where the dictator is a fat football coach." A writer from Los Angeles was surprised to see how many middle-aged men at Ohio State games even looked like Woody. It was enough to make one ponder how the faithful—in football or elsewhere—might, over time, share appearances, like long-married spouses who had chosen one another because of some common attribute.

WHAT HAPPENED AT THE END OF THE 1970S WAS WHAT HAPPENS WHEN ONE IGNORES THE EARLY STIRRINGS OF ONE'S MORTALITY: young women still smile bountifully at us, surely they do; that lost quick step is merely held in abeyance; no wrinkle that, but merely a mark of character; the waistline remains taut, it is the trousers that have shrunk. Football is so attractive because no one ages. It is a game played by the perpetually young, and each autumn holds its promise. Only the coach ages; he is the Dorian Gray figure whose portrait, season by season, assumes loss, overwork, the abuse of media, the fickleness of fans, the disappointments of time.

Woody's last three years were a slow descent: Ohio State slipped from sixth in the country to eleventh, then it was unranked. There were those who traced Woody's tenuous hold on the zeitgeist back to the 1960s when he was still piping Mitch Miller into the locker room. Picture Mitch Miller in the evolution of 1960s rock, amidst the Grateful Dead, Jimi Hendrix, and the Rolling Stones. Mitch and Elvis. Even Mitch and the Beach Boys. Mitch Miller who gave rise to karaoke, so out of touch with the then-current generation that his music was piped into shopping malls to discourage teenagers from gathering.

By the time Woody was fired after the 1978 Gator Bowl, Columbus was no longer the relatively sleepy place he'd inherited. It was larger, more nuanced, even—dare the word be used?—cosmopolitan. Ohio State had achieved its goal of becoming a national institution and things once condoned or at least tolerated could no longer be ignored. The university's status, its reputation, were at stake. Football was no longer a game for the idiosyncratic. Frank Howard was long gone, Bear Bryant would last only another few years. A new circumspection was on order, and none of them would fit into it. In the culture of modern, corporate college football, coaches would be CEOs, caretakers of image as well as wins.

Jim Stillwagon tried to tell Woody about how things were changing, but his old coach couldn't hear. "A lot of guys were hosing him, but he never thought that way," Stillwagon said. "At the end of his coaching…you can't believe how bad it was. He didn't even think there were drugs going on. There were the biggest drugheads in the world during the end. Woody would just say, 'That doesn't happen, not here.'

"Someone would say, 'That guy's fuckin' you.'

"'He wouldn't do that to me.'

"He wouldn't even comprehend anybody not doing what he was supposed to do. It was really out of control. You could just see it. It was public. Guys were drugheads. He just couldn't fathom it…"

Of course he couldn't. He had come from another time, and he worked assiduously to bend time and history. He loved history because he felt historical himself. He could have bound himself in vellum and buckram and stuck himself on a shelf in every coach's office, easy reference for when people wanted to know how things were done as they should have been done, when they were at their best, when everything in America was best.

He said he wanted to die on the field, and so he did, only it wasn't Ohio Stadium. It was in a second-tier bowl game in Jacksonville, Florida, and when he slugged Clemson middle guard

Charlie Bauman, Woody was sick with heart disease and diabetes. And so quickly, he was dead to the game he had given his life to. He'd won 205 games at Ohio State, won or shared thirteen conference and five national championships, and coached fifty-nine All-Americans. He came home to gall bladder surgery and a marquee on a Columbus porno house that read "Bye, Bye, Woody."

In firing Woody, Ohio State had done what it had to do. Behavior tolerated even a decade before would no longer be. Woody's behavior on the national stage had become a liability. Yet locally, he was still a valuable asset. No matter his dismissal, his enthusiasm for his school—and his skills as salesman—would remain undiminished. And he remained a revered figure for much of the alumni. Almost reflexively, he became the university's minister without portfolio, working almost as tirelessly as before.

The university named him professor emeritus. He had a campus office, and in 1986 he gave the commencement speech at Ohio State's graduation. The street outside the stadium was named Woody Hayes Drive. Upon his death in 1987, dozens of checks from any number of charity dinners were found uncashed in a drawer. His way of giving back. Former president Richard Nixon, his old friend, gave his funeral eulogy. Ten thousand people attended a service in Ohio Stadium and the fans piled roses on the stadium turf.

In all his time, then and since, an odd thing: he has never been satisfactorily catalogued. As he fades from view, there has still been no proper accounting of his tempestuous reign in Columbus. Only that it is unlikely to be duplicated, in either wins and certainly not in temperament. For he lived on some perilous edge no one else could see nor understand. His impulses ran from the beneficial to the banal, and along with an astounding generosity he was also brutal, petty, and reactionary. His rages cost him both wins and his health. "He was always frighteningly—even pathologically—at the mercy of private demons," said *Time* magazine.

In spite of the demons, there was a kind of greatness in him although, finally, it was greatness thwarted. He lived publicly, wholly on view, and he would never have survived the advent of

YouTube and Instagram. And yet, because he lived so fully, we forgive him his trespasses. For do not most of us wish to live in a manner that is so unapologetically, authoritatively ourselves?

Section Four
The post-modern Buckeye: in pursuit of a new legend

It was the ultimate tribute to Woody that his passage marked an era unlikely to be repeated, at home or elsewhere. The Old Man had, in essence, outlived the game as he knew it, and when his former subaltern Earle Bruce opened the new decade undefeated and in the Rose Bowl, it seemed that a proper order had been returned to Columbus.

As fate and football would have it, though, it was Earle's finest moment, not to be revisited. At the end of the 1980s, he was followed by John Cooper, an outsider who no speaka da native language, and whose vital work on Ohio State's infrastructure seemed to be appreciated only in hindsight. (He had two great one-loss teams, in 1996 and 1998, being denied Abraham's bosom each time by the state of Michigan.)

The quarter of a century that came after Woody was an era defined by very good coaches—even the near-great—and success almost any other program only dreamed of. Jim Tressel, with his careful style and caretaker quarterbacks, won a national title in 2002 (the first consensus one since Woody's in 1968) played for two more, and reduced Michigan to an also-ran on the schedule. Then in 2010, he lost his job (and a stellar 12–1 season) over a scandal that history has since—in the evolution of scandals—relegated to a misdemeanor.

And so Ohio State, by that measure established long before by Woody himself, was just short of perennial greatness. The university's philosophy department was surely intrigued by the conundrum of the football program, which appeared to be a perfect example of what is known as Zeno's dichotomy. This is the 2,500-year-old paradox described by *Wired* magazine as "moving from point A to point B requires that you first cover half the distance, then half of the remaining distance, and so on—an insurmountable infinity of almost-theres that keeps you from point B."

Wasn't this exactly what bothered the most fervent of the fan base? It was the notion that space seemed to be infinitely subdivided, with one's goal(line)—save the rare title years—always at a distance, even if tiny. While it may have been the nature of life near the top of the national polls, the diehard Ohio State fan did not approve of conundrums.

It was hard to imagine what Jim Tressel might have done had he remained in Columbus. There was already some disenchantment with Tressel's offense, and the best guess was that his inherently conservative nature would have eventually caused more. Perhaps, in that constantly inclement personal coaching weather over Ohio Stadium, he'd gotten out just in time.

When Tressel fell, OSU's timing was exquisite: Urban Meyer was emerging from burnout after two championships at Florida and ready to get back in the game. What better fit for Ohio State than a pedigreed Ohio guy who'd begun at Ohio State. His fast start presaged legendary status, but as that self-proclaimed deity Father Divine once said, "Bein' God ain't no bed of roses."

We begin the new era in an inconspicuous place—with a small disquisition on two of the most remarkable athletes ever at Ohio State. One of them, the ill-used Paul Warfield, belonged to the previous era. The other, Cris Carter, practically announced the new era at Ohio State as his own.

Watching Warfield play at the next level—when Warfield was finally allowed to play—Carter first understood how he, himself, wanted to play. By the time he left his abbreviated time at Ohio State, he'd so dramatized the receiver position that offense at Ohio State would never be the same again.

They bridged the two epochs neatly. Warfield was a symbol of opportunities the old era had not seen; Carter was a symbol of the new one, impossible not to be seen. The post-modern period would see its best expression with Urban Meyer, who was a young coaching assistant for Carter's final Ohio State season.

And thus the seasons evolved.

End game

A tale of two generations

THE RELATIVELY SHORT LIST OF GREAT OHIO STATE RECEIVERS IN THE LATTER HALF OF THE TWENTIETH CENTURY is neatly accented by two of the at-large greatest—although greatness for neither Paul Warfield nor Cris Carter was wholly obvious until they became professionals. The subsequent illumination of their craft reflected back to Columbus only when Ohio State was a footnote on their weighty professional résumés. Neither, for instance, are in the College Football Hall of Fame, yet both are in the pro hall.

Warfield came late to the receiving game because he played for Woody Hayes in the early 1960s. About which, enough said. (In Warfield's sophomore year, OSU averaged ten passes a game, and his statistics didn't get a lot better.) His college tenure was one of omission; Cris Carter's was commission: in 1986 he was OSU's first All-American wide receiver but ruled ineligible after secretly signing with a sports agent, and his absence in the lineup led—somewhat more than indirectly—to Earle Bruce's firing.

Warfield and Carter were separated by a generation and quite a few style points. Warfield—old-school, mild-mannered and uncomplaining had been one of the best high school runners in the country. On the varsity, he scored from 60 yards out the first time he touched the ball. He set an Ohio record in the 180-yard hurdles and won the state long jump title. And he played basketball.

When the Warren G. Harding High basketball team came to Columbus to scrimmage Columbus East over a Thanksgiving weekend, Woody showed up at the team's breakfast with a cake for Warfield's 17th birthday. Woody collected Ohio athletes, and he wanted Warfield. But once he had him, he didn't seem to know exactly what to do with him.

Warfield's athleticism was such that it was hard to keep him off the field, though. So he stayed on it all the time. Players did that then, because unlimited substitution didn't reappear until the 1965 season. He made the All-Big Ten team twice—but largely for his talents as a defensive back. As a junior, he led the Buckeyes in receiving—eight catches, 139 yards. That would be, in time, the work of merely one autumn afternoon. It might be said, not inaccurately, that the only thing containing Warfield on the football field was Woody's offense.

In three years at Ohio State, he caught 39 passes. His numbers at running the ball weren't gaudy, either: he had 1,047 rushing yards. One Big Ten scout explained Warfield's limitations as an Ohio State running back. "Coach Hayes doesn't like a back who ducks and darts all over the place," he said. "He wants the back who puts his head down and heads straight for the goal line on an off-tackle play. Warfield isn't big enough to run over people."

Paul Warfield was simply an athlete. But that position didn't exist back then. He never lamented—publicly anyway—how Woody played him. He even thanked his coach for teaching him how to block, for at Ohio State blocking was where the repetitions were. "For my capabilities," Warfield said, "running the wing T may have been better, but I have no regrets. I learned how to block, and blocking became the skill I needed when I evolved into professional football…"

Before his senior year, though, he'd flirted with giving up Ohio State for a baseball contract from the Pittsburgh Pirates, who wanted him in spite of the fact that he'd only played a little sandlot baseball after high school; Warfield, it seemed, could play *anything*. He was, for instance, the fifth-ranked long jumper in the world while still at Ohio State, even though he competed only in the spring. He related long jumping to football, measuring his stride precisely, looking on the field for that invisible grass takeoff board.

In 1964, he went to Cleveland, the eleventh overall pick of the NFL draft. While scouting Warfield, the Browns' personnel had already noticed how nervous the opposition was at the mere prospect of what he might do, and it didn't take Blanton Collier, the Browns coach, long to notice Warfield's athleticism.

Moved to receiver, he caught 52 passes for 920 yards as a rookie, and the Browns won their first NFL championship in nine years. He was still playing on a running team, however—the Browns had perhaps the greatest running back of all time, Jim Brown, and after him, Leroy Kelly, another one almost as good. So Warfield's rookie numbers, in terms of catches, were his career best. But that early scouting report was consequential: Warfield's very presence on the field was sometimes as good as a catch, because he always had to be accounted for, sometimes with a double team. Thus, as would be the case throughout his career, Warfield's numerical sacrifices were laid on the altar of the running game.

It was big news in 1970 when the Browns traded him to the Miami Dolphins. In five of his six Cleveland years, Warfield helped lead the Browns to the playoffs. They won one NFL championship and played in three NFL title games—twice one game from the fledgling Super Bowl, which was first played in January of 1967. In those halcyon days, though, the Browns were used to winning it all: they'd dominated the NFL in the 1950s. They were Green Bay before Green Bay was Green Bay. But Otto Graham was long gone and they needed a healthy quarterback. Their answer was to trade Warfield for the third pick in the 1970 draft, and that was Purdue quarterback Mike Phipps. The solution, though, was worse than the problem; Phipps never won a playoff game for them.

"The only thing I'd say about Mike is I think he'd rather have gone fishing than play football," said one of his teammates. It wasn't the most fair appraisal of Phipps's abilities, but there it was anyway. A larger consideration was the trade itself, for as Cleveland sportswriter Tony Grossi pointed out about Phipps, "He never escaped the giant shadow left by Warfield's departure."

Warfield, meanwhile, found himself on another run-oriented team. Miami's backfield was one of the best ever—Jim Kiick, Larry Csonka (another Ohio guy), and Mercury Morris—but Warfield loosened the defenses with his big-play capability. His first season in Miami he caught only 28 passes but he gained 703 yards—more than 25 yards a catch. The opposition simply could not contain Warfield and Miami's backfield.

The gonzo journalist, Hunter S. Thompson, wrote the best description of Warfield: "There is an eerie kind of certainty about Warfield's style that is far more demoralizing than just another six points on the scoreboard," he said. "About half the time he looks bored and lazy—but even the best pass defenders in the league know, in some nervous corner of their hearts, that when the deal goes down Warfield is capable of streaking right past them like they didn't exist…" Thompson said that watching Warfield float into the heart of the defense was the most beautiful sight in football, for Warfield caught the ball without seeming to notice its arrival.

In the entire history of the sport, there have been few so defined by such grace. His teammates, once watching him walk down a street, laughed at how he seemed to be reading the sidewalk for clues as to where he might step next, an instinctive suppleness and balance denied to mere mortals. At the same time, he was a devastating blocker—a blue-collar skill he'd learned from Woody back in Columbus. "He would knock you right on your ass," said one of his old Browns teammates, linebacker Dale Lindsey, describing how Warfield once took out Los Angeles Rams' 6-foot-7 defensive end Lamar Lundy. "Laid him out like a tree."

In Miami, Warfield was known as the most dangerous receiver in pro football. He was a perennial Pro Bowler, played in three Super Bowls (the Dolphins won two of them), and scored once every five times he touched the ball. His numbers weren't necessarily Hall of Fame numbers, but numbers don't always tell the full story. There was *this* one, however: Warfield is the only NFL player to catch 400 passes and average 20 yards per catch (427 catches, to be precise, for an average of 20.1). No one else has come close. Paul Warfield was one of the few receivers who didn't even have to touch the ball to alter the game. And students of the game still regard his trade to Miami as worst in Browns history.

THE OTHER FOUNDING OHIO STATE RECEIVER CAME ALONG TWENTY YEARS LATER, and he would influence the game in an entirely different way. By the time Cris Carter arrived in Columbus in 1984, Earle Bruce actually had some affinity for a thrown ball, and although Earle had been a trainee at Woody Hayes's spartan dinner table, he still liked a little dessert. Carter was dessert.

He came from not very far away—Middletown, Ohio, where he was a prep legend in two sports, and basketball almost claimed him. His older brother, Butch, had starred at Indiana and gone on to the Indiana Pacers, and Cris saw himself in the NBA, too. That is, until his high school coach, Bill Conley, explained to Carter the scarcity of 6-foot-2 guards in the NBA. So football it was.

When Cris told his brother he was going to Ohio State, Butch asked him, "Why you want to go there? They don't throw the football."

And Cris said, "Well, they've never had a receiver like me."

And they hadn't. Conley called him the most versatile athlete he'd ever coached. He was Ohio State's first All-American wide receiver. He was also the first to gain 1,000 yards in a season (1,127 in 1986). He didn't have the greatest speed but he was remarkably sure-handed, had uncanny body control, and the traffic around him didn't seem to exist.

(His high school teammates laughed about his speed. "I would be looking downfield for him, and he'd be over there, yelling for the ball," said his Middie quarterback, Al Milton. "You had to throw him the Hail Mary because he couldn't get behind anybody. He was never open. But he caught it, anyway.")

Even then, Carter was perfecting his trademark sideline moves—planting his toes just inbounds and stretching himself to catch passes impossibly out-of-bounds. There was a Carter catch in the 1985 Citrus Bowl so improbable it took film to verify it. First, he leaped impossibly high, reached out of bounds so far he appeared to catch the ball on top of the BYU bench, then came down on his toes just inside the chalk mark. The quarterback, Jim Karsatos, thought he was throwing the ball away, and he couldn't believe what he saw. "He (Carter) caught the ball left-handed by the point of the football at least a yard out of bounds," Karsatos said. "Then he somehow levitated back in bounds to get both his feet in..." Karsatos still calls it the greatest catch he ever saw.

"Carter was the brash, talented kid who ultimately did more to help the Ohio State offense evolve than any quarterback who had ever played there, Art Schlichter included," said sportswriter Joe Menzer. Carter turned down the NFL draft in the spring of 1987, intent on returning for his senior year—and a shot at the Heisman. Ohio State was the preseason No. 5, then came the troubles. An FBI investigation turned up a postdated agent's contract Carter had signed with the controversial Norby Walters, who, according to one report, threatened clients who left him by telling them, "I'm going to talk to my people in Las Vegas and get them to break your legs."

Carter was declared ineligible for the 1987 season, leaving quarterback Tom Tupa without his main receiver, and Ohio State fell to 6-4-1. Earle Bruce was fired the week before coaching his players to a 23–20 win over Michigan in Ann Arbor. If you have to go, that's the way to do it, but most Buckeye fans believe Carter's transgression with Norby Walters doomed both the season and Bruce. Even without his senior year, Carter left OSU with the school record for career receptions, 168, which—more than thirty years later—has been topped only twice.

He went to Philadelphia in the supplemental draft and began a classic journey of wandering in the wilderness, failing three drug tests and ending up with Minnesota, who claimed him off the waiver wire for $100. (His old teammate Keith Byars said of him, "Cris has always been an all-or-nothing kind of guy…when he was doing drugs and alcohol, I'm sure he was trying to be the best addict out there.")

That hundred bucks was the best bargain in pro sports since a sandlot player named Johnny Unitas signed with the Baltimore Colts for $437 a week back in 1956. A decade later, Carter had been to eight Pro Bowls and was named the Walter Payton NFL Man of the Year. It was an impressive example of righting one's personal self, especially as he'd reinvented both himself and the receiver position.

Carter caught thousands of balls, using the Jugs machine dialed up to fifty-five miles per hour while he stood sideways from ten yards away. ("I wouldn't try that because I'd break my fingers," said the other Viking receiver, Jake Reed.) His work habits translated into a career of catching the uncatchable. "I catch everything that the normal people catch and I catch a few things that no one catches," Carter said. He caught passes over the heads of defensive backs, in the back of the end zone, one-handed, falling down, and—during warmups—behind his back.

His Minnesota offensive coordinator Brian Billick said Carter's uniqueness came from being able to catch the ball in tight places. "Not many can make the full-speed cuts Cris can in such small space," Billick said. "He has tremendous body control." Billick contended that Carter invented the modern slot receiver. "Basketball on grass," Billick called Carter's abilities, fitting for the Middletown guy who once wanted to play NBA basketball.

When he left the game after sixteen years, he had rendered the unprecedented as commonplace, and he had become prince of the highlight reels. ("They don't pay us to be insurance anymore," he said. "They expect us to alter outcomes.") He was second only to Jerry Rice in catches (1,101) and touchdowns (130). He had caught nearly eight miles of passes, gone to the Pro Bowl eight times, and been named to the NFL 1990s All-Decade Team.

It was only a matter of time before he made the Hall of Fame. That happened in 2013 where he apologized to Ohio State fans and to his old coach, Earle Bruce. Not playing for Ohio State his senior year, he said, "was the only regret I have in my athletic career." Canton, he noted, was a mere 241 miles from the housing project he'd grown up in but, he said, "It felt like ten million miles."

Odd that Ohio State—not the first place people thought of as a training ground for wide receivers—had produced two of the NFL's most accomplished. And both had pushed the envelope. At Ohio State, Carter was the first of the high-octane receivers who'd follow him, and he gave the passing game parity after the miserly aerial offenses of OSU's past. The Buckeyes would heretofore recruit the receiver position as never before. His play at the next level set a standard for those who came to Columbus after him. He was so good at what he did, he shamed the impossible; watching him, one could no longer tell how difficult it was to catch a thrown ball. As for Paul Warfield, he made evaluators change the way they graded receivers, for his greatness—obvious to his contemporaries—couldn't be measured statistically. He played the prime of his career in the deadball era, and he still redefined the passing game.

Between the two of them, a generation apart, their supreme athleticism announced to all: *This is what you can now expect.*

> One of the worst things about coaching football at Ohio State was the 90,000 assistant coaches you had at every home game.
> —Earle Bruce

The man who followed The Legend

Earle suits up

EARLE BRUCE HAD BRASS ENOUGH FOR A FULL ORCHESTRA, BUT IN THE END HE NEVER HEARD THE DIRGE IT WAS PLAYING FOR HIM. He was nervy enough to follow The Legend into Columbus, and at the end of his first season, in the 1980 Rose Bowl, he was two points away from being one himself. There, the unbeaten No. 1 Buckeyes were underdogs to a USC team so talented it featured six future All-Pros and one Heisman winner who was backed up by a future Heisman winner. Early in the game, with Ohio State on the USC two-yard line, USC defended the series perfectly. USC linebacker Chip Banks, on fourth down at the one-yard line, stopped Art Schlichter on an option keeper—the determining play in a 17–16 USC win.

"If I had pitched it to Cal Murray," Art said afterward, "he probably would have walked into the end zone." Bruce agreed with him, and such is the hindsight that corrects history's misdeeds. Rose Bowl dinner for Bruce and his staff was pastrami and corned beef sandwiches, eaten off the hood of the car in a Sunset Boulevard parking lot. "This is what happens when you lose," said Bruce, ruefully. If he'd won, he said, there would have been a tablecloth.

His quarterback, Schlichter, looked back years later and remembered the game with a canny observation. He recalled how the field looked, a telling moment, given what was to come in his own life, and he said, "It was as green as money." He saw it as the one game that would have changed everybody's life forever. "It would have elevated us all to hero status," he said, "a lasting legacy as an Ohio State national championship team. The impact of a national championship in Earle's first year, I'm sure, would have changed his career as well."

Even the USC coach, John Robinson, understood his win was as much luck as Trojan talent. "Ninety times out of a hundred, they would have scored on us," he said. And: "There's not a coach in the country who doesn't think he can make two yards in four tries."

Bruce was an interesting study, an outsider whose Maryland-bred blue-collar comportment never quite seemed to fit Columbus. Perhaps after three decades and what appeared to be half the history of Ohio State football, the place was just accustomed to Woody Hayes, the old magician who, even as the forces of anarchy threatened to unseat him, would pull off yet another season in the national limelight.

It was mollifying to some of the fans that Earle was Woody's invention; Woody had kept Earle at Ohio State after Earle blew out his knee as a freshman, even creating a student assistant position for him. (In those days, injured players usually lost their scholarships.) He loaned Earle his car to get to his first job interview, and he gave Earle his first college job, even if Earle did take a pay cut moving from Massillon to Columbus. He came in as defensive secondary coach, which he felt secure about because he thought Massillon's pass coverage strategies were ahead of Ohio State's. He was used to the football culture, too, as Massillon at the time had what many thought was the No. 2 football program in Ohio, even if it was a high school. (The town was so fervent that fans might stone the team bus after the infrequent loss, which might help explain why Earle was unbeaten in his two years there.)

When Earle first saw Ohio Stadium he thought it was one of the ancient wonders. That was before he coached for Woody, who was the genuine ancient wonder. Student assistant was one thing; staff assistant was something else. He knew how peculiar Woody was, but he didn't know the extent of it until he found himself rooming with Woody on a recruiting trip to western Pennsylvania. Earle turned on the television. Woody turned it off. Earle went to the bathroom. So did Woody. "The room seemed to be shrinking," Earle said. "He was everywhere."

When Woody finally went to bed and turned out the light, Earle heard him say, "Fuck 'em all." He wondered what Woody was talking about. He worried about what he might be missing. Finally, after what seemed to be hours, Earle drifted off. The next morning, he asked Woody who he was talking about. "The alumni," Woody said. It was his method of maintaining a notion of control over what Earle would later refer to as "the 90,000 assistant coaches." Said Woody, "Take their money, but you don't have to answer to those bastards for anything."

Earle spent an entire season in Woody's doghouse and never knew why. Once, introducing his assistants to the players' parents, Woody forgot Earle's name. Earle got chest pains (most of the assistants did; the quarterbacks got ulcers). He thought about returning to Massillon and opening a pizza restaurant, and he dreamed about sitting on top of the practice facility and dropping a cement block on Woody. "Woody lived in my subconscious," he said.

Woody never complimented Earle's coaching until Earle left for Tampa in 1972. Of course, Earle had only been at Ohio State for six years. Yet it was the most impressionable experience of his coaching life, and it prepared him for all that was to come, including his return to Ohio State.

And so: two points from the immortality bestowed by winning a national title, Earle began 1980 as top Columbus dog. He was tops in the AP poll, too, which put Ohio State at its preseason No. 1 spot. Two weeks in, though, and the honeymoon was over. Art

Schlichter, unhappy because he wasn't throwing enough, threatened to transfer, then the Bucks lost to UCLA. They lost to Michigan, too, and to Penn State in the Fiesta Bowl. It was the first of Earle's six 9–3 seasons. How was such seasonal congruity even possible? Imagine the Vegas line; even a seasoned odds-taker like Schlichter wouldn't have touched it.

Earle's record was exemplary—most anywhere but Columbus, that is. For three decades, Ohio State had been constantly in the national picture, and the fans now perpetually dreamed of empire. No coach—not even Woody—was larger than the empire. Thus, coaches visited Columbus; it was never quite home to them. Only when they were, as Earle would put it, "undefeated or dead."

For reasons never fully articulated (or even understood), Columbus did not warm to Earle. He was always a little bit suspect. "Bruce has had a debilitating problem—his personality," said *Sports Illustrated*. And: "Despite the kind of record he has, people just don't rush to his support." (That from the director of alumni affairs, which surely let Bruce know exactly what Woody was talking about when they were stuck in that Pennsylvania motel room recruiting Pennsylvania.)

No Ohio State coach seemed to fail expectations in so many small ways. He was criticized for not being glib, for telling the same jokes, for not dining—as Woody did—at the faculty club. Woody's personality was such that he could lecture you on Sherman's tactical warfare and you'd come away thinking you'd been included in an intimate, personal moment. Earle had none of this; moreover, he wasn't interested. In essence, Earle was criticized for not being Woody. (The hazy fan memory had already forgotten how easily Woody himself yo-yoed up and down in their glib affections.)

Earle was called "roundish and frayed looking, as if handled fondly but a lot." One publication or another always seemed to be writing that Earle's shirttail was sticking out, as though the shirttail was an infraction and might cost Ohio State some yardage. His friend and supporter, athletic director Rick Bay, suggested that Earle show up on game day wearing a tuxedo. Bruce didn't, of course, but he did start wearing a jacket and tie, along with a fedora, which someone said made him look like Bugs Moran going to Al Capone's funeral.

The *Plain Dealer* quoted a university official calling Earle "whiny, grumpy, greedy." Bay said he didn't understand why Earle had a problem with popularity. "Everybody who knows him likes him," said Bay, who hated coming to work on Wednesdays because that was when the letters written at halftime on Saturday got to him. "Maybe he needs to get out more."

Some of it was simply that losing three games a year was at least two too many. Bay recalled a top booster telling him not long after he had arrived in 1984, "Earle's done a great job. But you're new in town and let me give you some friendly advice. No one in Columbus wants to be told that 9–3 is acceptable…" There it was again: dreams of empire. Earle was neither undefeated nor dead, and those seemed to be Columbus's only choices for him.

He won a lot of games but not a lot of influence. The latter, he said, wasn't his job. He wasn't a man of nuance, which, in his blunt world, was a virtue. "I was fired because I pissed off the Columbus power structure," he said. Or as the *Los Angeles Times* said, analyzing Earle's departure, "he wasn't one of the fellas," noting that the Columbus downtowners apparently wanted someone who could both tie a Windsor knot and beat Michigan.

In his near-decade in Columbus, Earle won four Big Ten titles, four bowl games, and beat Bo Schembechler five times (something even Woody couldn't do). When he was fired during the week of the Michigan game in 1987, he had the best record in the Big Ten, then he beat Bo—in Ann Arbor—on his way out the door. "I always mind losing to Ohio State but I didn't mind so much today," a sympathetic Schembechler told him after the game. (Ohio State wouldn't win again in Ann Arbor for fourteen years; it was though Earle's firing had somehow cursed the university.)

The firing wasn't pretty; for weeks, there was more dirty laundry in Columbus than a finals-week frat house. Upset and angry at both the firing and the handling of it, Earle used the nuclear option: he sued the university for wrongful dismissal. Earle contended university president Edward Jennings had made malicious statements about him, that he'd implied Earle was too old to be head coach. In the ensuing (and very public) brouhaha, reports were flung around about Jennings's own job being in danger because of "carousing and excessive drinking."

It was suddenly *Scandal*, in which the U.S. president had been replaced by the university president. "Money, Sex, and Football: A Tale of Bungling and Chaos, Honor and Revenge," read one national headline. With Jennings's heavy-handed treatment, Earle, never a fan favorite, was now a martyr. The Ohio State Marching Band serenaded him in front of his Worthington Hills house and *Columbus Monthly* said Ed Jennings had just done something even Earle Bruce couldn't do—"make Earle Bruce a sympathetic figure."

Earle demanded to know exactly why he was fired, but Jennings said he didn't have to give Earle a reason. Even *Sports Illustrated*'s writers couldn't pin Jennings down, and when they asked him what he wanted in a football coach, he said, "I know it's a fair question. But, ah, but, ah, I, ah, I, and I'll answer it to some extent, but very briefly because I, ah, don't want any implication about the, ah, current coach. But, ah, you're, ah, gonna, ah, see a coach, as, who does, ah, represent the university well. Ah, and, ah, is, ah, ah, is a part and parcel of the institution." And thus one gets some idea of the difficulty of being head coach at Ohio State. Or its president.

The lawsuit itself was settled and quickly; Earle got a lump-sum payout of $471,000, which was more than triple the salary left on his contract, but the settlement bought out some of his retirement benefits and included a stipulation that he return a portion of the payout if he found a new job before the end date of the old contract.

His coaching career was not yet over: the next season he was coaching at Northern Iowa, and he went on to Colorado State. (There, he was then fired in another scandal in which he was charged with abusing players, as well as discouraging them from taking classes that conflicted with practice, all of which must have gladdened the cold hearts of the anti-Bruce faction back in

Columbus.) He finished his career with five seasons in the Arena Football League. None of it says that the Ohio State firing wasn't the formative event in his career, for it was. Whatever Earle's personal culpabilities (both at home and abroad), it was clear he'd disobeyed—unwillingly, of course—the essential mantra in Columbus, which was to win. Not often but always.

WHILE HE DID NOT BECOME A LEGEND AT OHIO STATE, HE DID LEAVE A LEGACY. College football history is filled with examples of programs that faltered after a legend stepped down. Earle didn't allow that to happen at Ohio State. And though he did not claim college football's biggest prize, his former assistants did. At least eight of them became college or pro head coaches, and among them they've—as of 2018—won fifteen national titles and a Super Bowl. (Dom Capers, as defensive coordinator, helped Green Bay win another one.) Earle didn't take any credit for their success but surely he had some small part in it. There was another, more painful legacy: no other coach would be dismissed like Earle was. Many thought the nature of Earle's firing kept John Cooper employed for at least an extra season or two. Or as Earle put it, "I was a godsend for John Cooper."

Columbus has never been a place with much talent for irony, but part of Earle's legacy was exactly that: when his coaching career was done, he found himself at home in Columbus. He was a radio commentator, and in 2016 he was asked to dot the "i" in Script Ohio during the halftime of the Rutgers game. He was, in other words and at long last, the paterfamilias. He'd become the elder statesman, as though all that had gone on before had been merely a rite of passage. No matter, the pain of it. He'd loved Ohio State since the first time he saw it well over half a century before. Now—finally—it had returned the love.

About the time you're feeling pretty good about yourself, be sure and check your hole card.—John Cooper

The outsider

The man who followed the man who followed the legend

JOHN COOPER WASN'T THE SAME KIND OF OUTSIDER EARLE BRUCE HAD BEEN, but they both had trouble settling down in Columbus. Earle was blunt, single-minded, and didn't much care for what passed as the social niceties in downtown C-bus. Cooper, on the other hand, was extremely affable, the kind of guy who, in the words of one of his assistant coaches, "could sell a pair of white gloves to a woman eating a ketchup popsicle." And he came to Columbus with a splendid résumé. His Arizona State team had just beaten Michigan in the 1987 Rose Bowl, which was all the résumé he needed. (Although as every Ohio State fan knows, a Michigan win is a Chinese meal; after a brief time, you're hungry for another one.)

His difficulty was that it took him forever to understand the peculiar passions of the native population. His particular sociological dilemma was described best by Alan Natali in *Woody's Boys* when Natali said of Cooper, "He seemed never to consider that entering into such an intricate system of customs and beliefs was like inheriting a classic automobile—Great-Grandfather's Duesenberg or Pierce-Arrow—a vehicle impressive to drive but difficult and expensive to maintain." The population did odd things like date important occurrences by the Michigan game, as in, "My son was born a week before we beat Michigan in '94." (Being as how 1994 was Coop's first win over Michigan in seven tries, it was an auspicious occasion, and this particular newborn was surely blessed, perhaps in the manner, say, of an infant born in China with long ears, a feature that promised longevity.)

Cooper thought Michigan should be nothing more than another important game, although not one upon which the fate of Western civilization would be foretold. Even some of his assistants felt the same way. They thought the undue pressure tightened up the players unnecessarily, rather than imbuing them with the proper helter-skelter primitivism they needed to vanquish Wolverines. Unlike Cooper, though, they knew better than to say so.

Cooper was geographically suspect, too: he wasn't from Ohio, he hadn't gone to school in Ohio, and he hadn't been an assistant coach at Ohio State. His Tennessee accent charmed the media (for a time, anyway), and some of the boosters. Early on, he was having lunch with some prominent Columbus businessmen and they asked him how many games he was going to win.

"The way I figure it," he said, "the coaches can win two or three games, the players are good for three or four, and you fans can win two. From you, I want LSU and Michigan." The guys laughed; it'd been a while since they'd been jollied, "jolly" not being much of an OSU coaching attribute.

And yet Cooper was still something like the Cincinnati bluegrass musician who, touring the East Coast for the first time, said, "They knowed right off we was from out of town." Cooper used phrases like "I wasn't born on third base, I bunted my way on" and "that dog won't hunt," although by late in the century, people in Columbus had mostly yard dogs.

One of the Cleveland *Plain Dealer* columnists said that if you sounded like Cooper and lived in Columbus, people wanted to see if you're wearing shoes. So John Cooper, a good church-going guy with a bit of down-home patois, found himself criticized for being bucolic by people who, until fairly recently, lived in a place known as Cow Town.

To top things off, Cooper called Ohio Stadium "Buckeye Stadium" (forget your wife's name and you can always call her "sweetcakes," but surely you cannot misspeak about the Horseshoe). Then he made a hot tub commercial. He immediately became, as someone said, "the coach who got into hot water for getting into hot water." One could appreciate the difficulty of understanding the Columbus dress code: whatever it was, both Bruce and Cooper seemingly violated it—the former for under-dressing, the latter for undressing. And, as Cooper might have known but didn't, a hot tub commercial just wasn't something a good Ohio guy would do.

The early ads for hot tubs and grocery stores were also perceived as grasping, although Cooper saw it as simply making up for his relatively modest base salary of $98,000. Coaches were becoming accustomed to perks, and it was unlikely that any other modern coach would die—like Woody—with uncashed checks lying around the house.

Next, Cooper got into trouble for being candid. After losing to Pittsburgh in his second game, he said the problem was "too many slow white guys." The truth hurt but first it irritated, and some of the truth was that, unlike Earle, Cooper had inherited a pauper's cupboard. Chris Spielman, Eric Kumerow, William White, and quarterback Tom Tupa were gone, and Vince Workman—the Bucks' best running back—was ruled ineligible.

So there wasn't much of a honeymoon. Ohio State lost six games in 1988, something that hadn't happened since 1947. In Cooper's first five years, his Michigan record was five losses and a tie. The 13–13 tie in 1992 occasioned President Gordon Gee's widely heralded remark that it was "one of our greatest wins ever." (Gee later apologized. "Perhaps I didn't realize football is almost a spiritual experience at Ohio State," he said, which led fanbase diehards to think Coop and the president had arrived in town on the back of the same turnip truck.)

The year before, Gee took a hit square in the popularity when, on the eve of the 1991 Michigan game, the university extended Cooper's contract. Then, in probably the most egregious example of bad timing in the program's history, Cooper's Buckeyes went out and lost 31–3—the worst Michigan loss in forty-five years. Local columnist Bob Hunter said OSU athletic director Jim Jones "must have felt like the guy who gave the *Titanic* captain a raise just before the iceberg." When Michigan's stellar quarterback, Elvis Grbac, heard about the contract extension, he said, "Give him five more years!"

President Gee was inundated with several thousand letters, most of them opposing the new contract. "Sometimes I think we get a little too intense around here," he said, sounding almost wistful, as though he were imagining the old days when the kids at North Dorm were tossing a rugby ball around and trying to figure out Walter Camp's rulebook.

THAT 1991 GAME PROVIDED EVEN MORE LOCAL IGNOMINY WHEN PLAYERS SAID COOPER READ HIS PRE-GAME SPEECH. There were two constants before the Michigan game, reported *Plain Dealer* columnist Bill Livingston: (1) recite the Lord's Prayer (you really want Him on your side) and (2) hand out the really inspirational stuff which, as Livingston put it, "has the players hopping around like they just ate something out of a chemistry lab dish."

This was also the game of the end zone histrionics by Michigan receiver Desmond Howard, who concluded a 93-yard punt return by striking a Heisman Trophy pose, then went out and actually won the Heisman. (He called his posing "a little shout-out to the people back in Ohio.") Both Howard and Grbac were Cleveland boys who had known each other since the tenth grade, and—sacrilege!—they had chosen Michigan over Ohio State; Grbac wanted to be a Buckeye but the Earle Bruce firing scared him north. Both had sterling college careers and decent pro ones. Cooper took note: here were two Ohio boys who surely would have helped him, but through no fault of his they got away.

Thus things went, obscuring the work Cooper was actually doing, which was rebuilding the football infrastructure. He transformed Ohio State's rather plodding offensive culture, he upgraded the strength and conditioning program into the envy of other D-I programs, and—most important—he expanded recruiting in prospect-rich places like Texas and Florida. Soon, Ohio State was getting elite players, and in number. (He found a Heisman Trophy running back in Philadelphia, a Rose Bowl quarterback in Arizona, and some five dozen future NFL draft picks in fifteen different states.)

Between 1993 and 1998, Ohio State had a near-unprecedented run: three of Cooper's teams were undefeated going into the Michigan game (don't ask), three of them were ranked either No. 1 or No. 2, and the Buckeyes were a small handful of points from two national title games. OSU historian Jack Park called it "one of the best eras in the history of the program." In 1995, Eddie George won the Heisman, and Orlando Pace, the most decorated lineman ever at Ohio State, won the Lombardi Award (which he'd do again the next season). Pace was an overwhelming blocker and, publicizing Pace's own Heisman run (he finished fourth), the sports information department sent out refrigerator magnets with Pace's name atop a picture of pancakes. If he hadn't invented the pancake block, he'd certainly defined it.

Cooper's best—as well as most devastating—season was 1996 when the Buckeyes were once again unbeaten and No. 2 heading into the Michigan game. They had already knocked off two top-five teams (Notre Dame and Penn State), and Michigan was a lowly three-loss No. 21. Surely the Wolverines couldn't knock Ohio State out of the title game a second year in a row. No question to ask in this freighted decade. The 13–9 loss—played in Columbus, a further indignity—encompassed all of John Cooper's six earlier losses, said *The Plain Dealer*, "into one colossal headache." The Buckeyes had gotten to the Michigan 2-, 4-, and 19-yard lines and come away with only field goals.

There was some small validation when Ohio State upset Cooper's old team, Arizona State, in the 1997 Rose Bowl. It was his best win. But after the euphoria ended, the memory of the

Michigan loss returned and with it, the lost national championship. Even in winning, the coach had lost. The 1996 team was roundly acknowledged to be one of the best Ohio State teams—maybe the best—of the century. "'Ninety-six was as good of a football team as I've been around," said Luke Fickell, who played that Rose Bowl game with a torn pectoral muscle, then went on to coach at OSU before becoming head coach at the University of Cincinnati. He said it was a better team than the Ohio State title team of 2002.

Cooper was back on top in 1998 when both the AP and ESPN/USA Today ranked the Buckeyes as the top college football team in the nation. The previous year's Butkus Award winner, linebacker Andy Katzenmoyer, was returning, as was Antoine Winfield, the player who would win the Thorpe Award as the nation's best college defensive back.

On the other side of the ball, Joe Germaine, the most efficient quarterback in the Big Ten the previous two seasons, would be throwing to David Boston, a wideout many believed was the best receiver in college football.

The talent made the national headlines, but not in the most accommodating way: in late August, *Sports Illustrated* featured a cover photo of Katzenmoyer proclaiming "Ohio State is No. 1"—but with an asterisk that added "If Andy Katzenmoyer Makes the Grade." Once again, distraction ruled the day.

Katzenmoyer wasn't the only OSU player who needed to improve his GPA, but the article featured his situation and pinned OSU's title hopes on him. The Big Kat, as a summer school student, was taking such courses as Golf 1, Music 140, and AIDS: What Every College Student Should Know, and university president William Kirwin had received complaints about what was called the The Big Kat's special treatment and "academic integrity." (One late night show retort went: "What's the midterm in golf? Nine holes?")

The dispute between athletics and the academic mission of the nation's universities was as old as football itself, and it had been debated at OSU for at least three quarters of a century. The official position at OSU was that athletes should at least appear to be students, and that nothing was done for players that wouldn't be done for any other student. What regular students didn't receive, however, was the support of the athletic department: athletes had people looking out for them, people who knew the university rules.

Still and all, it seemed a bit disingenuous to place the fate of college academics on the shoulders of a Westerville, Ohio, kid, no matter how broad they were. Television stations had begun following him to class, and *Sports Illustrated* wrote, "The last time the republic so concerned itself with the academic performance of a few undergrads, Dean Wormer had just placed Delta Tau Chi on double-secret probation."

Cooper had a firm grasp of Katzenmoyer's situation, even if—as usual—he was undone by his own candor. "He's a bright guy who has no interest in school," the coach said. "He's here to play football." Even Katzenmoyer's mother—an educational consultant and community college teacher—understood: "You can get a degree in ballet, in vocal music, sculpture—even in tuba," she said. "Maybe you should be able to get a degree in football."

Cooper didn't sell education quite like Woody had—Hayes promised mothers their sons would get a good education and he'd harass (sometimes years after their playing days) those who didn't get their degrees. Cooper just promised them the chance. It was only a decade after Woody but the culture had moved light years, and Cooper knew that. He understood that for some of his recruits, the only education they were interested in was the one that graduated them into the NFL.

Meanwhile, after the preseason brouhaha in which Katzenmoyer had become the poster jock for the ills of big-time college football—no matter that nearly every Division I school in America had courses in basket-weaving and elementary canoeing (what some called "the soft options")—The Big Kat was soon excelling with his personal GPA (Ground Pounding Average), and the Buckeyes remained the No. 1 team in America through the eight games in September and October, winning by an average of 29 points.

Then the tripwire: Michigan State, a 28-point underdog at home. The Buckeyes held a 24–9 point lead early in the second half but, unfortunately, they wouldn't score again. The Spartans, coached by Nick Saban, who had spent a year in Columbus as Earle Bruce's assistant, ran off 19 unanswered points. "When you don't put a team away," Cooper said, "they start to think, 'Hey, we can win this game.'"

The Buckeyes had two late chances: they reached the Michigan State 19 but failed to convert on fourth-and-one, and on the final drive, Joe Germaine passed the Bucks to a first down on the MSU 15. He threw three more passes—all incomplete—before completing the fourth to Renaldo Hill, who happened to be a Spartan defensive back. It was Michigan State 28–24, with Ohio State one good break and single-digits away from the national championship game.

Ohio State finished No. 2 in the country, so close to the national title as to smell the bronze on the trophy. At Ohio State, though, No. 2 is the mile-long miss. Whatever marginal goodwill afforded Cooper—and the residual university concerns about the Earle Bruce firing—was winding down. Or as *Cincinnati Enquirer* columnist Tim Sullivan said, "His reservoir of goodwill was hardly big enough for a decent-sized drainage ditch."

The end-of-season failures allowed other factors to creep into the conversation. A graduation rate of 28 percent (the NCAA average was 56 percent) might not look so bad when the team goes 11–1, but Cooper's teams of 1999 and 2000 were 6–6 and 8–4. So "academic integrity" was being bandied about again. And these teams were also being criticized for lack of discipline.

The 2000 season—Cooper's unlucky 13—was a fraught one. He was criticized for being aloof with his players, and *The Plain Dealer* said, "They don't play their Buckeye leaves off for him." One of the starters was dismissed after accomplishing a 0.0. GPA, another sued a teammate for assault, and team captain Ken-Yon Rambo was accused—by his own players—of being a poor leader and late for meetings. "They knew what kind of dude I was when they elected me captain," Rambo said. "Sometimes I'm not going to be on time for things." It was what *The Plain Dealer* called "a mass conniption."

Cooper needed a big season, and he didn't get it. His last game came on New Year's Day of 2001, in the Outback Bowl. There, the Buckeyes were beaten 24–7 by South Carolina, the only unranked team in a bowl game. The MVP was Ryan Brewer, a kid from Troy, Ohio, a former Mr. Football who'd been passed over by Ohio State. He was responsible for 214 all-purpose yards, three touchdowns, and, according to the Columbia papers, "the firing of a coach." Not quite, but good copy.

Ryan Brewer was in the game but not the bigger picture. He was simply one more ironic footnote that cluttered John Cooper's biography, and much of it had little to do with Cooper himself. He had won 111 games for Ohio State, second only to Woody, but as the *Cincinnati Enquirer* reported, "No football coach in America wins more and is loved less." His sins—strange accent, hot tubs, overt candidness, Andy Katzenmoyer's GPA—were venial sins, not mortal ones. Michigan losses, however—and so many of them; where was the law of averages when you needed it?—those were mortal sins.

WHILE THERE IS USUALLY A LIFE AFTER FOOTBALL FOR COACHES, MOST OF THEM DIE ON THE FIELD, their records permanently attached, like nicknames, ill-considered tattoos, felony convictions, and cellulite. In such a manner, they are forever marked. Ask "Old 9–3 Earle Bruce," for instance. Ask Cooper about Michigan: "Old 2-10-1." It was perhaps the highest irony that the team he beat to get the Ohio State job—Michigan in the 1987 Rose Bowl—was the team he couldn't beat once he got to town. He was, as someone slyly remarked, Ohio State's finest September coach.

In such, his true legacy was obscured. He had returned Ohio State—after a decade and a half of near-anonymity—to its rightful place among the elite. Bruce Hooley, a Columbus radio talk show host, said, "If John Cooper, over the course of his career, had gotten the same fortuitous bounces that Jim Tressel got in 2002, there would be statues of John Cooper outside Ohio Stadium. But he lost the one game you can't lose at Ohio State…" (The closest Coop came was the life-sized butter sculpture they made of him for the 1997 Ohio State Fair—no small honor in itself but still a perishable dairy product.)

He was Ohio State's first administrator, a novel approach in Columbus. (Although Paul Brown had aspects of it in his program, which he fully developed in Cleveland.) Cooper delegated, perhaps too much, for there were flaws in being so hands-off, and no matter whose hands, the coach was always blamed.

He was still an outstanding coach—one of the best of his century—and he lifted expectations back onto talk of national titles. He missed two of them by the smallest of margins, and his recruits helped Jim Tressel win his 2002 title. His real feat, though, was that he created the transition between the past and the future—between the old-fashioned offenses of Woody and the high-octane ones that would, in time, be Urban Meyer's.

He was never going to be an "Ohio guy," and being a sanguine man, he understood. "They weren't happy with Woody," he said once. "They weren't happy with Earle Bruce, they're not happy with me." He knew that at Ohio State, they were seldom happy with anyone. Happiness in Columbus was nearly always in retrospect. Or as he would say, embracing his Tennessee patois, "One week you're drinking wine; the next week you're stomping grapes."

But in time, he came close to being an Ohio guy. He had an office at the football complex, occupying space beside Earle Bruce—two outsiders who'd been granted native status. In 2008, Cooper was inducted into the College Football Hall of Fame, and in 2013, the Ohio State Athletics Hall of Fame. Nearly three decades before, Columbus had chosen him. Then it hadn't. Now, though, he'd chosen. Columbus wasn't Tennessee, but—finally—it was home.

Titletown, U.S.A.

Out of nowhere came the most improbable season

THE OCCASION OF THE 2002 NATIONAL CHAMPIONSHIP WAS MADE EVEN MORE GRAND BY HOW UNLIKELY IT WAS. If ever a team had been favored by the gods, it was this one. The entire season was an old-fashioned movie serial that ended with a cliffhanger every Saturday. It gave Jim Tressel, its self-effacing, newly-arrived coach from the provinces, favorite son status and launched one of Ohio State's great eras, even if it would ultimately be marked by an asterisk.

Preseason prognostications gave little hint as to how the season would unfold. The AP poll placed OSU at a respectable—but auspicious—No. 13 just behind Michigan, and even the Big Ten championship was a long shot. The best thing in OSU's favor was the schedule—no Michigan State, no Iowa, Michigan and Penn State at home.

Quickly, though, an unlikely cast of characters began to assert themselves: a freshman running back soon to be labeled "a me-too mercenary," a two-way superman with a propensity for spectacular plays on both sides of the ball, and a nervy egghead quarterback who'd pull off more hair-breadth escapes than Houdini (who'd once gotten himself out of a locked canvas mailbag).

The Buckeyes opened with Texas Tech, an early test for a passing defense that was suspect, as they were facing Kliff Kingsbury, the Red Raiders' Heisman candidate who'd win that season's Sammy Baugh Trophy. Kingsbury threw for near his seasonal average of 350 yards that afternoon in Columbus but Texas Tech's defense hadn't anticipated giving up 175 yards to Maurice Clarett, the OSU freshman prodigy, and the Bucks won handily, 45–21. After the traditional mauling of one of their shirttail Ohio cousins (Kent State this time) and a solid win over No. 10 Washington State, they moved up to No. 6 in the polls and headed south to play the University of Cincinnati at Paul Brown Stadium.

The UC game represented for most Ohio State fans an in-state breather before going into Big Ten competition. It was the ninth in a series of football contests begun a decade earlier between OSU and other Ohio schools willing to go into the Horseshoe and take their lumps for a big payday, and it made economic sense to keep some of this money in-state. (In 2014, Ohio State paid more than $2 million to Kent State, Cincinnati, and Virginia Tech; UC's guarantee was nearly a million dollars whereas Tech's was $350,000, which we now know is the price of an upset—it was OSU's only loss of the season. OSU's athletic director, Gene Smith, had already said he thought a million dollars would be the market price, and so it seemed, although it prompted debate about how much big-time programs should pay their early-season victims.)

Often, these in-state games were met with disappointment and derision from season ticket-holders, who didn't care to see the Buckeyes run up the score on Toledo or Ohio. Yet the truth was, the Mid-American Conference teams tended to play at least as well as OSU's other early warm-up invitees such as Rice, Fresno State, and Pittsburgh. (And no MAC team ever lost 72–0, like Pittsburgh did in 1996.)

The UC game was unusual in that it was OSU's first road game against an in-state team since 1934 when the Bucks beat Western

Reserve in Cleveland's League Park, 76–0. Ohio State fans traveled well, though, so UC had small home-field advantage. More than 10,000 of its fans bought tickets through OSU ("If it was up to me we wouldn't have sent them any tickets," Bearcats coach Rick Minter said, recalling that UC had received only 4,000 tickets from OSU for its 1999 game in Columbus.) With an attendance of 66,319 at Paul Brown Stadium, it was the largest crowd to attend a football game in the city. Not Horseshoe numbers but impressive nonetheless.

Ohio State came into Paul Brown Stadium as 17-point favorites, but it wasn't unusual for the in-state underdogs—riding a wave of emotion—to play well for a quarter or so before the Buckeyes' overwhelming talent kicked in. In 1992, the eventual Mid-American champs Bowling Green lost 17–6 in a moral victory for the upstate school; Miami of Ohio and Ohio University also played Ohio State relatively close; and in 1999, UC jumped out to a 17–3 lead before losing 34–20. A few of the Buckeyes recalled that UC had the ball 37 out of 60 minutes and gained 475 yards. Therefore what happened over the next few hours shouldn't have been a surprise.

Ohio State was facing another good quarterback—and even they didn't know quite how good. Gino Guidugli had come to UC from across the river where he'd taken Highlands High to two Kentucky titles, and Sports Blog Nation called him "the comeback kid," saying that the Bearcats lived and died on his right arm.

UC led with less than four minutes remaining when Craig Krenzel—called by *Cincinnati* magazine "the poster child for succeeding in sports without any athletic ability"—scored from six yards out: Ohio State, 23–19. However, an earlier Ohio State play, Krenzel's 29-yard scamper on the second play of the fourth quarter, which led to a field goal and cut UC's lead to 19–17—proved to be the little noticed game-changer. For when Ohio State took the lead at last, then returned the ball to UC with 3:39 remaining, it meant UC needed a touchdown and not merely a field goal. Unathletic or not, Krenzel's run may have been the play of the game.

Guidugli quickly took the Bearcats into OSU territory where, with 1:21 left, he had a first down on OSU's 15. Next came the first—but not the last—Buckeye miracle of 2002. Two of Guidugli's passes were dropped, and on fourth down, he threw over the middle where OSU linebacker Matt Wilhelm tipped the ball to Will Allen in the back of the end zone.

"Thank you, Jesus," said OSU safety Mike Doss.

"I feel like I just watched a train wreck," added his teammate, tight end Ben Hartsock.

Small consolation, but UC had just become the only Ohio team in the last eighty-one years to take a lead into the fourth quarter against Ohio State. Somewhere, a goat had been sacrificed to OSU's season, or perhaps an old ritual enacted in Columbus's Green Lawn Cemetery involving a dead cat at midnight.

As THE YEAR WAS SHAPING UP, the Buckeyes would have to put together a series of impressive wins and/or hope others would clear the table of undefeated teams. At the end of October, eight were still unbeaten and *Sports Illustrated* explained how being undefeated didn't get you into the championship. "Winning 'em all doesn't mean winning it all," said the magazine, asserting that even in the power conferences there were still teams of a lesser brand who'd have trouble qualifying for the national playoffs, even with a perfect record.

Democratic lip service was paid to the 130 some-odd Division I football teams, but in reality, some hundred of those teams would likely never occupy the Olympian heights of AP's annual poll. Even fewer than half of those would ever find their way into the College Football Playoff. Football democracy thus existed essentially for those who could afford it. Or as that noted Italian sports commentator Mussolini had it: beautiful in theory, fallacious in practice. (On the eve of the 2017 playoffs, for example, the sixteen total slots awarded in its first four seasons had been filled by just nine programs. But thirteen programs played in the last four men's basketball Final Fours.)

Heading into November, Ohio State edged No. 17 Penn State in Columbus, 13–7, reverting to its earlier white-knuckled form (see University of Cincinnati), which would continue through the season. One of Tressel's more significant coaching moves was to start his sophomore flanker, Chris Gamble, at cornerback against Penn State, which made him the Buckeyes' first two-way starter since the iron man era of nearly forty years before. Although he'd practiced sparingly at the position, Gamble's third-quarter 40-yard interception return for a score was the play of the game. (Catch his zig-zagging run on YouTube.)

Andy Groom's fourth-quarter punt from his own end zone—*Sports Illustrated* called it "a 59-yard moon shot"—was another peak OSU moment. Groom was a Columbus kid who'd begun as a walk-on and ended as a first-team All-American. His punt, said the magazine, "helped ice an ugly-as-sin win." So ugly the pollsters moved Ohio State from No. 4 back to No. 6.

Of Ohio State's last seven games, six were won by a whisker and providence, including three come-from-behind wins and two that went into overtime. There would surely be no providence left for future Buckeye teams, for it had been exhausted in perpetuity. The games were tottery and precarious, yet the Buckeyes prevailed week after week. It was as though the law of averages had been mothballed, and it became an entire season of waiting for the other cleat to drop.

Against Purdue, trailing 6–3 with 3:10 left, Chris Gamble, apparently feeling invalidated by only playing two ways, joined the special teams and ran a punt back to the Purdue 46. This set up Krenzel's fourth-and-one, against-the-wind pass to Michael Jenkins for a 37-yard touchdown and the 10–6 win. The TD play was one of five nominated by ESPN as "best play of the year;" and *The Plain Dealer*'s Bill Livingston said it was the play that put OSU in the title game. Illinois was won in overtime, 23–16, with—once again—Krenzel providing a crucial third-down scramble that set up Maurice Hall's game-winning touchdown.

"There was no plausible explanation for what was going on, how the Buckeyes always seemed to be living on the edge but never fell off," wrote *Columbus Dispatch* columnist Bob Hunter. His question to linebacker Matt Wilhelm about why was answered simply. "Who cares?" Wilhelm said, implying that being 12-0 was reason in itself.

"How do you explain an undefeated team that has barely survived four of its last five games?" *Sports Illustrated* asked, rhetorically. The article described the original skepticism of the players who saw "a 5-foot-9 Mr. Rogers dress-alike who kept a recording of the Ohio State band in his car's tape deck." Yet Tressel converted his skeptical players, "hardened by infighting and bad press," as the magazine put it, and soon he had them gathering in the end zone after home games to sing the school song, *Carmen Ohio*. (It was a kind of ironman glee club that dared you to criticize the fact there were no sopranos.)

Thus 105,539 spectators showed up in Columbus for the 2002 Michigan game—the largest crowd in Ohio Stadium history. (Chris Gamble, in honor of his seasonal yeomanry in playing several positions, was the subject of a local television spoof that portrayed him as reporter, public address announcer, and drum major. After selling concessions and tickets, he finishes by sweeping the stands when a supervisor tosses him some keys, and says, "Chris, can you lock up when you're done?")

With prescience born of the event, officials greased the goalposts in an attempt to keep them upright, given an OSU victory. As with most of November's games—and half of October's—no such thing was assured. An injured Maurice Clarett managed to account for 119 yards anyway and, per usual, the game came down to the last second, with Michigan driving for the go-ahead score.

"My only thought was, 'Who's the guy running the clock?'" said linebacker Matt Wilhelm. "I mean, one second left? What is that?" Nickel back Will Allen preserved the 14–9 win with a goal-line interception, a fitting reenactment of his save in the last seconds of the Cincinnati game back in September. (He celebrated this one by running the football up to his parents in the stands.)

The goalposts survived, but fans pulled up stadium turf then went out into the city where they overturned cars and set at least a hundred fires. "The behavior was criminal and unacceptable," said university president Karen Holbrook. "And unfortunately, most of those responsible appear to be our students." The over-the-top festivities made *The Tonight Show* where Jay Leno announced, "Yesterday President Bush signed a law to create the Department of Homeland Security…their first job: protect Americans from Ohio State football fans."

"Jim Tressel seems to be too good to be true," said *The Plain Dealer*. The coach said that he was proud—"Not only that we won, but because of the way we've won." It was a phrase that would return to haunt him. But not during this charmed season, which was still unfinished: the national championship game awaited. The Buckeyes were facing a powerful University of Miami team that had won the 2001 title and, favored by 13 points, it was bringing along a 34-game winning streak.

For the title game, most of Columbus was either in Arizona or huddled in front of their television sets and the entire city, spookily empty, looked like a backlot studio set for a post-apocalyptic movie. (The Buckeyes captivated so much of the entertainment audience that the Palace Theatre canceled a performance by the Muppets.)

There had been so many gridiron Lazarus moments from this team that the fans regarded such moments as ordinary and paid scant attention to the oddsmakers, for the Buckeyes had been trashing the odds all season. Paul Daugherty of the *Cincinnati Enquirer* said the championship game was like watching open-heart surgery—"your own."

It lasted for three hours and fifty-seven minutes, including two overtimes. Miami had five turnovers, four of them forced, and the Bucks held Miami three times from the one-yard line. It was, as Bob Hunter of the *Dispatch* pointed out, "Ohio State football your father always told you about."

Maurice Clarett's five-yard touchdown in the second OT delivered the winning score—31–24—but his premier moment came in the third quarter when he ran down Miami's Sean Taylor, who'd just intercepted Krenzel, and plucked the ball away. This led to an OSU field goal—its only points of the second half—and what proved to be the 17–17 regulation tie. (Bill Livingston said Clarett's recovery was "a novel lesson in how it feels to have your lunch money taken away on the playground.")

The game's major dramatics came in the first overtime, with Miami taking the lead, 24–17. On the subsequent drive, Ohio State faced fourth-and-extinction. But Krenzel saw that the Miami cornerback wasn't playing a true "under" technique—which would have placed him between Krenzel and receiver Michael Jenkins—and so he calmly tossed a 17-yard comeback pass to his receiver for a first down on the Miami 12. (Chris Gamble, his other receiver, said that Krenzel was so calm that he was "a little weird.")

Three plays later, the Buckeyes found themselves at fourth down again. "Here's the play," Krenzel said to Gamble. "Fade stop. If you got one-on-one, I'll put that bitch right on you. No thinkin' about it."

The ball hit Gamble in the hands, falling incomplete. Then, after an interminable moment with fireworks already celebrating Miami's win, the back judge tossed a flag. The subsequent pass interference call on Miami's Glenn Sharpe put the ball on the two, with an automatic first down. Krenzel scored on third down, and after the first overtime the game was tied 24–24.

The call raised an epic controversy: "You felt like you could've assembled a ship in a bottle in that time," complained *Sports Illustrated's* Rick Reilly. The judge, Terry Porter, said he waited because he was going over the play in his mind. Reilly said he choked. *The Plain Dealer* said the call was "iffy…but you need breaks to win something this big."

No one from Miami believed the interference call; Ohio Staters saw it as divine intervention. In a recent interview, Glenn Sharpe was still protesting his innocence. "To this very day I still truly in my heart believe I didn't commit pass interference on this guy," he said. "I truly believe that." As for Gamble, who was in on 117 plays for the evening, he said he should have caught the ball, which would have rendered the entire controversy moot.

In the broadcast booth, Dan Fouts turned to his partner, Keith Jackson, and asked, "Having fun yet, big boy?"

"I'm worn out," Jackson replied.

The game ended—finally—when OSU linebacker Cie Grant saw no tight end in front of him and understood that he had a straight shot at Miami quarterback Ken Dorsey. "I got one of my better jumps," he said. His blitz disrupted Dorsey's last-second, fourth-and-one, end zone pass, and the Buckeye faithful had yet another hero. Grant was an unlikely one, a choirboy—literally—from New Philadelphia who'd flirted with both Michigan and Michigan State before heading for Columbus, then played four positions, as well as sing *Carmen Ohio* after the title win. (His *a cappella* rendition is a YouTube staple, 191,000 views.)

Krenzel was the game's offensive MVP (sharing team MVP with Chris Gamble). He, too, originally favored Michigan—he was from Sterling Heights, Michigan, and the only Michigan guy on the 2002 roster—but when Michigan began to favor Drew Henson, Krenzel looked south, setting aside the natural enmity of the natives who quickly adopted him as one of their own. Studying molecular biology, he was regarded as something of a bookworm, but his cerebral nature spilled over onto the playing field where his ability to finish off critical plays gave him a princely status. His inherent modesty didn't hurt, either. Once, commenting on his team's seemingly preordained season, he said, "I think it has a lot more to do with everything but me."

They were called the "Luckeyes," and while fortune was surely their twelfth man throughout the season, ball-control game plans, unflagging poise, and impressive big-play capacity counted for more. "For once, Ohio State, playing in that gigantic stadium, the repository of a whole state's hopes and dreams, went all the way," said Bill Livingston.

Jim Tressel's reign was just beginning, and it was filled with promise. He would never again have a season like 2002, though, and the conclusion of his time in Columbus would be even more unpredictable than what had just transpired.

> It's a wonderful feeling to see the confetti coming down—Jim Tressel

Tresselball

A period of grace and the subsequent fall

HE WAS THE SENATOR, A MAN ALMOST TOO BUTTONED-DOWN AND WELL-SPOKEN TO COACH SOMETHING AS ROWDY AS FOOTBALL. With his tidy appearance—and the vest, which quickly became iconic—he could have passed for an economics professor. And yet, at his untimely demise in 2011, his body of work was surpassed only by Woody Hayes.

He arrived in town with an uncertain pedigree; he'd coached Youngstown State to four national titles but that was, after all, Youngstown State, and there were few precedents for traversing the distance between a place such as Youngstown and The Holy City. There were the usual skeptics, of course, but any criticism was quickly laid to rest. In his first season, in 2001, Tressel beat a ranked Michigan team, and the next year, he did it again, on his way to a 14–0 season and the national championship. It was the first fourteen-win season in major college football since Penn did it in 1897.

He had the advantage of an inheritance from his predecessor, John Cooper, who bequeathed Tressel a goodly crop of recruits but not, fortunately, his tendency to die at Michigan. Then in Tressel's second year, he'd managed an outlandish season in which his Buckeyes appeared almost supernaturally favored by fortune—something Cooper never had. Half the 2002 wins were by a touchdown or less and two were won in overtime, including the double-overtime dogsweat classic against Miami (which was only the Hurricanes' second loss in three years).

Tressel was the American Football Coaches Association Coach of the Year (he'd now won it at two different schools), and he was thus the crowned monarch of Ohio. Only Paul Brown had shown so much early promise, but unlike Tressel, he'd taken his promise elsewhere. Tressel was polite, sincere, never forgot names, and believed in the correct Ohio virtues: motherhood, manhood, and beating Michigan, which he proceeded to do with astounding frequency. Unlike John Cooper, Tressel was a neo-Copernican and believed—as most Ohio State fans do—that the Earth and the planets revolved around the Ohio State–Michigan game.

Not even Woody had Tressel's winning percentage over Michigan, although in fairness, Tressel did not have to contend with Bo Schembechler. Tressel approached Michigan almost clinically. He called The Big House "a fun place," which it seemed to be, as he only lost there once, and he even liked its acoustics. "You close your eyes and think they're rooting for you," he said. The *New York Times* wrote that "no one else has ever owned the spotlight on its biggest stage so securely while being so low-key. No one else came in so underestimated and raised expectations so abruptly. No one else in the modern era dominated The Game so thoroughly."

Always circumspect, he said when hired only that the fans would be proud. It's doubtful that even he knew exactly how proud. After the perceived looseness of the latter Cooper years, Tressel told his players there'd be "strict accountability," and quoting his father, Lee, the former Baldwin-Wallace coach, he said, "The only excuse for missing a class is a death in the family—your own." Soon, as *The Plain Dealer* pointed out about Tressel the younger, "he owned Saturday in this state."

The 2002 title was money in the psychological bank, thus the fans forgave the relatively undistinguished seasons that came before 2006. (It was, after all, Ohio State, which posited its own definitions about what was distinguished.) The university had not fielded such a canny, unflappable coach in quite some time, especially one that so regularly beat Michigan. *Columbus Dispatch* columnist Bob Hunter memorably described Tressel by saying that if he ever blew up during his OSU tenure, "it would have happened only because somebody slipped a hand grenade into his suit coat while he was smiling and nodding. And if he had survived the blast, he would probably have calmly described it as an 'excellent explosion,' said he 'has always had respect' for people who make hand grenades, and might have even added, evenly and without a change in tone, that 'we all come to Ohio State to participate in excellent explosions like this.'"

His 2006 team was No. 1 from start to finish—including a classic win over No. 2 Michigan that clinched the Heisman for quarterback Troy Smith. Ohio State fans had once again assumed their birthright, which was, of course, the undefeated season—and playing for the national championship.

TRESSEL WAS BACK ON TOP WHERE HE'D BEEN IN THAT FORTUITOUS SECOND SEASON when he'd so quickly assumed a place among the school immortals. He employed something they called "Tresselball," which featured good defense, special teams play for field position (he said the punt was the most important play in football), and an unerring, run-oriented offense. It was in essence "Woody 2.0," but Ohio State's recruiting prowess—like Woody's—kept the Buckeyes among the very best teams. (The mantra at good football schools like Ohio State was that the institution itself gave you nine wins, which explained why Earle Bruce was fired; those nine annual wins weren't really regarded as *his*.)

There had been a chaotic finish to the 2006 season; the computer polls had Florida and Michigan tied at No. 2, the human polls had them separated by .0101 points. No one seemed to want a Michigan–Ohio State rematch, however, so Florida—coached by former Ohio State grad assistant Urban Meyer—backed into the finale with Ohio State, who'd beaten four ranked teams during the season (including two No. 2s) and were favored by a touchdown.

There was an initial flash of brilliance by Ted Ginn Jr., who returned the opening kickoff 93 yards for a touchdown, then was gone to an injury. Troy Smith, routinely and roughly bookended by Florida's defensive ends, had 35 yards passing, an interception, and a fumble. The Buckeyes had no answer for Florida's speed nor its strategy.

"Desert Disaster," read *The Plain Dealer* headline, in type large enough to be seen in Columbus. Its gimlet-eyed columnist, Bill Livingston, summed up the game in this manner: "Without Ginn, his speed receiver, with his bodyguards in front of him overwhelmed, with Gators shadowing his receivers when he did have time, with the demystification of his coach, with nowhere to run or hide, Smith had become the one thing no one expected college football's biggest difference-maker to be—ordinary." Adding insult to injury, the Gators wouldn't even use Smith's name. "First time I hit Heisman, it was so hard I heard him grunt," said defensive end Derrick Harvey.

Tressel had a chance at redemption the next year, bringing Ohio State back to the 2007 title game. No. 1 OSU had been upset by Illinois, dropped to No. 7, then beat Michigan and—amidst a chaos of upsets among the front-runners—found itself back at No. 1 and facing No. 2 LSU in the finale. The French Quarter's Preservation Hall Jazz Band opened with the national anthem, played as a funeral dirge, which proved prophetic for the Buckeyes who were buried, 38–24. Said *The Plain Dealer*, "It looked more like the Buckeyes were sentenced to this game." SEC teams had now beaten Ohio State nine consecutive times in bowl games, and the perception was firmly set that Southern college football in general—and SEC teams in particular—were superior to the Big Ten.

The back-to-back title games were followed by a spate of geopolitical theorizing about the losses, which ranged from sunspots to southern compensations for losing the War between the States. The theories generally involved speed, giving rise to such epithets as "SloHio." It suggested speed was a quality enhanced by sunlight and occurred only below the Mason-Dixon line. (General Sherman's sprint qualities in Georgia and South Carolina, neither of which were in the SEC at the time, were conveniently overlooked.) In the 2006 title game, the fastest player on the field—before his injury—was Ted Ginn Jr., the Cleveland kid who ran the opening kickoff back 93 yards. Ginn, with the Carolina Panthers in 2015, was timed at 22.44 miles per hour on a 74-yard touchdown catch against Atlanta, which was deemed the fastest foot speed on an offensive play in the NFL that season. (Usain Bolt's top speed in his record 100-meter dash, for comparison, was 27.80, but he wasn't wearing shoulder pads.)

THERE WAS AN UNORTHODOX THEORY ABOUT THE PROPERTIES OF SPEED IN A GIVEN GEOGRAPHY, and it went like this: for decades, Big Ten teams had to adapt to rain, wind, mud, sleet, and snow. This brought about the plowhorse lineman, physically imposing but not necessarily fleet of foot because he didn't *have* to be. The southern teams, meanwhile, weren't mudders because *they* didn't have to be. Southern teams only came north for early non-conference games, and most bowl games were played in the South.

There was a natural cause-and-effect: all that salubrious weather led the South into a more wide-open offense. (There was a memorable speech given by Frank Leahy of Notre Dame who, during practice in a blizzard, challenged his complaining players to be like the Great Northern Buffalo. "The Great Northern Buffalo," he said, "sticks his head into the wind and braves the cold, not like the puny Southern Buffalo, who turns his back to the storm." The Great Northern Buffalo, of course, was a mudder.) The North and its weather fostered a culture of power running and slugging it out in the trenches; northern offenses tended to contract, as if the linemen drew heat from one another. In the South, because of the heat, its offenses grew more expansive and used more of the field. It wasn't speed that caused the difference; it was the *perception* of speed. Spread offenses simply *looked* faster.

"There's the Big Ten imagination gap," wrote the *Chicago Tribune* back in 1992 after the famous Ohio State–Michigan 13–13 tie—and after the conference had lost fifteen of the previous nineteen Rose Bowls. "Conferences like the Pac-10 long ago switched to a wide-open speed-based style of play that is not only more fun to watch but devastating when used against plodding Big Ten teams..." That tie game, said the *Tribune*, "looked more like mace-and-truncheon combat among armored knights than modern college football."

There were bigtime OSU losses in 2008: a blowout against No. 1 USC, and close ones to Penn State and Texas, both of whom were No. 3 at the time. There was another loss to USC in 2009 (as well as one to unranked Purdue). Increasingly, the faithful began to wonder if Tressel could bring in the talent and run the schemes needed for the Buckeyes to once again compete on the national stage. The perception was that Ohio State could by virtue of its superior talent win nine, ten, even eleven games a season, but when faced with a team that put equal talent on the field—such as those from the South—the Buckeyes' contracting offense couldn't compete. Or so went the criticism.

Tressel was the latest in a long line of good coaches about whom it was beginning to be said, "He can't win the Big One." It disregarded the fact that you had to win some *other* Big Ones to get to *the* Big One, at which time you might be known for not winning *that* Big One. The thinking presupposed not losing. Ever. Given Ohio State's reputation, *every* loss was a bad one, and there was even such a category as "a bad win." (If such unthinkable standards were applied to our own professions, most of us would be filing for unemployment benefits by week's end.)

THIS WAS THE OLD OHIO STATE BUGBEAR: YOU'RE ONLY AS GOOD AS YOUR LAST TITLE. Earle Bruce had demonstrated that nine wins weren't enough; John Cooper demonstrated you needed double-digit wins and one of them had better be Michigan; and Jim Tressel was being asked for national titles. (His difficulty was revealed by those fans who were never happy; they said they wished Ohio State had not played in the back-to-back title games because their fervent nature was such that they'd rather be a little disappointed by not getting to the championship game than be a lot disappointed by getting there and losing.)

If Tressel was about to be passed over by the game's evolution, though, he was still capable of surprise and good game-day coaching. In 2002, for example, he had won the Michigan game on Craig Krenzel's flip to tailback Maurice Hall—an option OSU hadn't run all year. In the 2006 classic with Michigan—No. 1 vs. No. 2—Ted Ginn Jr. lined up at tight end and scored on the ensuing pass. Tressel was once quoted as not wanting an offensive coordinator because, he said, "What would *I* do? Eat bon-bons?"

In 2008, Tressel pleased his fan base by swiping Terrelle Pryor—the first player in Pennsylvania history to run *and* throw for 4,000 yards—away from Penn State. Pryor was the top-ranked quarterback prospect in the country, big and fast, with "game-changer" emblazoned across his jersey where other players had their names. For a brief moment, it looked as though Pryor might bring about Ohio State's offensive renaissance, but it wouldn't happen. This was never clearer than in 2009 when the Buckeyes faced Pete Carroll's University of Southern California Trojans in the Horseshoe. The 18–15 loss was close but only due to the Buckeye defense, and the perception was that Pryor was in the wrong offense. Tresselball played well in the Big Ten, but could it compete with the country's other national brands?

The 2010 team began the season at No. 2, then briefly occupied the top spot before being derailed in mid-October by a barely-ranked Wisconsin team. The Buckeyes finished the season at No. 5 after beating Arkansas in the Sugar Bowl. The singular moment—finally beating a SEC team in a bowl game—was then undone by an unholy sequence of events that became known as "Tattoogate."

In late 2010, five players—including Pryor—were suspended for the first five games of the 2011 season because they'd received "improper benefits," meaning they'd signed autographs for tattoos, as well as selling Ohio State memorabilia. In the spring of 2011, Tressel resigned after the NCAA found he'd not only known about the player improprieties but had signed a statement saying he *didn't* know. The 2010 season—and the bowl win—were vacated, which left the Buckeyes with an 0–1 record, their only official game a loss to Wisconsin.

Tressel's statesmanlike demeanor had heretofore kept him above the fray, although improprieties always seemed to be lurking in the underbrush, even back at Youngstown State where his quarterback had been flagged for receiving "improper benefits." There were other off-the-field penalties, i.e., Troy Smith (disorderly conduct and improper benefits) and Maurice Clarett, the poster boy for inadvisably bad form. After a sensational freshman year in 2002 in which he helped win the national title, Clarett lost his early promise in a dose of public relations fiascos that required a double course of penicillin.

A biographer was needed to chronicle Clarett's misdeeds, which ranged from yelling at his position coach to skirmishing with school administrators and receiving—allegedly— preferential classroom treatment and illegal benefits, as well as filing a false police report. Clarett went on to one season in the United Football League where he gained 154 yards, then ended up in prison. Unfortunately, in off-the-clock behavior for players, the head coach is still the man in charge, and as such he receives only marginal sympathy for his impossible work in exercising any real control over his young charges and their hormonal overloads.

As for "Tattoogate," the crime was largely in the aftermath. (At least one commentator called it "a scandal that had no victims.") Disregard, for the moment, the fact that the items players traded for tattoos actually belonged to them. Shelve, for another moment, how dishonorable it might seem to Ohio State fans that a player would sell his Gold Pants Club pin for beating Michigan. The pin still belongs to him. It's not equipment swiped from the locker room.

Tattoogate became *another* story when Tressel learned what had happened, didn't tell his athletic director, then falsified an NCAA document saying he didn't know. Was he trying to help his players?

Or was he the minister caught *en déshabillé* with his choir director? That is, was he trying to protect his record and saw—with Pryor, his emerging quarterback—an undefeated season looming?

The critics, less forgiving than Tressel's fans, picked up on the coach's perceived rectitude, for when the university called a news conference to announce Tressel's initial suspension and fine, he had to cancel a signing for his book, *Life Promises for Success: Promises From God on Achieving Your Best*. The book, suggested *The New York Times*, was a reminder of *true* success—how to evade the NCAA rules.

THERE DID SEEM TO BE SOMETHING ABOUT OHIO STATE FOOTBALL THAT BROUGHT OUT THOSE who applauded its difficult moments. Possibly it was football's own celebrity, or simply human nature and the rejoicing that often occurs at the misfortune of others. (This quality was evidenced wonderfully by radio comedian Fred Allen who once wrote a friend, "The only good news I have heard of late is that the man who wrote *Happy Days Are Here Again* committed suicide last week.")

Ultimately, Tressel's fall from grace was an ambiguous one: half the fans might have believed the coach was untruthful and self-serving, but just as many—maybe more—thought the punishment didn't fit the crime. To most, he was just a guy who'd made a bad decision (or two), which simply showed he was very much like the rest of us. ("We didn't think he'd behave like the rest of us. Not until he did," wrote the *Cincinnati Enquirer's* Paul Daugherty.)

When Tressel returned to Ohio Stadium in 2015 to be inducted into both the Ohio State and College Football halls of fame, he received, said Bob Hunter, "his usual rock-star treatment" and was paraded around the end zone on the shoulders of his former players. Of course the fans forgave him. He'd given them a title, and he'd beaten Michigan. Losing to Michigan, *that* was the one unforgivable sin.

The Plain Dealer said the scandal had simply happened too soon, for not long afterward there was "walking around" money for athletes at the Power Five schools, and football players were suing to be treated as employees. It all made Tattoogate look relatively trivial. That—and time—soon softened the original verdict that Tressel was "a rogue coach hiding behind a phony image." The sale of memorabilia, wrote Bill Livingston, "seems like a prissy, persnickety violation."

After Tressel came the forgettable year of 2011, Luke Fickell's interim year when he managed as well as he could from a most difficult place, and Ohio State was once again at a crossroads. It needed more than a football coach; it needed a savior, one who could bring the program into the modern era.

It needed Urban Meyer.

The miracle of 2014

And you thought the last title was unexpected

Urban Meyer arrived in Columbus with all the fanfare of a victorious general returning home and, in a way, he was. Thoroughly an Ohioan, his origins were secure, and he demonstrated his formidable prowess with a 12-0 initial season in 2012 and the nation's longest win streak, even though it ended unexpectedly at the hands (and elbows) of Michigan State in the 2013 Big Ten championship game.

No respecter of persons, Michigan State. The Spartans had ruined two of Woody Hayes's perfect seasons (1972 and 1974); dashed John Cooper's 1998 season; and now in 2013, here they were again, using their same old gris-gris. (There was, too, the Orange Bowl game at the end of the season in which Ohio State lost to Clemson, 40–35, although after Michigan State, it was simply anticlimactic.)

After such, the faithful deserved a miracle, yes? And what better pathway to a miracle than by making one seem impossible, which is exactly what the early 2014 loss to Virginia Tech did. In its own way, that 35–21 loss might have been worse than the previous loss

> Don't give me theory. Give me testimony.
> —Urban Meyer

to Michigan State, for it seemed to dash Ohio State's hopes just as they were being newly established.

It was an unhappy home debut for quarterback J.T. Barrett, who'd just taken over for the injured Braxton Miller. Barrett was sacked seven times in what was the most dispiriting opener since Art Schlichter's against Penn State in 1978. (Schlichter threw five interceptions, into what *Sports Illustrated* called "a bewildering scaffold of double coverages.") In similarities to Penn State, Virginia Tech also threw an unpredictable defense at Ohio State: the Hokies stuffed the middle and brought up their safeties, pressuring Barrett into quick reads and gambling that he couldn't make the throws. And he didn't, completing only nine of 29 and throwing three interceptions.

When sportswriter Bill Rabinowitz asked Meyer how—after the VT game—he would have answered someone asking about Ohio State's chances for the playoffs, Meyer said, "I'm going to escort that person out of the facility." The Buckeyes dropped to No. 22 in the polls, and the doubters were in ascendance. It seemed only the players themselves maintained belief. "Everybody was saying, 'We can't, we can't, we can't,' said tackle Taylor Decker. "The fact that people said we couldn't meant we had to."

What followed was a series of lesser contests—Kent State, Cincinnati, Maryland, and Rutgers—in which the Buckeyes averaged 56 points and quarterback Barrett honed his craft. Then the season's turning point: Penn State in Happy Valley. While the Buckeyes appeared decidedly mortal in Happy Valley, escaping with a 31–24 double overtime win, they demonstrated two of the qualities all champions possess: good fortune (ten OSU points came on controversial calls for which the Big Ten would apologize) and perseverance.

Barrett played with a strained knee and threw two interceptions but his plucky guidance kept Ohio State poised, even after Penn State erased its 17–0 deficit and forced the game into overtime. A 17-yard run by Barrett in the first OT set up his own score, and in the second OT, he scored the winning touchdown (which probably should have been accredited to guard Pat Elflein, who drove him into the end zone). Said Meyer afterward, "Freshman quarterback, freshman lineman, freshman this, freshman that…" *The Plain Dealer* noted that the Buckeyes were "not back-in-the-playoff-conversation good," but they'd done what Meyer said all great teams did—survive.

There was a breather against Illinois (55–14), then up next was the Buckeyes' old scourge, Michigan State in East Lansing, who seemed to be making a case for being Ohio State's No. 1 Michigan rivalry. There were twenty-six Ohioans on the MSU roster, including quarterback Connor Cook, the MVP of last season's victory over OSU in the Big Ten title game and a good Parma Heights boy. That loss to the Spartans had ended the Buckeyes' historic win streak and cost them the Big Ten trophy and a shot at the national championship, any one of which was incentive enough for an Ohio State team haunted by the Virginia Tech loss and needing a quality win. A strong win over the No. 7 Spartans would be a grand place to exorcize the demons.

MSU's secondary called its turf the "No Fly Zone," but OSU's receivers, who'd studied hardily each Spartan defensive back, weren't impressed. With three minutes left in the half, Barrett tossed a slant to Michael Thomas, which resulted in a 79-yard score that tied the game at 21–21. (In the media session afterward, Thomas would say, "Where the No Fly Zone at?") Then with a minute left, Barrett threw perfectly to Devin Smith on a post pattern for a 44-yard score and the lead, which the Buckeyes never gave up. Barrett finished the day with 300 yards. It was his best game so far, prompting *USA Today* to call him "a star on the rise."

The Washington Post was more perceptive. It reminded a national audience that Ohio State deployed formidable athletes, played formidable football, and was formidably coached. "It still maintains the capacity to lose a starting quarterback (Braxton Miller) when his shoulder tears in August, then develop a freshman replacement (J.T. Barrett) with big-game prowess across the months that follow," it wrote. And more important: "It still has the wherewithal to capitalize on its own orneriness over being scorned eleven months prior." The Buckeyes had just done unto Michigan

State what Michigan State had done unto them last season, said the *Post*—"They capsized expectations."

The Bucks leaped from No. 14 to No. 8 in the College Football Playoff rankings, and as befitting their new station, satisfactorily dispatched Minnesota (31–24) and Indiana (42–27), taking a No. 6 ranking into Ohio Stadium for the Michigan game. The Wolverines were 5–6, and the Bucks, who'd lost to Michigan only three times since the turn of the century, were 20-point favorites. Even so, tradition was honored, in that the letter "M" was blanked out all over the campus. The Wolverines put up a gallant front—on both sides of the ball—before falling, 42–28. The game, though, was more notable for the season-ending injury to quarterback J.T. Barrett, which happened on the first play of the last quarter.

Barrett's earlier touchdown pass to tight end Nick Vannett had just broken Drew Brees's Big Ten record of 42 touchdowns in a season (he added two more on the ground), he'd soon be named first team All-Big Ten, he'd finish fifth in the Heisman voting—and he was gone. "Seriously? That happened?" said Ohio State's culture consultant, Tim Kight. "The guy who came from nowhere is gone? And now the *third* guy has to go in there?"

Ohio State had now been officially reported dead three times in the season. The first was in August when Braxton Miller (a two-time Big Ten MVP who'd finished fifth in the 2012 Heisman voting) went out with a shoulder injury. The Virginia Tech loss was another death. Then Barrett.

THE REPORTS OF A BUCKEYE DEATH WERE WILDLY EXAGGERATED, THOUGH, and here began one of the great, redemptive stories in the history of Ohio State football. It was one of those legendary moments that pulled the fans from their ordinary lives and bound them forever to the possibility of grand spectacle. It was, in short, the very reason why they *were* fans. The progenitor this time was an unlikely prospect from the Cleveland ghetto named Cardale Jones. He'd played a total of 39 snaps, thrown one incomplete pass, and his previous moment of note occurred when he made his infamous freshman tweet, "Why should we have to go to class if we came here to play FOOTBALL, we ain't come to play SCHOOL." (Like much about the late-blooming Jones, it proved to be somewhat misleading, as Jones had a 3.0 grade point average. And a sense of humor: when he graduated in 2017 with a bachelor's degree in African American studies, he inscribed the quote on his graduation cap.)

Jones was an unusual prospect, physically imposing, with an arm so strong his teammates called him "12-Gauge." He was a ghetto kid who'd never met his father, growing up so poor he wore bags over his worn-out shoes to stay dry and turned his dirty shirts inside out to give himself another few days of wear. Needless to say, he had a bit of adjustment problem at Ohio State. His coaches found him smart and likable but, as *Sports Illustrated* succinctly put it, "out of shape, not interested in hard work, and academically indifferent." As a redshirt freshman in 2012, he was so unprepared he not only failed his first workout, he didn't get through the *warmup*. Even Meyer admitted that Jones was "a guy who had one foot out the door."

Awaiting him in his first start—the Big Ten championship game, no less—was Wisconsin and its Heisman candidate, Melvin Gordon, who'd just set the major college single-game rushing record (408 yards against Nebraska). Undaunted by Gordon, the Buckeye defense dented Gordon—and his Heisman ambitions—by making him "go horizontal," as OSU cornerback Doran Grant called it. Gordon ended the day with 76 yards and a fumble that resulted in a Joey Bosa touchdown. "When it came down to it," Gordon said, "we just wasn't playing Wisconsin football." (Gordon's subject-verb agreement difficulty was supposedly caused by the Buckeye defense.)

The game was a 59–0 blowout that finally allowed the Bucks to think about the national title picture. Jones was 12-of-17 passing for 257 yards while Ezekiel Elliott got almost that much (220) on the ground. Jones was named the game MVP and was seen afterward scampering about with a rose behind his ear. When he tweeted "Holy Shit," *Sports Illustrated* said it was the precise sentiment of everyone who had seen the game.

The emphatic win was exactly what Ohio State needed because there was so little separation among the top six teams, and, as the magazine pointed out, "college football's selection process involves both unfortunate math—four teams from five major conferences—and serious consequences: teams that get in earn $6 million for their conferences." In a week, no one would remember who No. 5 was. Ohio State had just sent the College Football Playoff selection committee a not-so-subtle message: *What else do we have to do?* Or, *You can't ignore us.*

When the news broke on Sunday that Ohio State *was* one of the four best teams in the country, not everyone was happy. The Vegas oddsmakers were disappointed that TCU and Baylor had been surpassed by Ohio State. "They had one good game and they ran the score up on Wisconsin to get style points," said one bookie. The problem, of course, was the system, which having only four slots, was designed for unhappiness.

Coach Meyer had a sip of the 2004 Dom Pérignon ($180 a bottle) brought in by his Dublin neighbors, then went back to work, worrying about Alabama. The Southeastern Conference had won seven of the last eight national titles, and three of them were by Alabama—2009, 2011, and 2012. Fortunately, the Alabama of 2014 was not one of *those* teams. The Tide had trouble surviving its own conference: it lost to Mississippi, nearly lost to Arkansas and Auburn, and beat LSU only in overtime.

Nick Saban's team was still the No. 1 team in the country, a nine-point favorite, and coasting on the SEC's mantle of transcendency, which suggested that the Big Ten was your father's Oldsmobile. Scott Kennedy, *Scout.com's* recruiting expert, said, "Very rarely is Ohio State going to butt heads with someone as talented as they are, and even more rarely are they going to butt heads with someone *more* talented than they are. But this is it. This is Alabama." Forty-two out of forty-three ESPN analysts picked Alabama to win. And Ohio State was playing in the Sugar Bowl, in "the voodoo-hexed city of New Orleans," which amounted to home turf for the Tide. The southerners may have lost that original contest with the North, but they'd since made up for it in hype.

There was one voice of reason, and it belonged to Alabama's defensive coordinator, Kirby Smart, who said, "We've talked to several coaches in their league and every coach to a T said—these are coaches that have been in the SEC—without a doubt, they've got an SEC team, they've got SEC speed, and SEC size. They just don't play in the SEC."

The game was billed by *The New York Times* as a contest between two of college football's best coaches—"Saban the defensive genius versus Meyer the offensive savant." Meanwhile, there were questions—apparently serious—about the advantage held by Ohio State because Alabama had only one game film of Cardale Jones: not only did the Tide not know who Jones was, they had no idea what he could do. (The Ohio State staffers were in almost the same situation; *they* didn't have but one game film of Jones, either.)

Ohio State's game was late in the day, which meant the Buckeyes got a boost from watching the earlier Outback Bowl in which Wisconsin beat Auburn—a month before, Auburn had led Alabama by nine before eventually falling, 55–44. Meyer was elated. He immediately addressed his team on what he called "the whole perception-versus-reality thing," and pointed out the Wisconsin win as the reality. "The reality just happened," he said. Jones, having good practices, was aggravated by all the hype. "We were hearing what we couldn't do, all these great players they (Alabama) have, that this was a scrimmage for them for the national championship game. All that stuff pissed me off…"

Ohio State immediately moved the ball on the Tide but was thwarted by turnovers. With eight minutes left in the half, Alabama was ahead 21–6. The Buckeyes, though, played with such equanimity they made a two-touchdown deficit appear part of their game plan. Jones, with five-of-seven passing for 68 yards, brought the Bucks to the three-yard line, and with 2:55 left Elliott made the score 21–13. The OSU defense forced Alabama three-and-out, and Jones again moved the Buckeyes downfield. With twelve seconds left, Jones handed off to Jalin Marshall, who pitched to receiver Evan Spencer in what appeared to be a double-reverse. But Spencer stopped and threw a 13-yard pass to the gymnastically-inclined Michael Thomas in the left corner of the end zone where Thomas made a highlight reel catch, leaving the game 21–20 at the half.

On OSU's opening drive of the second half, third-and-8, Jones unloaded deep to Devin Smith for a 47-yard score and a 27–21 lead. The Buckeyes' contention was now manifest. Alabama coach Saban—who'd been defensive backs coach at Ohio State for Earle Bruce—would say afterward that he hadn't seen on film that OSU receivers could burn defenders all over the field. (It was suggested that maybe no one *could* until Jones and his big arm got on the field.)

There was a bit of touch-and-go yet remaining, but Ohio State was playing with the panache Alabama usually reserved for itself, and "the tourists from Ohio," as the OSU fans were called, had made the stadium their own. Twice overcoming near-disastrous field position (punting twice from their own end zone), the assured Bucks, in a final dominant gesture, handed Elliott the ball and, making one cut and breaking an arm tackle, he went 85 yards on the longest play from scrimmage the Tide had permitted in the entire season.

"When Elliott went all the way to the end zone for a 42–28 lead," said the *Washington Post*, "Ohio State had gone all the way from September, and that had been one considerable climb." A little over three minutes remained, but for all practical purposes Alabama was done. Elliott was the Sugar Bowl MVP, with his record 230 yards (20 carries and a 11.5 average), and ESPN said Jones's performance (called "alternately brilliant and maddening") might have made him one of the greatest replacement players in college football history.

After the Alabama game, which carried all the hype of the Second Coming, Oregon was almost anticlimactic. The Bucks were now headed for Arlington, Texas, to play a game that would mark their twenty-fourth week of football, this one against Heisman Trophy winner Marcus Mariota, who'd finish his season with 42 touchdowns and only four interceptions. Vegas, of course, favored Oregon, and the Buckeyes, having confounded expectations so many times this year, found their underdog status comforting.

The Ducks were another up-tempo team, boasting that only sixteen seconds elapsed between their offensive plays. "Their whole system is that they want you to go run around the house three, four times and then go play," Meyer said. "It was 'the fatigue factor.'"

The Buckeyes were undeterred. Their practice theme was "Eliminate 16." Meyer set the play clocks on the practice field to "16." He even put two shot clocks—the number frozen on "16"—in the hotel dining room. They worked at Oregon's pace, and they knew that they, themselves, were faster. And they were no longer worried—if they'd ever been—about their quarterback, even if Jones's backup was H-back Jalin Marshall, who'd been an option quarterback in high school and spent most practices throwing the ball into the dirt in front of his receivers. (He'd have an important game, but not at quarterback: he had a good early catch, then a first down on fourth-and-two to keep the Bucks' first touchdown drive going, and set up another touchdown with a 17-yard punt return.)

The Buckeyes once again ignored their multiple turnovers and held Oregon at bay. In the final analysis, it was Ohio State's own offense that set the tempo. Going into the final quarter, Oregon was marginally down, 28–20, but languishing. Ezekiel Elliott scored twice more, making the final score 42–20 and finished the day with four touchdowns and 246 yards—enough for his second straight MVP trophy.

The Buckeyes had put together a season some said was the best college football season ever by a coaching staff. Meyer had lost two Heisman candidate quarterbacks; his tailback, Elliott, broke his left wrist in August and could carry the ball only in his right hand; and his offensive line had been raided by the NFL. "We weren't supposed to be here," said the new quarterback, Cardale Jones, as cornerback Doran Grant and some of the linemen made snow angels in the deluge of post-game confetti covering AT&T Stadium. (Back in Columbus, fans broke into Ohio Stadium and pulled down a goalpost. They filled the streets around the campus with so much fervor and animation that the Columbus police felt compelled to douse them with pepper spray.)

It was the eighth title recognized by the university, and it came after a season in which the Buckeyes set or tied seventy-four records, including the NCAA, the Big Ten, and the championship and bowl games. The National Championship Trophy carried the Bucks' 2014 schedule and, appropriately enough, rendered "Michigan" as simply "TUN"—Team Up North.

Sportswriters, who had begun the season by positing Ohio State as being "moored with a vague irrelevance," were now certain that the SEC's dominion over college football was at an end and that it would not command the next decade as it had the previous one. The Buckeyes, having survived near-impossible odds, appeared set for the near future. Cardale Jones was returning, along with J.T. Barrett and Braxton Miller, both of whom would soon be healthy.

As usual, though, the future—as grand as it appeared on paper—would bring its own unpredictability. Having splendid quarterbacks to choose from might not be the blessing it seemed, and there was always that pesky Big Ten upstart, Michigan State, looking to build on its reputation as spoiler.

They came squalling into existence with their formula delivered in kegs and their mamas proudly diapered them in tablecloths. They were big when they were little, and they grew from there.

The lost man

What ever happened to Ohio State's once most-vaunted position?

In the happy circumstances of Urban Meyer's arrival, there was also a departure. It was only a loss of a kind, unhappy mostly in its historical sense, of small note when compared to the culture's larger losses, to wit: the phone booth, home delivery of milk, and the last episode of *The Sopranos*. Still, we might rank it with the disappearance of other large species like the northern white rhino, with which it shared such characteristics as size, foot speed, and a fondness for wallowing in mud.

We speak here of the Ohio State fullback, for decades poster boy for Ohio's blue collar values, an unwitting symbol for the things many Ohioans held dear: strength, manly purpose, and forward motion, no matter the opposition. He, too, was a working man, righteously pugnacious in his cause, dependable in a crisis (fourth-and-one, say), and in all, a good man to go downfield with. He was an oversized vertebrate with what seemed to be perpetual grazing rights to Ohio Stadium. He was also, as were most of them, a sturdy homegrown boy, and we imagined him and his brethren suckled by full-figured Norwegian types who split firewood one-handed and raised their sons on beef and biscuits. They came squalling into existence with their formula delivered in kegs and their mamas proudly diapered them in tablecloths. They were big when they were little, and they grew from there.

When they reached Columbus, they inspired the next generation of small boys who spent their waking hours chasing each other across vacant lots, returning at dusk with the badges of fullback honor: skinned knees, various bruises, and sometimes the real article—a fat lip. They called themselves Otis, Brockington, Henson, Johnson, Broadnax—any of Ohio State's legion of major appliances who dominated the Big Ten for years and earned Ohio State the sobriquet "Fullback University."

THE FULLBACK WAS WOODY HAYES'S CREATURE, BECAUSE WOODY MADE HIM. But they'd actually been around long before, obdurate fellows who needed little in the way of praise or publicity, seemingly content with their proletarian role in the old single wing offense. The first OSU fullback of note was Gene Fekete, a chiseled specimen from Findlay who'd perfected his running technique by sprinting crossways in newly-plowed farm fields. It made him pick his knees up so that he didn't fall on his face, a style that proved detrimental to Big Ten defenses.

Fekete was a mainstay of OSU's first national title team, in 1942, when he led the Big Ten in rushing. Against Pittsburgh in Ohio Stadium, he got the ball three times and ran for 139 yards, including a fullback spinner trap that went for 89 yards and a school record that may—or may not—still be a school record, depending upon one's sources.

He finished eighth in the Heisman voting that year—the first time a sophomore made the top ten. (The trophy was won by another Ohioan, a Croatian kid named Frank Sinkwich, who'd grown up in Youngstown and played for the University of Georgia.) Unfortunately for Columbus, Fekete never played for Ohio State again. First, he was in the army, then a knee injury thwarted his pro career with Cleveland before it had begun.

Ohio State's first consensus All-American at fullback was Bob White, a rawboned bundle of unpleasantness who'd started off at center, although he seemed at home wherever Woody put him, which was almost anywhere. In one game, he played six positions, including guard, center, fullback, and linebacker. There are some old-timers around who still cite his performance in November of 1957 as one of the signal acts in school history. That was when Ohio State played fifth-ranked Iowa for the Big Ten championship—and a trip to Pasadena. Down 13–10 with less than eight minutes left, White carried seven of eight plays, gaining 66 of 68 yards and the go-ahead score as OSU won 17–13. Then after scoring he returned to center, blocking for Frank Kremblas's three straight quarterback sneaks before Kremblas, with thirty-six seconds left, punted the ball away.

White was called "a startling facsimile of the great Bronko Nagurski," which made for great publicity, and posited him for a stellar 1958 season which he began on the cover of *Street and Smith's Football Yearbook* and ended by finishing fourth in the Heisman Trophy voting (won that year by Army's Rhodes Scholar halfback Pete Dawkins). He wasn't Bronko Nagurski, but his replacement in 1959 came close.

That was Bob Ferguson, Ohio State's first great modern fullback, a fireplug from Troy, Ohio, and an early evolutionary precedent for what college running backs would become. He was almost the size of Ezekiel Elliott—who wouldn't come along for another half century or so—and he could run like a tailback except that wasn't what Woody wanted him to do. He hunkered down in Woody's split-T backfield, resembling something large and burrowing, and at the snap he plunged off-tackle, carrying half the defense downfield. *That* was what Woody wanted him to do.

"He was reliable as a Swiss watch, carrying the ball more than four hundred times and losing yardage on only four occasions," sportswriter Mark Rea said about Ferguson. The bull of the campus put up running back numbers, both as a junior (853 yards) and again as a senior (938), nearly all of them difficult. In 1961, he was second in the Heisman voting, behind Ernie Davis of Syracuse, the first African American winner. The vote is still one of the closest in Heisman history.

If you want to know what that circa-1960 Ohio State offense looked like, look at film clips from OSU's championship 2014 season with Elliott's powerful running and J.T. Barrett keeping the opposing defenses off-balance with his own running threat. Take most of the creative offensive symbiosis away and you'll have Ferguson and his quarterback, Tom Matte, who rushed for 682 yards in 1960 (behind Ferguson's 853).

Ferguson thus began a remarkable run of Ohio State fullbacks who appeared big, powerful, and quick enough to play running back in today's offenses. There was Matt Snell, relegated to blocking for Ferguson until he inherited the position as a senior in 1963. He was team MVP but seemed mostly relieved when his college career was over. "You've got to remember, playing for Woody Hayes wasn't a lot of fun," he said. "You were beat up. You were tired. You just wanted the season to end." In 1964, Snell was the AFL Rookie of the Year, then helped the Jets win Super Bowl III where many thought he, not Joe Namath, should have been the MVP. (These days, though, he's more famously known as the first guy to make a Miller Lite beer commercial. And he ended up on OSU's All-Century Team as a defensive end.)

Woody's fullback meridian, though, probably occurred in the Michigan game of 1962 when his three fullbacks teamed up for 260 yards, led by a homegrown import named Dave Francis from Columbus West High who had 186 of them. They beat Michigan, 28–0, and helped disseminate the notion that Ohio State was the eternal home of the fullback. "Hayes's use of them," the *Plain Dealer* wrote, "is believed revolutionary in college football." Woody, surely, was in his element.

Before the 1968 season, he wanted to recruit three fullbacks, but they were also being courted by Indiana. When they visited Bloomington, the Hoosiers' coaching staff rolled out films of the 1967 Ohio State–Indiana freshmen game, in which

John Brockington and Jack Tatum played fullback—and ran magnificently. Woody's prospective fullbacks, seeing faint possibility in Columbus behind Brockington and Tatum, were no longer Woody's prospective fullbacks. Indiana signed all three. In 1972, Hayes outdid himself by using *four* fullbacks in a 44–7 romp over Indiana, although that was less about strategy and more about simply letting everyone in the game. "If I were a fullback, there's only one school in the country I'd consider," Woody said afterward, and *Sports Illustrated* reported that it was a win earned the Woody way: "pure power into the center of the Hoosier line by four different fullbacks who perceptively chose the right school."

In the late 1960s, Woody had a pair of back-to-back All-Americans: Jim Otis, who was the first OSU back to gain 1,000 yards—a fullback!—and John Brockington, who backed up Otis for two years, then in 1970 became a 1,000-yard gainer himself. Champ Henson led the nation in scoring as a sophomore in 1972 (20 touchdowns) but his career was thwarted by injury. And in 1973, Pete Johnson arrived—Ohio State's last great, pure fullback. Johnson was Archie Griffin's lead blocker for Griffin's two Heisman seasons, but he was also a surprisingly agile runner himself.

He broke Henson's national scoring record in 1975 (25 touchdowns) while rushing for 1,059 yards, and had a decade-long career with the Cincinnati Bengals. His coach, Forrest Gregg, called him "a refrigerator with feet," and although Johnson weighed at least 260 pounds, he once reeled off a 57-yard run—and 112 yards—then said to reporters, "That wasn't me out there. Fat men can't run that fast."

It was a remarkable, if short-lived, run for fullbacks, but college offenses were evolving, even at Ohio State. The first death throes came when Ohio State went to the I-formation. The new formation *did* not happen over Woody's dead body, but when it did happen, he wasn't exactly his old spit-and-vinegar self. Listening to his assistants was never his strong suit, even when they were as good as his 1968 ones, but that year he *did* listen. Hence, the I-formation, and as Woody feared, it made the fullback more of a blocker. (Or as one scout said, "Fullbacks were guards whose brains had been knocked out.") For a time, though, Archie Griffin's success masked what was going on, for while Archie got most of the carries, it was still Johnson who got the ball inside the twenty—and the touchdowns. Even so, he rushed for 1,059 yards in 1975 (behind Griffin's 1,450) and left OSU with 56 rushing touchdowns, still a school record.

Woody kept the fullback on life support by insisting on running his old Robust-T offense inside the 20. The fullback scored and stayed in the headlines, otherwise he would have been just another blocking back. But Hayes was fighting the future, for the fullback had become something of a fireman on a diesel locomotive. Offensive coordinators were already finding ways to build a ground attack without a fullback. Coaches were moving the fullback into the slot, whereby an extra dimension was added to the offense. Was he then a fullback or a receiver? And who covered him—a linebacker or a defensive back? With zone blocking, the lone back in a single-set offense didn't need—nor want—a fullback in front of him. With his speed and size, he was the show.

At Ohio State, there were transition guys like Keith Byars, who in 1984 should have won the Heisman but didn't, and Eddie George in 1995, who did. They were big all-purpose backs who could do most everything, and they set the coaches' future sights on their own formidable skill sets. Byars and George were the incarnation of the near-forgotten Bob Ferguson, although running in more updated offenses, just as Beanie Wells and Ezekiel Elliott would be in the new century.

The fullback, nonetheless, was becoming a new man. Once he had been moved outside, he found himself reborn as a tight end, or a motion tight end, and thus an H-back. The old fullback usually blocked an inside linebacker; the new one blocked an outside one. And he might be a receiver. It was just another evolution, and it forced the defense to figure out what to do with a player who didn't line up where he was supposed to. He was no longer the bad boy of Woody's mulish offenses, though. He had become, God forbid, a *concept.*

Most observers thought the old definition of the fullback was pretty much gone. No less an authority than The Big Tuna himself,

Bill Parcells, who won two Super Bowls with the New York Giants, said it was like the Pleistocene Epoch. "They had all these different types of large animals roaming the earth, but the majority, I know, are extinct," he said. "That's what is happening to the fullbacks."

In 2012, halfway through Urban Meyer's first season, the Buckeyes squeezed out a 52–49 victory over Indiana. While the victory preserved Ohio State's undefeated run, the staff, finding itself short of linebackers, tapped fullback Zach Boren for the middle. There was little mention of the move being the end of an era: Boren, though, was the last starter listed at fullback on the OSU roster. Woody's glamour position, which had once defined the program, was seemingly gone, another victim of progress.

Boren was a tough kid from Pickerington, Ohio, who'd come to Ohio State as a linebacker, then found himself at fullback. An uncomplaining team guy, he remained there for most of his career, although he seldom saw the ball—in 2011, he didn't get a carry. There could have been no better final act, though, for Boren was the exemplar of the old-time Ohio State fullback, in both size and temperament. Behind his blocking, OSU's running backs put up more than two dozen 100-yard games, and that, if nothing else, would have endeared him to Woody.

It was, after all, what the fullback was supposed to do.

The football library

And you thought coaches weren't bookish fellows

SOON AFTER THE TURN OF THE CENTURY, OHIO STATE'S COACHES were the principal managers of large, complex systems, and the most visible of them were celebrities with huge social media followings. Instead of X's and O's, they talked "leadership," an all-purpose word meaning their team just made the playoffs. The first of these in Columbus was Jim Tressel, whose *Winners Manual: For the Game of Life* was a mélange of sloganry, soapbox, and Bible study. It was an earnest huzzah for the supremely disciplined athletic life, and by honoring its admonitions to the letter, one should be able to walk on the Olentangy without getting one's socks wet.

The author(s) admit it was assembled as much as written, and we see little of Tressel himself. We do learn that as a graduate assistant he ate cold SpaghettiOs from a can and made a hundred dollars a month. And talking to his players about temptation, he said, "When I was in school, there were never any girls knocking on my dorm-room door." And then, in parenthesis, he wrote, "I'll admit that may not be just a product of the era I'm from."

Otherwise, though, it's an intense examination of the eternal athletic verities—responsibility, discipline, attitude, love, excellence, etc.—all of which appear on the page in raised and gilded letters, overwhelming all but the most dedicated reader with their sobriety. One longs for more of the game's riveting specifics to lessen the abstraction, but the book's real agency is missionary zeal, and its piety is probably what bought out the critics when Tressel seemed to fall athwart his own teachings. (When he wrote about his players, "We're giving them more tools to help them develop and putting them in learning situations that take them further down the same road they've been on for eighteen years," some saw it as instruction to Terrelle Pryor and his teammates on the proper acquisition of tattoos.)

No matter the voice, it was apparent coaches had joined that old ruling class from whence most of our wisdom came: monarchs, priests, and the various titans and moguls. A new industry had been born. (Amazon, by one count, offered some fifty-seven thousand books with "leadership" in the title.) There was now an audience beyond those who wished to know about the run-pass option. *This* audience already knew what the coach did; now they wanted to know how he did it.

Urban Meyer's 2015 book, *Above the Line: Lessons in Leadership and Life from a Championship Program*, is similar in concept to Tressel's but enlivened by its conciseness. It's highly readable, perhaps because Meyer's co-author was Wayne Coffey, an award-winning sportswriter who'd already been on *The New York Times*' bestseller list (as was *Above the Line*). There's less pontification in Meyer's book; he simply presents and gets on with it. We also get small personal glimpses. There's a picture of Meyer sending text messages during Mass, for instance, which displeased his wife, Shelley, and a recognition of his overly-animated self as a young coach (his own description being "raving lunatic").

The surprise is how quickly one recognizes that the book's instructions apply to all his readers, not just as athletes but in whatever they might be doing. It's essentially a template for personal management. Meyer, too, has an unerring sense of converting a cliché into a practicum. One of his formulations is "event plus response equals outcome." It's uncomfortably close to a cliché until he explains how the response becomes both well-considered *and* second-nature. "What does the situation require of me?" Meyer asks.

It's clearly a question for all manner of events other than third-and-long.

Despite the intervening half century, there's a connection here going back to Woody Hayes—Ohio State's first celebrity coach—who wrote one of football's first leadership books. It wasn't called that back in 1973 when *You Win with People* was first published yet amidst its meandering text was one of the major elements of the successful leadership book: the character of the people you hire. Or in Hayes's case, *recruit*. He may have been the first coach to think people wanted to know the secrets beyond the X's and O's. (Or perhaps it was simply what he wanted to do, which is more likely.) And he understood that his successes lay primarily with the people he put on the field.

It was Hayes's third book, and no one is surprised to learn that he wrote his own books—no ghostwriter, no collaborator, not even a publisher. He did them himself and they look like it. The design and presentation lack the professional look of a book put out by major publishing company—one of them is spiral-bound—but what would you expect from Hayes? If he was going to put his name on something, it had to be authentic.

He was probably the most widely read of the last-century OSU coaches, certainly in Ohio. He followed two of his national championship seasons with books. The first, *Football at Ohio State*, was published in 1957 at the height of Hayes's "three yards and a-cloud-of-dust" offense, and it demonstrated in mighty detail his punch-'em-in-the-face style. The second, *Hot Line to Victory*, came after the 1968 championship season. *Hot Line* had a little more personality, including a history lesson on the relationship between William Tecumseh Sherman and Rex Kern, two generals from Lancaster, Ohio, who—in Woody's mind, anyway—were of the same stripe. Woody saw himself utilizing the techniques of Sherman, Heinz Guderian's Panzer units and the *blitzkrieg*, as well as George Patton. (Military historians, however, might have seen a closer kinship between those guys and Tiger Ellison, whose own *blitzkrieg*—the run-and-shoot—was seldom deployed at Ohio State.)

THE BOOK ALSO GAVE A NOD TO O.J. SIMPSON'S FAMOUS 80-YARD RUN IN THE 1969 ROSE BOWL that put USC up 10–0, which Woody said was "the only long scoring run in ten games against the best defense at Ohio State in eighteen years." After a quote or two from that other famous offensive strategist, Sun-Tzu, Woody dispassionately analyzed Simpson's shifting speed and reaction to the OSU defense. That in itself was surprising, as Woody was not customarily dispassionate about anything, and there is ample—and famous—documentation of his initial reaction to Simpson's run. His defensive secondary coach, Lou Holtz, said Woody "took a strategic grasp of my jugular and screamed: 'Why did O.J. go 80 yards?' I told him: 'Because that's all he needed, Coach.'"

Woody also provided an intricate diagram of O.J.'s demoralizing play, showing the position of every player on the field, with O.J.'s run highlighted. Woody was particularly impressed by USC's left guard, who sealed off the man in front of him, then took out the backside linebacker. Simpson made two great cuts in the open field and, according to Woody's exacting diagram, ended up in the Pacific Ocean, the waves carefully drawn into Woody's playbook.

Unlike the book written by his friend Tiger Ellison, Woody's books didn't change the game, but each had a large impact on other coaches. There was a time when it seemed as if every coach in Ohio had a copy of *Hotline*, and it became part of the collective knowledge of the coaching community: everybody, for instance, knew how Ohio State ran the 27—the fullback off-tackle. Even the spectators in the stands could see it coming.

In terms of influence, though, it would be hard—this side of Walter Camp's *American Football*—to find a football coaching book that has had more influence on all levels of the game than Tiger Ellison's book, *Run and Shoot Football: Offense of the Future.* In it, Ellison chronicled the birth and development of a football system he created in the late 1950s while coaching at Middletown High School in Southwest Ohio. He had already shared his offense with other high school coaches, but his innovations, such as spread formations and receivers adjusting their routes on the fly to the defensive coverage, did not become widespread.

In 1963, Ellison was inveigled to Ohio State by Woody Hayes to coach the freshman team. There was new hope for Ellison's Run-and-Shoot, but he should have known better, for he was working for "the most non-passing coach that ever lived." (This was Woody's own evaluation, found in the foreword to Ellison's book.) The best Ellison managed was sneaking in a few plays for quarterback Rex Kern in that glorious 1968 championship season.

It was a tribute to the mutual respect between Ellison and Hayes that Hayes's aversion to Ellison's offense never seemed to interfere with their friendship, and perhaps in the last analysis he did Ellison a favor: he made him write a book, for it was the only way Tiger's offense would find an expression. It might have been Woody's most notable moment in support of the arts.

Published in 1965, the book became an interesting curiosity among high school coaches but practically unknown in the higher levels of the game. Even in 1975's *Guide to Football Literature*, Tiger's book was listed under "High School Offenses." Few coaches were willing to risk their livelihoods on the radical offensive philosophy Ellison put forth. Few, that is, until the book fell into the hands of "Mouse" Davis, a high school coach in Oregon.

While traveling the Northwest coaching circuit, Davis came across a copy of Ellison's book and saw an approach to football that few others—outside of Ellison—saw. Using Ellison's basic approach, Davis won state high school championships in Oregon then took the concept to Portland State where, on Neil Lomax's arm, the offense rewrote a sizable portion of college football's passing records. Davis found that the best answer to critics who said, "You can't run that crap," was to show them he could. He continued to synthesize Ellison's ideas as he rose through the football ranks, all the way to Jim Kelly and the Houston Gamblers of the United States Football League.

"When the book first came out, we sold about 30,000 copies," Ellison said, "mostly to high schools. They finally let it go out of print. Some years later they called me again and said, 'Those Houston Gamblers have got everybody in the country calling us… let's do it again.'" Ellison and Davis never met, but Davis always acknowledged his debt to Ellison. "All I did," he said, "was read Tiger's book." And they communicated from afar. When Ellison learned Davis had lost the copy that years earlier had inspired a football movement, he sent Davis a new copy with the inscription, "Every time you score a touchdown, I sell another book."

THERE ARE EARLIER BOOKS BY OHIO STATE COACHES, THE MOST NOTABLE ONE BEING JOHN WILCE'S *FOOTBALL: HOW TO PLAY IT AND HOW TO UNDERSTAND IT*, published by Charles Scribner's Sons in 1923. Wilce is one of the forgotten Ohio State coaches, even though his legacy includes Ohio State's first win over Michigan and the Buckeyes' first trip to the Rose Bowl. More important, though, was his offensive thinking in the early 1920s when the game was almost wholly run-based. He was one of the great early students of the game when, as they said about the time before Paul Brown, "the ball was merely tossed out on the field."

Wilce didn't have Knute Rockne's South Bend public relations machine working for him, and it was easy for his accomplishments to be overlooked. He was also a reserved man, a bit of an academic in a tough-guy profession that still communicated by way of the primitive grunt. But he and Illinois coach Bob Zuppke were pioneers in the development of the forward pass, and it was Wilce who gave Ohio State national standing with his offensive ingenuity. Not only did his teams throw the ball, but throwing was wholly integrated into his offenses. His 1920 team won the conference title by passing. The old football sage, Walter Camp, saw Ohio State beat Wisconsin and he called Harry Workman's two late touchdown passes to All-American Pete Stinchcomb, which won the game, "the most thrilling I have ever seen."

The strategy of using one's running game to set up the pass had not yet become the all-encompassing mantra of the century, mostly because the pass was used so sparingly. (By the turn of the next century, the run-to-set-up-the-pass had become so imbedded in the language that it was an *Urban Dictionary* entry, an extended sexual metaphor for foreplay and its happy conclusion.) Wilce, though, took what was about to become the prevailing offensive notion of the game—and reversed it: he may have been the first coach so prescient as to use the pass to set up the run. For early on, he recognized that the threat of passing loosened up the defensive secondary, which in turn provided the likelihood of more open running lanes.

He was innovative on the other side of the ball, too. Some credit him with being first to employ the strategy of rushing the passer, as well as using a five-man defensive line. *The New York Times* called him "a modern of moderns," and his book outlined strategies that wouldn't be part of mainstream football for more than a decade. Still and all, Wilce was foremost an *educator*. He even looked the part in his thick-rimmed glasses, which gave him an owlish appearance, the result of omnivorous reading habits—by candlelight—as a boy.

Wilce extolled the virtues of cleanliness, fresh air, and what he called "proper thoughts," the latter being particularly problematic for his teenage charges. His spartan regime even extended to nutrition where he told his boys to avoid pork, gravy, and cake. He was earnest, a bit cerebral, and he fretted over his own use of the phrase "intestinal fortitude," which he had inserted into one of his team lectures. The phrase came to him while riding the streetcar to campus, and he wondered if by using it he might be regarded as pretentious.

The 1920s weren't kind to Wilce. While his teams validated the building of OSU's enormous new stadium, they never reclaimed the glory of the Chic Harley-Pete Stinchcomb years. Ironically, the game he helped build and expand was, for him, getting too big, too business-like. His early teams, though, had given birth to an eager new audience, one that would never again be satisfied with anything other than wins and titles.

And so Wilce, with little complaint, demurred; the game he'd helped create was no longer *his* game. He'd finished his medical degree in 1919 (while coaching Ohio State to a 6–1 season in which only 12 points had been scored on the Buckeyes). So it wasn't as though he had no fallback position. When he resigned after the 1928 season he turned to what might have been—all along—his true calling, becoming a professor of preventive medicine at Ohio State and one of America's leading heart specialists.

After Wilce's book came another seminal text, published in 1957, the same year as Woody's *Football at Ohio State,* this one by former Ohio State All-American Gomer Jones, who'd played in the early 1930s then turned down the pro game to be a Buckeye assistant to Francis Schmidt. Jones's book, *Modern Defensive Football,* which he wrote with his coach, Bud Wilkinson, quickly became the definitive guide to football defenses, even though it seemed somewhat incongruous that the offensive tactician Schmidt had somehow godfathered a book on defense.

By 1947, Jones had arrived at Oklahoma where he quickly became what one writer called Wilkinson's "jovial lieutenant," just as the Sooners went on an unprecedented 47-game winning streak, winning thirteen straight conference titles and three national championships. It was Jones's work as much as it was Wilkinson's and Wilkinson knew it. "Gomer and I work as partners," he said. "All we do at Oklahoma is as much Gomer's thinking as mine."

Jones's other book, *Offensive and Defensive Line Play,* published by Prentice Hall in 1961, achieved a similar status as his first book. Although it appealed to a narrower audience, it remained a basic text for aspiring line coaches through the 1960s and 1970s. In it Jones acknowledged the influence of Francis Schmidt, whom he called "one of America's truly great coaches." He also acknowledged longtime OSU assistant Ernie Godfrey, saying that

Godfrey's theories were the basis for his own, which produced sixteen Oklahoma All-American linemen. (Godfrey, of course, was the dean of OSU assistants, coaching for thirty-three years in Columbus with seven different head coaches.)

When Wilkinson retired in 1964, Jones became Oklahoma's head coach, but he made no secret he was taking the job as a temporary assignment. He'd regularly turned down other offers and once said, "I've already got an ulcer, why do I need to be head coach?" Some said he took the job because his players lobbied so intently for him. ("He wanted every guy he coached to love him like a brother or a dad," said Norman McNabb, the co-captain of the 1950 national championship team, "and we all did.") Jones was the author of two undistinguished seasons after which he became athletic director. Some speculated that his lack of success was due partly to the fact that as head coach Gomer Jones no longer had Gomer Jones as his line coach.

His books have been superseded by the game's evolution and a countless array of football titles ranging from books on scouting methods to life lessons from athletic trainers. Nothing is overlooked, even when it should be. The best published efforts by Wilce, Jones, Ellison—even Woody himself—are now museum pieces. But their plays, techniques, and strategies are valuable references, giving us important insight into the game as it was played. And there's always value in seeing how some of the game's most successful coaches organized, presented, and coached football.

The titles can still be found, largely untouched, in libraries around the country and sometimes online, in places like eBay. The books, like the coaches' personalities, are now officially recognized as rare and historic, selling for prices ranging from $70 to more than $800. Woody and his old freshman coach, Tiger Ellison, would probably be amused. Given Woody's temperament, however, he might simply be outraged.

OHIO STATE

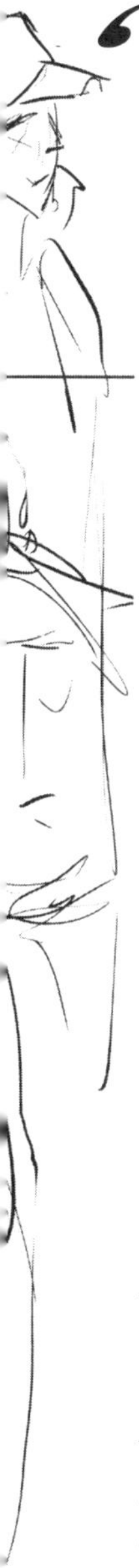

“Do you know many people who wake up in the morning and say, ‘Today, I am committed to being mediocre’?—Urban Meyer

Urban’s legend

He surpassed the others to become one of his own

IN THE ANNALS OF OHIO STATE FOOTBALL WAS THERE EVER A MORE SERENDIPITOUS MOMENT? When Jim Tressel left in the spring of 2011 after being tattooed by an NCAA investigation, the tears of a weepy Buckeye Nation fell only briefly. They lasted through a 6–7 record that autumn and its accompanying season of rumor and speculation, most of it involving Urban Meyer, an Ohioan fresh into a coaching sabbatical after winning two national titles while slumming in Florida. Even Florida’s Alligator Army was predicting—as early as June of 2011—that Meyer would go to Columbus. “Members of the Earle Bruce coaching tree tend to be loyal to Ohio State,” one of them wrote. (In the late ’80s, Meyer was Bruce’s receivers coach.) “So I’ve resigned myself to seeing Meyer in scarlet windbreakers.” And before the 2011 season was out, the Alligator Army was, indeed, seeing red. Or to be exact, scarlet, as in scarlet and gray. Urban Meyer and Ohio State: kismet. Meyer was once again a Buckeye, but this time he was *the* Buckeye.

He arrived in Columbus like some potentate, his triumphal entry missing only a carriage procession onto the university Oval.

He came rested, recovered from the intensity of Florida (two national championships and 104 games won over the previous decade), as well as an unfortunate excess of bad publicity about his roster of miscreants who were, depending upon one's perspective, the devil's spawn or merely typical college kids violating the open-container laws.

His Buckeye bona fides were impeccable: native son (was there a more representational Ohio place than Ashtabula?), two-sport star, Ohio State coaching cred. His origins were designed by providence and Bud Meyer. The elder Meyer was an honor graduate of the mid-century's School of the Unregenerate Hardcase, a demanding overseer in whom both bark and bite were coequal. He was as upright as a stalagmite and made of similar elemental minerals. He was legendary for having made Urban run home—some eight miles—after taking a curveball for a third strike, although it was just that: a legend. The run was Urban punishing *himself*, for what he saw as letting his team down. (He finished by spending an hour hitting balls off the backyard batting tee.) Yet Bud's world *was* essentially black and white, and it would be years before it acquired a color palette.

Bud was also a Woody Hayes fan, and like father, like son. Urban had come of age wearing "45"—Archie Griffin's number, and he recalled the Ohio State-Michigan game being played on store loudspeakers in Ashtabula (punctuated by Christmas carols). In a state lacking any larger identity, Columbus was the polestar, receiving the veneration of Ohio's faithful. One did not often rebel from such devoutness (particularly as the Meyers were good Catholics), thus Bud and offspring made the journey together.

Sometimes the journey was quite literal, as when Urban was an assistant at Illinois State in 1988 and his parents drove to Terre Haute—nine hours—where they joined a throng of several hundred to watch ISU play Indiana State. These were, after all, the résumé-building years. Meyer had survived a couple of years in minor league baseball then became a walk-on defensive back at the University of Cincinnati. This was followed by another two years as a grad assistant on Earle Bruce's Ohio State staff. They were insufficient, near-breadline years in which Meyer, in addition to his football duties, once drove a midnight shift forklift for $16 an hour.

There were other sojourns at Colorado State and Notre Dame—then his first head coaching job: Bowling Green, a graveyard of a place in 2001, staggering from a two-win season. He told his mentor Lou Holtz that it wasn't a good job. "Of course it's not," Holtz said. "That's why they're offering it to you."

THE HIRE PROVED TRANSFORMATIONAL. When the BG president showed up to voice his pride in the team before its first game—at Missouri, no less—he told the players the scoreboard didn't matter. Meyer said it did (as soon as the president was out of earshot), and BG won, 20–13, even after losing some twenty players who found Meyer's regimen too intense. (The trashcans around the practice field, receptacles for vomit, were an early tipoff.) The Falcons finished 8–3 that year; ESPN said it was the biggest turnaround in Division I football. And it was here that Meyer and his staff, laboring under a leaky roof that occasionally dripped rainwater on their meeting room table, "practically sequenced the genome of spread football," in the words of Cleveland writer Bill Livingston.

It was now Meyer's game, and there was an early moment that foretold the kind of offense his teams would run: his old coach, Earle Bruce, watching a BG practice, expressed acute dismay at one of Meyer's formations.

"What the hell is happening?" he yelled. "What the hell *is* that?"

"Coach," said Meyer, "it's off-tackle power, your base play."

There were recognizable elements to Meyer's offense, surely, but there was no model for what he was doing. "It was," as Meyer said, "'Go build something.' But there was no book to build it..."

Other coaches were asking the same questions Bruce asked. Their defenses were having to stop something they hadn't seen before. In 2002, meanwhile, Bowling Green was briefly ranked No. 20 nationally and ended the season at 9–3. At Utah, Meyer's unbeaten 2004 team was the original "BCS buster," that is, the first time one of the non-automatic qualifiers—football's scruffy second-class citizens—played in the Bowl Championship Series. (The Utes, as if to display their umbrage, beat Pittsburgh in the Fiesta Bowl, 35–7.) At Florida, it took him only two seasons to win a national title—courtesy Ohio State, which brought mixed reactions in Ashtabula, Meyer's hometown and a Buckeye stronghold. At the Crow's Nest Restaurant and Lounge, the normally Buckeye-partisan owners were sanguine: "If Ohio State has to lose to anyone, who better than Florida?" asked one of the regulars.

The one-sided game (41–14) brought back the old arguments about SEC speed vs. those plodding Big Ten'ers (Ted Ginn Jr. notwithstanding). This time, though, the speed seemed to reside with Florida's defense, which stymied Ohio State's newest Heisman winner, quarterback Troy Smith.

It was a sobering Buckeye moment: Ohio State, No. 1 in the country for the entire season, had not only lost the title but was now responsible for a nation's perceptions regarding foot-speed. Worse, the loss had been dealt by one of their own. (And "SEC speed" had been introduced into the *Urban Dictionary*'s lexicon as a noun meaning "the mythical advantage that the SEC has against other conferences in college football.")

"It was as clear a moment of arrival as football had seen in years," said *Sports Illustrated*, even as Meyer was being credited with the SEC's modern day vigor. (His 2006 title began a streak of seven consecutive national titles won by the Southeastern Conference, including Meyer's second, in 2008.) The key to SEC success was evident in the Ohio State game. It wasn't necessarily speed on the edges where even the fans in the high bleachers could see it; it was speed in the trenches. *That* was what Ohio State hadn't been prepared for. OSU linemen couldn't consistently block Florida linemen.

It was no small amount of irony that Meyer's homecoming brought the Buckeyes into a successful defense against that old shibboleth, SEC speed and dominance. For in the incandescent season of 2014, Ohio State beat Alabama in the College Football Playoff semifinal, then vanquished Oregon for the title. It was another superlative moment, and for those who were looking for the superlative itself, it was that Meyer had become college football's leading practitioner of the spread offense.

Ohio State's hiring of Meyer was, in large part, because it was thought Meyer could close the gap between the SEC and the Big Ten. It was something like the old Packard ad: "Ask the man who owns one." For Meyer had owned the SEC, and he would soon own the Big Ten. It was a happy circumstance that it took an Ohio guy to do it, and his offense was surely a large part of it. For those who thought the spread offense was all about passing and finesse, Meyer said otherwise: his offense was built around the run. "Power football with spread sets," he described it.

MEYER'S OFFENSE OWED AT LEAST A MINOR DEBT TO THE OLD SINGLE-WING, in which the tailback had serious multitasking duties—he had to both run *and* pass (he also blocked and, upon occasion, even punted). His quarterback, almost without exception, was the modern incarnation of this guy. From Josh Harris (Bowling Green) and Alex Smith (Utah) to Tim Tebow (Florida) and J.T. Barrett, Meyer was so good at developing these guys that he essentially traded one Heisman candidate, Joe Burrow, for another—Justin Fields. (That's a joke but not quite.)

His quarterbacks were such a threat that they gave the offense a numerical schematic advantage against the defense. "Equating numbers," he called it. "If you can make the defense account for the quarterback, that meant one guy you didn't have to block." It was never Joe Tiller's "basketball-on-grass" at Purdue, which was said to be the first team in the Big Ten to run a spread.

Tiller might have five receivers and his offense was called such because Indiana was a basketball state—although it probably wouldn't have worked as well if Drew Brees hadn't been running it. (Meyer wanted nothing to do with the term and once said to his coaches, "You won't coach here very long if I hear that come out of your mouth, basketball on grass. It's power football with a spread set.")

Meyer brought the spread along in a different package, and the ghosts of Ohio State's past came with him. There was Francis Schmidt's creativity, Sid Gillman's precision, Paul Brown's organization, and Tiger Ellison's imagination. And even some of Woody Hayes's ground game but, as *The Plain Dealer* pointed out, "with thinner resistance because the spread used the whole field, not merely the bloody ground between the tackles." Meyer didn't invent the spread, but he made it his. (There were light bulbs before Edison, too, but no one remembers who made them.)

No one was better at taking an idea and improving it. Meyer had an intuitive sense of football's edges, and he liked it out there. He was also a masterful recruiter, and he knew how to find skill people. But in 2012, he was shocked at the national perception of the Big Ten.

"I remember looking for other Big Ten teams on the recruiting rankings when I first got here. I said, 'Wait a minute, where is everybody?'" When early commitments didn't stay home and migrated instead to Ohio State, the other coaches kvetched about Meyer's aggressiveness; they saw it as violating the rather courtly gentlemen's agreement regarding their chattel. Meyer, though, was simply showing the Big Ten how the SEC did things, and in so doing, he'd bring the conference along with him.

When he arrived back in Ohio, the Big Ten had won but one consensus national title in nearly fifty years—Ohio State, 2002. This terrible drought was, of course, contrasted with the almost embarrassing fecundity of the SEC, which had just won *seven* consecutive titles (two of them Meyer's). Early in the 2014 season, *The New York Times* bemoaned, "The Big Ten is not what it used to be." The *Times* suggested the Rust Belt now girdled Midwestern football, pointing out that Texas and Florida each turned out twice as many D-I footballers as Ohio and that Big Ten teams had been overseen by "a succession of mediocre coaches."

The SEC sold excellence, the *Times* said. The Big Ten sold tradition. All in all, it was a gloomy picture inferring the conference was made up of dewlapped old-timers sitting in front of spiderwebbed trophy cases while lamenting the passing of the Notre Dame Box offense.

Meyer, though, would have both tradition *and* excellence, and he'd been aiming for his old SEC adversaries since his first season in Columbus, in 2012, when his Buckeyes were unbeaten but ineligible for the postseason. They'd begun that spring when Meyer and his coaches were working through practices but without the players. "We practiced *practice*," he said.

As an analyst watching Alabama win the 2012 title, he was asked how Ohio State would have fared against the Crimson Tide, and he answered circumspectly. "We could have competed," he said. "I would never say we could beat them because I don't know if we could…" To *Dispatch* writer Bill Rabinowitz, though, he revealed what he was really thinking: *They're so much better than we are right now. We're not even close.*

There had been the brief lapse at the end of 2013 when the unbeaten No. 2 Buckeyes were upset by Michigan State, 34–24, in the Big Ten Championship game. The 2014 title was thus surprising and redemptive, won as it was with a third-string quarterback, the quintessential sleeper Cardale Jones, who'd once been given a dunce cap by his exasperated coach. The CFP semifinal was in the Sugar Bowl against none other than No. 1 Alabama, whom the Buckeyes beat 42–35. "Ohio State overcame the hardened, years-old notion that it couldn't keep up with the Southeastern Conference at big-stage football," said the *Washington Post*, pointing out how Ohio State had overcome everything from "vague irrelevance" to losing its quarterbacks.

For the fervent believers in manifest destiny—the notion that Buckeyes were destined to expand across the Big Ten and beyond—more titles were surely in the offing. And they nearly were. In the first five years of the College Football Playoff rankings, Ohio State finished No. 4, No. 7, No. 3, No. 5, and No. 6. "The entire playoff has been about Ohio State," said the *Plain Dealer*, calling it "the complex code that freezes the playoff computer."

The Buckeyes won that first CFP title in 2014, then in 2015 went undefeated for eleven weeks before another of those inscrutable losses to Michigan State, which resembled the undead in the old horror movies. Critics said Ezekiel Elliott lost the game. Not because he played but because he *didn't*. (He was given the ball for only a dozen carries, gaining just 33 yards.) The Bucks recovered, handily beat Michigan (No. 12), then Notre Dame (No. 8) in the Fiesta Bowl. "Obvious top-four talent," said the *Plain Dealer*. But the playoff committee didn't know what to do with a team that hadn't won its own conference. Michigan State went on to play Alabama in the CFP semifinal, losing 38–0, and the playoffs had shifted football's major argument. For most of the season now, it is no longer "Who's No. 1?" but "Who's No. 4?"

Meyer's 2016 team probably shouldn't have been in the playoffs at all. It failed to win its conference—again—but this time the committee reversed itself and invited a non-champ (perhaps restitution for its 2015 choices). Ohio State's 31–0 loss to Clemson suggested the committee should have invited the old 2015 team.

His 2017 and 2018 teams were both on the cusp, each derailed by inexplicable losses. First, there was the No. 3 Buckeyes' 55–24 loss to unranked Iowa in 2017 ("the apocollapse," said the *Plain Dealer,* and a headline in the *Cedar Rapids Gazette* read: "Welcome to Woodshed, Iowa"). Alabama, although losing its final game to Auburn, was taken instead (then vindicated the committee's choice by beating Georgia for the title). The next year, with the Buckeyes at No. 2, there was the 49–20 loss to Purdue, equally unranked. "What Has Made Ohio State Particularly Prone to Blowout Losses?" asked *Sports Illustrated* but offered no answers, other than to point out the Buckeyes were one of the most penalized teams in the country (8.3 per game, through the first eight weeks).

IN 2018, AN ALBATROSS IN A TINY SCARLET-AND-GRAY VEST HUNG OVER THE SEASON. In August, Meyer was suspended for three games over the depredations of his receivers coach, Zach Smith, who'd been caught up in a domestic abuse imbroglio featuring enough dirty linen to swamp a laundry franchise (a reported favorite: sex toys delivered to the Buckeye football offices). A university investigation found that Meyer had mishandled allegations against Smith but, as *SBNation.com* pointed out, "they didn't think he *intended* to mishandle allegations."

All of it was complicated by the fact that Smith was the grandson of Earle Bruce, Meyer's early mentor and close friend. Ohio State issued a tortured on-the-one-hand-but-on-the-other statement, followed by the resignation of one of the school trustees over what he perceived as Meyer's too-lenient three-game suspension. This, in turn, was followed by a lather of sanctimony from various sportswriters, particularly the eastern ones, who lacked any imposingly large national college to take on, which fact seemed to incite them all the more.

USA Today called the coach a "reckless personnel manager" (among less favorable things) and suggested the school rename itself "Urban Meyer State." ESPN's headline read, "As society has evolved, Urban Meyer hasn't," and *The New York Times* said he was "the most radioactive coach in the game." Closer to home, the *Detroit Free Press* reproached the school itself. "If you read the report from the Ohio State investigative committee," it said, "you realize that having a university determine its football coach's fate is like letting a grandmother judge her granddaughter's beauty contest."

None of it was great news for the university, already caught up in *another* scandal, this one involving more than three hundred former students who contended they'd suffered sexual abuse by a team doctor between 1979 and 1997. All of this occurred just as the national cultural zeitgeist had been recalibrated by Harvey Weinstein, the film mogul who'd seemingly imposed himself on half the actresses in Hollywood. (The allegations prompted the #MeToo campaign and resulted in what came to be known as "the Weinstein effect.")

The stormless figure in all of this was Meyer's offensive coordinator, Ryan Day, who stepped unassumingly in and led Ohio State to its first three wins in the 2018 season, including an impressive one over nationally-ranked TCU. It's doubtful anyone knew it at the time, but it turned out to be Day's unofficial audition for the head coaching job. Meyer was back on September 22, but so were his headaches, an affliction that had followed him for most of his career. They were the result of a congenital arachnoid cyst on his brain, discovered back when he was a Notre Dame assistant and agitated by stress, anger, and excitement—the very emotions that fueled the sport.

The cyst wasn't life-threatening; it only felt like it was. And, oddly, it seemed to be a kind of governor capable of regulating the Meyer outbursts for which he was known (by his players and coaches, if no one else.) There was the practice session at Bowling Green called "Black Wednesday" (so bad it presupposed there were no more days in the week) and blocking drills known as "Vietnam." Tables might be flipped, and playbooks and remotes launched across a meeting room in those early years when he himself described his coaching style as "lunatic." (*Sports Illustrated* said he was "a leashed Doberman, straining to get kitty.") At one point, Meyer mused tellingly about finding himself on the autopsy table. "They're going to open me up," he said, "and go: 'What is that? What is that?' 'That's the loss against Michigan State. *That's* the one against Alabama.'"

He once said one of his fears was becoming "THAT guy." It was "the guy who had regret. 'Yeah, we won a couple of championships, but I never saw my kids grow up. Yeah, we beat Georgia a couple of times, but I ruined my marriage.'" By all accounts, he *wasn't* "THAT guy." His regrets were more likely just as he described himself on the autopsy table—manifested by the calcified remains of egregious losses (which meant any of them).

By midseason of 2018, on the sidelines, he seemed to be in physical pain and/or perplexed by what was happening in front of him. And no wonder: at Purdue the unfathomable Buckeyes were in the red zone four times and came away with only two field goals. The secondary allowed 378 yards, while roughing penalties kept two Purdue scoring drives alive. The best Purdue commentary came from an unknown poet on the internet:

Even the stars
seem to be laughing at me, at my fandom,

unaware that they too are drifting
in someone else's orbit,
that they too will run out of fuel,
that one day entropy
will do something
about their everything,
their superficial forever.
I tell them so.
What am I doing
with my life,
starting a fight with the sky?
Man, fuck Purdue.

Three weeks later, at 5–5 Maryland, Meyer's headaches were displayed nationally in a struggling 52–51 overtime Ohio State win. His Buckeyes never led in regulation and his defense gave up 503 yards to an offense led by a backup quarterback. ABC's cameras, meanwhile, focused on the coach, rubbing his head and bent painfully over on the sidelines as though he were stricken with more than Maryland's offense.

THEN WITH NO. 4 MICHIGAN IN THE HORSESHOE, the No. 10 Buckeyes demolished the northern invaders, 62–39. Jim Harbaugh had just become the first Michigan coach to lose his first four games to Ohio State (the Detroit newspaper suggested Harbaugh had become Michigan's John Cooper). ESPN said Meyer's rivalry games might as well be money games, pointing out that he was now 38–5 against his major rivals at Utah, Florida, and Ohio State. *Sports Illustrated* said Ohio State was better because "Urban Meyer's program is built to win games like this, and Harbaugh's isn't."

Ohio State believed it was still in the CFP race, but after beating Northwestern for the Big Ten title and moving to No. 5. The playoff committee thought otherwise. The Buckeyes had the most prolific passer in school—and conference—history in Dwayne Haskins, but they also had the worst defense. And they'd lost to the subaltern

Purdue. So the Buckeyes were off to the Rose Bowl where they beat No. 9 Washington, 28–23, and finished No. 3 in the country.

There were worse consolations, but the partisans were steamed: for two years now, the Big Ten Conference champion hadn't been in the playoffs. It was still up against that abiding perception of itself as a middling conference, which suggested that a loss within such second-fiddle company counted for more. (*How long, O Lord? Will you forget me forever?*) In the imperial SEC, on the other hand, a loss at the hands—or arms—of such celebrated adversaries counted for much less and, all in all, was to be expected. (Even so, Alabama hadn't lost to an unranked opponent since Nick Saban's first year in Tuscaloosa, way back in 2007.)

The more cynical fans—there *were* some—thought that after Ohio State's Purdue loss, the selection committee was merely choosing which team would lose to Alabama. (It was the Oklahoma Sooners, before Alabama itself was blown out by Clemson in the final.) The cynics' logic was that the fans got to complain about the inequity of the committee's choices while feeling silently relieved *they* didn't have to face Alabama (or Clemson). "The end of a confounding season for a wildly talented team," said *Sports Illustrated*—the most frustrating season ever by a one-loss team.

Two days after the CFP's final ratings were posted, Meyer announced his retirement. ("Merry Christmas, Jim Harbaugh! Ohio State's Urban Meyer is retiring," read the headline in the *Detroit Free Press*.) The basic reason: his health, an answer that may have contained more than one truth. It was clear Meyer had objected to his suspension, and the relationship between coach and university seemed frayed. Social media had been a season-long brushfire and the season had taken its toll, even for someone as tenacious as Meyer.

He told North Carolina coach Mack Brown (then an ESPN analyst) that he "couldn't be animated at the level he needed to energize his team." *His* word: animated. It was reminiscent of an old quote from *Sports Illustrated*: "Meyer loved the storm," the magazine said, "hell, he *was* the storm."

There was one final game—in the Rose Bowl, against Washington, and while it wasn't for that elusive fourth title, there was some foreordination to it. He'd never coached in Pasadena before, and the win over Washington gave his time in Columbus an appropriate closure. His early boyhood had been suffused with Ohio State and Woody Hayes's Rose Bowl teams. He was five when Woody's Super Sophomores beat USC, and by the time he was twelve, Ohio State had played in five more. A good bet is that Urban watched every one of them with his dad.

The win over Washington was an exclamation point on Meyer's impressive curriculum vitae. He'd elevated Ohio State into perennial contention, something that hadn't happened since Woody Hayes's streak between 1968–1975. Even a one-loss Buckeye team would now be considered a failure. In his seven years, he'd produced an undefeated team, won three Big Ten titles and a national title. Most notable in Columbus, he'd never lost to Michigan and, moreover, he'd essentially presided over the demotion of Michigan as the previous half of the conference's most eminent rivalry. (It was now Penn State.) He'd won 83 of 92 games, and only once had the Buckeyes been out of the Top 5. In addition, that fierce sense of Meyer competitiveness had spilled over into the entire conference. Nationally, he'd become the second-generation spread innovator, and his offense was a kind of influenza to a defense—too many emerging variants for any one application.

Even the eastern critics were more temperate now, oddly unified in their praise. "Brilliant mind, troubled brain, conflicted man: Urban Meyer puts football on the back burner," said *CBSSports.com*, calling him the offensive genius who perfected the much-copied spread offense. *The Washington Post* mused that Meyer was "a looming presence, a Rushmore figure, a rare sort and a mainstay hovering above Columbus." The writer, Chuck Culpepper, said Meyer, in spite of "the various transgressions" wasn't a bad man at all, and placed him in historical context with such titans as Osborne, Bowden, Bryant, Blaik, and, yes, surely, Ohio State's own man Hayes. Culpepper called them "unusual presences in the grubby vein of sports who existed somewhere between angelic and diabolical while well clear of both, men whose former players tend to speak of with a certain singular regard."

Still and all, he had become something of a cautionary tale to the profession he'd sat atop, even as his essential legacy was the impossible standard he set for future coaches in Columbus. *Sports Illustrated*, though, said you couldn't separate his coaching genius from "his problematic behavior off the field, both at Ohio State and Florida" and said Meyer's legacy validated the notion that "winning trumps accountability." (He'd once said that no one left the highest level of any endeavor "with every part of himself intact.") Columbus was having none of it. By the time Ryan Day took Urban's team—one of the most talented college teams ever—into the 2019 playoffs, Meyer's foibles had been wholly forgotten, in Columbus if not elsewhere.

AND THERE YOU HAVE IT, THE MAN AND HIS MOMENT, AT LEAST FOR *THAT* MOMENT, although no one actually believed Urban Meyer would not return to coaching. "I believe I will not coach again," he said. (See Jacksonville Jaguars, 2021-plus.) And in an interview with *The Plain Dealer*'s Doug Lesmerises in early autumn of 2019, Meyer said, "The morning is the hardest time of day. You're not in a fight. I've been in a fight for thirty-three years, and now you're not in that fight. So, how do you fulfill that fight? And I feel that every morning. Every morning…"

This was not the utterance of man intending to stay off the sideline. He was still relatively young, too. His appearance had always belied that of the traditional football coach, those slightly rumpled fellows sallow from long hours under fluorescent lights, most at home in the burrows of film and meeting rooms. He was trim, handsome, unaffected, even if somewhat contained. He was the one coach we most wanted to know, perhaps because he was the most unknowable.

No one wanted his retirement, it seemed. *The Washington Post* mused that the sport would be diminished, for college football was now "without a rare aura." Said the literate Culpepper, "It wasn't just one of those occasional auras that fills a room with such power that you swear you can feel it even when you're not looking at it. It would be without one of those presences that forges its way above the map, the way certain men always have across the 149 years of this oddball human endeavor."

That was something Columbus could buy. It was why we forgave the lapses. We forgave because his "rare aura" allowed us to forgive our own dailiness. We communally shared this transference, athletes by proxy, as our own cartilage remained intact. In his brief seven years, his transcendence—and that of his players—took our minds elsewhere, thereby fostering a small bright moment for ourselves.

A new Day dawning

The most excruciating season

In the late summer of 2019, no one in Columbus knew quite what to expect. But there were two things you could count on this time of year: humidity and optimism. The new coach had never been beaten, even if he'd coached only three games. There was a new gunslinger on the field who'd completed just twenty-seven passes in his collegiate career, and yet there were rumors he slept in a manger. A kind of happy, expectant tension governed the fan base, which was always awaiting the next spectacle.

Justin Fields's debut was so spectacular that Ohio State had quickly forgotten Joe Burrow, the Athens, Ohio, prodigy who'd spent three years waiting in the wings, only to be overtaken by bad luck (a broken hand) and spectacular competition (J.T. Barrett and Dwayne Haskins). Burrow had transferred out in 2018 and become an immediate starter at LSU, but he didn't have the year Haskins had, and there was no indication that he might.

Fields, though, scored on OSU's first four possessions (a 51-yard run and three passes) in the season opener against Florida Atlantic. Commentator George Eisner remarked that the visitors "were on a pace to give up over 180 points," and in one afternoon, Fields had become Ohio State's prime mover. Assuredly, he'd just earned his jersey number—he was the first starting quarterback to wear No. 1 since Stan Pincura back in the mid-1930s.

The Buckeyes moved on to the University of Cincinnati, who, *The Plain Dealer* pointed out, hadn't beaten OSU since the year Edison received a patent for the kinetographic camera. That was 42–0, followed by Indiana (51–10), who hadn't beaten Ohio State in thirty-one years. Ohio State's only loss thus far had been to the U.S. Patent and Trademark Office, which denied the university's application to trademark the word "The" in "The Ohio State University." The office said the word didn't function as a trademark and appeared in "merely a decorative manner," prompting a social media wag to say that the patent office now had "more wins against Ohio State than Jim Harbaugh."

The Buckeyes were in the midst of September's ritual sacrifice games, outscoring four teams 214-36, with the bones of the vanquished scattered in the end zone. There were, supposedly, some mid-season tests coming up—Nebraska, Michigan State, and Wisconsin—but they failed to materialize, giving rise to worried fan estimates of just how good the Buckeyes really were. Who was doing what to whom? Was Ohio State actually that good, or was the competition *not* that good?

Ryan Day, meanwhile, had slipped almost unnoticed into the Ohio State line of coaching succession. Governed by rules that were near immutable, one begat the next in an unending procession of football sons who, in turn, inherited Ohio's most exacting patrimony. This was, of course, a ferocious mandate to enhance the program, no matter how splendid it might have been. Arrestingly, every coach of the last half century has done exactly that, with the exception of Earle Bruce, who missed a national title by two points in his first year but never again came close. And they, presiding over the ancestral estate of Ohio Stadium, are the closest thing to royalty Ohio knows. (Three men coached the team for that half century, each went into the College

Football Hall of Fame, and each was fired, demonstrating how little the middling qualifications meant at Ohio State.)

Day, because of his brief reign—and his stalwart beginning—had yet to fall afoul of Ohio State's quicksilver critics. There was, of course, the charity afforded in one's initial season, but then Day had performed as immaculately as his quarterback. His strategical mind and quiet aplomb appeared to have won over both players and fans. It had been more than a hundred years since an East Coast immigrant, Yalie Harry Vaughn, had coached Ohio State, and Day—from New Hampshire—was a throwback, historically, anyway, to Ohio State's first decades when all their coaches came from the East.

"There is something different about Ohio State these days," said *Sports Illustrated*'s Laken Litman late in the season. "Hang around the Woody Hayes Athletic Center for a little while and it becomes evident. Players are looser and bouncier on the sideline before games. They're not as high strung or stressed out on a day-to-day basis. Everything was always 'fourth-and-1' under Meyer, said senior defensive lineman Robert Landers. "He has a similar intensity as Meyer, but his personality and his aura are more laid back and chill."

Nonetheless, the Bucks didn't get to No. 1 until early November, after thrashing No. 13 Wisconsin, 38–7, in a rainswept Ohio Stadium. J.K. Dobbins, ran for 163 yards against the No. 1 rushing defense in the country and his teammate on the other side of the ball, defensive end Chase Young, had four sacks, leading *CBSSports.com* to call him "the best football player in the country."

Unfortunately for both Young and the fans, Young, who was leading the nation in sacks, was suspended indefinitely for "accepting a loan from a family friend I've known since the summer before my freshman year." Young said he repaid the loan and sat down to await the NCAA's dispensation. *The Federalist*, a conservative online magazine, accused the NCAA of punishing Young for being poor and, with a certain amount of hyperbole, said it had basically ruined what could have been "one of the greatest seasons of any defensive end in the entire history of college football." Meanwhile, after the first snowfall of the year, rogue artists created a "Free Chase Young" mural on the quad outside the Siebert residence halls on south campus, complete with an enormous block "O."

The upcoming games were with Maryland and Rutgers, which didn't need Young—and at 73–14 and 56–21, they didn't need the first team. Concurring, Matt Tamanini at *landgrantholyland.com* came up with analytics that demonstrated Ohio State's *second* team would also be undefeated, although without the commensurate point spread. Young's suspension was the only moment of drama in a season noticeably free of it, another testament to Ryan Day, whose calm demeanor seemed to adhere to his players.

Ohio State held the No. 1 ranking for only a week before being ousted by LSU—and Joe Burrow—who had just dispatched major rival Alabama. (Adding injury to injury, Ohio pundits said that Nick Saban, Alabama's coach, was now 0–2 against third-string Ohio State quarterbacks.) Burrow, though, was no longer toiling thanklessly down on the depth charts and hadn't been since arriving in Louisiana where he had become an increasingly popular figure, particularly in the western part of the state where he was known as "Geaux Burreaux." His first year wasn't like Haskins's in 2018, but this year he was outdoing his old teammate (Haskins had 50 touchdown passes in 2018, but Burrow would finish the year with 60, breaking a single-season Football Bowl Subdivision mark set in 2006).

The Ohio State fans had always liked Burrow, and now they were anticipating a possible matchup between Fields and Burrow in the national title game. Two quarterbacks from Ohio State facing each other? A marquee moment, yes.

In the season's homestretch, the Bucks were outscoring opponents by 40.4 points per game, the second-highest point differential of the century, and nip-and-tuck with LSU for the No. 1 spot. Chase Young returned just in time for yet another test: Penn State. ("Welcome back, Monster," LeBron James tweeted.) *The New York Times* was calling the Bucks "a ruthless cyborg," but Penn State made them look momentarily mortal, coming back from a 21–0 OSU lead and scoring 17 unanswered points—all with Will Levis, a freshman quarterback. That was historically consistent with recent Penn State games, the past three involving what the *Times* called "palpitating comebacks" (PSU in 2016 after being down 14 points in the fourth quarter, and OSU rallying similarly in 2017 and 2018). In three seasons, the margin had been five points, making it truly a series for digitalis.

The Bucks finally scored on Fields's 28-yard pass to Chris Olave, then intercepted Penn State deep in Bucks' territory and came away with a hard-won 28–17 win in which Young got three more sacks. *Sports Illustrated* called it the battle Ohio State needed and painted a picture of Ryan Day driving down State Route 315 with his windows down blaring music. (The song was "Ballin'" by Mustard, song of choice in the Ohio State locker room.)

Next up: Michigan. The Bucks were already in the Big Ten championship game but it was still Michigan in the Big House, with all the foul chemistry both sides enjoyed. Earlier in the year, Michigan had been listed by one sportsbook as 6.5 favorites even though, as writer Matt Tamanini pointed out, the Wolverines hadn't beaten Ohio State since quarterback Fields was in the sixth grade.

NO ONE FORESAW AN END TO MICHIGAN'S PERSONAL DROUGHT, which was quickly extended for yet another season. The classic moment came in the third quarter after Fields's tight end inadvertently rolled up on Fields's left knee, sending him to the medical tent and the fans into apoplexy. Within minutes, though, Fields was back in the game, and on his first play he tossed a thirty-yard ad-lib pass to Garrett Wilson in the back of the end zone. Said Day: "I thought it was a Heisman moment."

The 56–27 game—four scores each for Fields *and* his running back J.K. Dobbins (211 yards)—prompted a sign in the stadium that read: "Eight in a row: is there a mercy rule?" All the while, Coach Jim Harbaugh's expression on the sidelines was one of constant perplexity, as though he'd been airlifted onto the Melbourne Cricket Ground. "Eight presidents have hailed from Ohio," said *The Plain Dealer*'s Doug Lesmerises. "Eleven Ohio State coaches have beaten Michigan. Ask your neighbor which is the more prestigious club."

In the Big Ten championship game with Wisconsin, the Buckeyes began the third quarter down 21–7. (Wisconsin, after that earlier 38–7 loss to Ohio State, was obviously aggrieved.) Then the Buckeyes scored on their first five possessions of the second half and its defense shut out the Badgers, winning 34–21. The suboptimal first half, though, denied the previously first-place Buckeyes the No. 1 playoff seed. LSU, who'd just beaten Georgia, 37–10, in the Southeastern Conference title game, was now No. 1 and, according to *The New York Times*, "its ambitions freshly enhanced and unchecked."

The Georgia game also near-guaranteed the Heisman for Burrow, who'd thrown for four touchdowns and set a SEC single-season record for TD passes, 48 as of the moment. The LSU spirit animal also proved himself good for a quote, saying that he didn't care who the Tigers played next. "You can take us to Canada," Burrow said with the moxie of youth. "We'll play on a gravel lot."

It was small comfort that in its own semifinal game, Ohio State had played one of the most thrilling contests in its long history. For Clemson had just repeated its semifinal playoff win of 2016 when it beat Ohio State, 31–0 (it was Meyer's first shutout through fifteen seasons and 194 games). The score, this time, was another matter—29–23—labeled by ESPN "an outright classic, a grueling battle of attrition, comebacks, overturned replays, and late-game regrets."

The comeback, unfortunately for OSU fans, belonged to Clemson; the regrets to OSU. Not your ordinary regrets, either, such as the regrets of 2016 when there was even a question of whether the Buckeyes, who hadn't won the Big Ten championship, should have been in the playoffs at all.

These regrets were bedrock regrets, the regrets of four o'clock-in-the-morning, hour-of-the-wolf, sleepless-dread regrets in which repeated trips inside the red zone were nothing more than field goals, a fumble return for a score ruled otherwise, and an end-zone interception. Any one of which might have meant victory. The coach-turned-commentator, Meyer, said about Ohio State's repeated trips into the red zone that he considered kicking a field goal a loss. "The mindset is: you've lost. On defense, you hold them to a field goal, you win. Clemson won the game because of that…"

Ohio State's 2019 edition is the most talented on-the-field team thus far this century, but the 2002 Buckeyes had the best luck. They had so much good fortune, they siphoned luck away from everyone else. This was a theory espoused by cheeky Catherynne Valente who said in *The Refrigerator Monologues* that luck was rare and finite, like palladium or cobalt. "To use it," she said, "you have to take it from somebody else." And so they did. They tried to lose at Cincinnati (two dropped UC passes in the end zone in the last minute); won at Penn State without scoring an offensive touchdown; beat Purdue with a fourth-down Krenzel-to-Jenkins pass that Brent Musburger called a "Holy Buckeye;" and beat unranked Illinois in overtime. They staved off Michigan with a last-second goal line interception, then went on to take what *The Enquirer*'s Paul Daugherty called "one last walk in a metal suit through the thunderstorm," winning the title game in—yes!—double-overtime.

The 2019 team didn't need luck; it relied on overwhelming prowess. It was so good, it seemed to stand apart. No superstitions for these guys, who scorned the old practices of snakeroot and alligator teeth and preserving the umbilical cord. Their helmets were covered in *buckeyes*. They didn't need luck; they *made* luck. That is, until Clemson. Ohio State, 2019, was the greatest team of the still-young century, but it was not a blessed one.

"A litany of excruciations," *The Washington Post* called it. And this most accurate summary from *Yahoo Sports*: "Emptiness from missed opportunity, rage for one crucial overturned touchdown call, and the aching void of unfulfilled potential," said Pete Thamel.

He was seconded by most of Ohio.

"The evidence suggests Day knows how to do the most important thing a man in a college town can know how to do according to the American public—hone a quarterback.. (The Washington Post)

And then there was 2020, the season that almost wasn't and perhaps shouldn't have been. There were opponents both on the field—when the Bucks actually got on it—and off, as the coronavirus operated under rules no one fully understood, which made it somewhat like the Big Ten itself. The conference, it seemed, thought other major conferences would follow its lead and cancel their seasons. When they didn't, the Big Ten scrambled to define itself; teams would play a conference-only schedule and institute virus protocols that, presumably, involved daily testing. The reactions fell predictably. Those closest to the program cheered while more distant critics contended they were seeing the true, grasping nature of big-time college football. (Another *Casablanca* moment, that.) "What the pandemic has done," said *The New York Times*, "is make even more clear how it is past time to replace the term student-athlete with a more contemporary one: essential employee."

The Woody Hayes Athletic Center closed down in March and players were sent home where they pursued their own creative venues. (Tackle Nicholas Petit-Frere pulled the house gutters down doing pullups, incurring the displeasure of his mother.) It was late October before Ohio State finally got back on the field, beating Nebraska 52–17. The game was notable less for the expected win than for the Buckeyes playing before the smallest crowd in the ninety-nine-year history of the stadium—1,344, which eclipsed the old record of 5,482 showing up to see the Buckeyes beat Wilmington College, 13–7, in 1926. (The score was close only because OSU played its reserves, a sportsmanlike salute to the WC coach, Shifty Bolen, who'd been an All-American end at Ohio State in 1917.)

Justin Fields went 20-of-21 for 276 yards and two touchdowns against Nebraska, all to the disappointing accompaniment of a seventy-decibel "murmur track" provided by the Big Ten, which is the equivalent noise of a loaded washing machine. (The track could go up to ninety decibels for the celebratory moments, i.e., scores or turnovers.) At Penn State, where Fields was a onetime PSU commit, he went 28-of-34 for 318 yards and four scores and the

Bucks won, 38–25. Against Rutgers (49–27), he tossed five scoring passes and ran for another touchdown, but played badly against previously unbeaten Indiana, throwing three interceptions—more than he had thrown in his entire college career. After leading 35–7 in the third quarter, the Bucks allowed Indiana to pull within one score before the Hoosiers lost, 42–35. Said *Sports Illustrated*, "Inside of an empty Ohio Stadium in the cold drizzling rain, we witnessed a football powerhouse carved through by a basketball school. It was quite shocking."

In essence, Ohio State exhibited flaws that would bedevil them later: inconsistency and poor defense (Indiana had passed for the fourth-most yards in a single game in OSU's entire history). Afterward, *@ImSeanByron* Twitter-posted: "Only The Ohio State Buckeyes get me from Happy to Xanax in a matter of fifteen minutes." Even so, the Bucks debuted at No. 4 in the first College Football Playoff rankings of the season—behind Alabama, Notre Dame, and Clemson.

Then games with Maryland and Illinois were virus-canceled, and Ryan Day himself tested positive. This brought in Larry Johnson to coach the Michigan State game. Johnson, the Buckeyes' defensive line coach, is considered the top defensive line coach in college football, and with his game day duties became Ohio State's first Black head coach. Fields complemented Johnson with his own best self, going 17-of-24 for 199 yards and adding another 104 rushing as Ohio State overwhelmed Michigan State, 52–12.

The drama in this cockamamie season was only beginning, though. For those anticipating the customary Michigan bloodletting, they would be denied, for between COVID-19 and injuries, Michigan was missing four entire teams of players. (Scarlet-and-Gray media wags pointed out that Michigan could actually have drafted a team or two and *still* not been ready to play.) The issue with losing Michigan, however (in addition to losing Ohio State's favorite annual spectacle), meant the Buckeyes had played only five games; Big Ten rules required teams to play six games to be eligible for the conference championship. Once more, the Big Ten contorted itself: In a "competitive analysis," it said,

Ohio State could have actually *lost* to Michigan and still finished ahead of Indiana. Therefore, the rules were changed to allow the Bucks to play No. 14 Northwestern for the Big Ten title.

Dabo Swinney, the Clemson coach, ranked Ohio State eleventh in his final Coaches Poll submission and said any team playing only six games should not be in playoff consideration. "It's like you've got to have 120 hours to get a business degree and yet these people over here only need sixty hours to get a business degree," he said mournfully. (He seemed genuinely peeved but was likely posturing for his own prospects after Clemson's loss to Notre Dame.) Whatever he was doing, it wasn't wise to give Ohio State such good bulletin board material when the two teams were likely heading for a rematch of the previous season's playoff game.

Which was exactly what was about to happen. Amid rumors of a COVID-19 outbreak (twenty-two players missed the Big Ten title game, including star receiver Chris Olave), Ohio State vanquished Northwestern 22–10, and in the process discovered Trey Sermon, the Oklahoma transfer who suddenly looked like J.K. Dobbins. (Or Eddie George, whose 1995 single-game rushing mark he topped.) Sermon ran for 331 yards, which was also the most rushing yardage in any college football conference title game ever.

No. 3 Clemson, meanwhile, won the Atlantic Coast Conference title by wreaking havoc on No. 2 Notre Dame. ("A thumping atonement," the *Washington Post* called the 34–10 Clemson win, avenging an earlier loss to the Irish.) Thus, in what ESPN snarkily termed "the Alabama-Clemson College Football Playoff Invitational," the CFP selectors put Ohio State and Clemson in the Sugar Bowl semifinal, while Alabama played Notre Dame in the Rose Bowl.

Thus Justin Fields and Trevor Lawrence, two of the country's best quarterbacks—who grew up near each other in Georgia—would face off again. Their previous game had been one of the CFP's best, and *The Washington Post* suggested it was "a clash that felt destined for a rematch." Fields, it seemed, had always been chasing Lawrence, whose *curriculum vitae* read slightly better. This time, however, Fields left no doubt as to who was chasing whom.

Even after suffering a devastating hit by Clemson linebacker James Skalski (who was ejected for targeting), Fields missed only one play then returned to toss a scoring pass to Chris Olave for a 14-point lead. For the night, Fields had 385 yards and six touchdowns—which was the number of his incompletions.

The 49–28 Ohio State win was one of the university's great victories. First, it was the program's first win over Clemson, who'd seemed to own game rights ever since that 1978 Ohio State Gator Bowl game in which Woody Hayes was called for targeting Clemson linebacker Charlie Bauman with a punch that cost the old coach his job. Second, it avenged the January 2020 29–23 playoff loss to Clemson, as well as solidifying a growing esteem for Ryan Day's stewardship.

Unfortunately, Alabama was having a transcendental season. Under new pandemic rules, the Southeastern Conference played a ten-game season, but all among its own members. Alabama scored more than 50 points a game in half of them, another 52 in the conference title game, and three of its players were among the top five Heisman candidates (including Tide wide receiver DeVonta Smith, who won it). There were so many awards, *Saturday Down South* said that non-CFP trophies were being used as doorstops in the Alabama athletic facility.

The stars were not aligned for Ohio State in the national championship game—indeed, they mostly seemed to be playing for Alabama, i.e., Smith, whose unholy speed got him 215 receiving yards by halftime. Football isn't much of a game for extenuating circumstances but there were some for Ohio State: Two starting defensive linemen were out, Justin Fields was banged up, and running back Trey Sermon—who had only come into his own during the last two games (524 yards)—was gone with a collarbone injury after one play. Even so, the Buckeyes were still present in the third quarter. Unfortunately, their defense wasn't.

It was masterful in containing Alabama's All-American running back Najee Harris, who bristled postgame when someone suggested it wasn't difficult to produce on the Ohio State defense. "You didn't see what they was doing?" he said. "They was blowing my ass *up*, what you talking about? That's why we able to throw so much bubbles and slants and all that. But, Bro, they was blowing my ass out…"

Harris ran for only 79 yards, one of his worst offerings of the season, yet Ohio State couldn't suppress wide receiver Smith and quarterback Mac Jones, who threw for 464 yards and five touchdowns. Given that, and a laid-up running game (Sermon's replacement, Master Teague, was good but the offense needed sublimity), Ohio State could no longer keep up.

It was accurately summed up by Cleveland sports columnist Doug Lesmerises: "Ohio State, at its best, may have had a chance Monday. Maybe not. But the Buckeyes weren't at their best. And this era's college football dynasty was as good as it has ever been."

Actually, it was better. In the previous decade, Alabama put up a paranormal body of work not seen since football's Paleolithic Age when Princeton and Yale won most of the national titles. Since 2009, the Tide played in the finals eight times and won six of them. Such a body of work elevated Nick Saban, a one-time defensive backs coach at Ohio State, into a pantheon with Jesus Christ, Mahatma Gandhi, and Bear Bryant. (Saban was fired by Ohio State after the 1981 season for—legend has it—not closing on the recruitment of Napoleon McCallum, the Milford, Ohio, running back who went on to become a two-time All-American at Navy. The Buckeyes then had to make do with their own All-American, the middling Keith Byars.)

Ohio State was now relegated to the periphery of the era's super teams. Both the Associated Press and the Coaches Poll put the Buckeyes at No. 2, which by Columbus's measure, *was* the periphery. (This was Urban Meyer's gift to Ohio State: seasons in which even a *playoff* loss was egregious.) Critics pointed out that no runnerup in the last three championship games had been within 17 points of a win (although they ignored the previous three titles games, which were decided by a total of 12 points). There seemed to be a perverse nostalgia for both a national playoff *and* elements of the 1990s when different teams held the final No. 1 rankings in the same year and ten different programs claimed national titles in the decade.

"The most important media outlet covering each program was the local daily newspaper," wrote *Slate's* Ben Mathis-Lilley. "If your favorite team won a big game, you might get to read a literary write-up in *Sports Illustrated.* The season took shape based on the outcomes of a series of rivalry games, which helped settle conference championships, which in turn determined the combatants in bowl games. A two-loss season, or even a three- or four-loss one, might be remembered fondly, if one of the wins was important enough."

Ah, the good old days of a mere twenty-five years ago. The newspapers are, by and large, gone, *ESPN* is the Goliath on the block, and coverage is essentially social media-based, which—like so much of social media—works toward opinion and controversy (Mathis-Lilley calls it "absurdist social media commentary").

So what is going on in Division I's stratosphere? Not much parity, certainly. Since the CFP began seven years ago, four teams—Alabama, Clemson, Ohio State, and Oklahoma—bullyragged twenty of the twenty-eight spots. What's going on is the same kind of power dynamic driving business, entertainment, and technology: them that has keep on having. Recruiting for talent to stifle the competition may be Google and Amazon; it's also the Power Five. To complain about the consolidation of teams at the top of the Division I ladder is to complain about the nature of the peculiar beast that is the American system, or as pundit Matt Taibbi said, "You need to be a bureaucracy in order to survive one."

The top echelon of college football's Division I is, indeed, exactly that. Put another way, it's an exclusive club, the rules being: (1) you have to get into the club; and (2) you have to be successful *inside* the club. Ohio State, meanwhile, has been at or near football's top echelon since the building of the stadium in 1922. The school's grand design was, in fact, at the forefront of converting an old school recreation into a formidable business.

Knute Rockne in the 1920s may have well been football's first celebrity coach and Notre Dame the first national program (out of necessity rather than design, it has been pointed out, because of the country's anti-Catholic prejudices). But Ohio State—at almost the same time—was building the modern institutional framework that made its football the best program "to consistently meet unreasonable expectations," as one observer put it. Even after Alabama's astounding previous decade, Ohio State and its .730 winning percentage through 1,311 games remains the NCAA's all-time leader. (Alabama is an infinitesimal notch back, at No. 2.) In addition, no other team has made more appearances in the Associated Press's rankings, which began in 1936.

With the evolution of the sport in the last quarter of a century, the expertise in recruiting, training, technique, and coaching is whackingly prodigious. Some contend the platform is so good that the recruiting base cannot supply enough top-caliber athletes. Which is why four teams dominate the CFP.

And those with slightly less talent remain underneath. The question of the moment is trying to discern whether Alabama will remain Alabama. Or, asks Chuck Culpepper of *The Washington Post*, "The sport always has breathed with a large handful of kingdoms, but if the handful dwindles and variety withers, does the sport wither alongside?"

Again, history instructs: In the decade before Saban, the Tide barely broke even, won one SEC title, and finished in the top ten only twice. There was a national title in the 1990s, but the 1980s were mostly uninspired. Clemson won a national title in 1981, but until Dabo Swinney arrived the Tigers were largely toothless. Oklahoma was in football's wilderness during the 1990s.

A bad streak in Columbus, meanwhile, was Earle Bruce going 9-3 for six straight years. With the exception of Luke Fickell's replacement year after Jim Tressel's departure, no coach in the twentieth century had a losing record; from Woody Hayes in 1951 onward, all had winning percentages of over 70 percent. In other news, Urban Meyer and Ryan Day kept the Big Ten from becoming an afterthought (like the Big 12 and the Pac-12). First, Meyer elevated the play. Now Day has kept it there. The irony is that such rapturous work has left the fan base unhappy with merely getting into the CFP; now they want it all. ("The College Football Playoff is great and makes everyone sad," read a headline in *Slate*.)

Ohio State is far removed from Michigan defining any season. Now it's Clemson and Alabama. Until the next time, fans of the Scarlet-and-Gray may mutter sarcastically along with Ben Mathis-Lilley, "Godspeed, you gumbo-addled, deep ball-chucking swamp freaks, Godspeed."

OHIO STATE

Section Five
Postscript: unfinished business

The topics in this postscript are dear to scarlet-and-gray hearts everywhere and surely deserve a passing moment. First, a contemplation of an old controversy: the national titles. Ohio State claims eight; Kent Stephens, the old hand at the College Hall of Fame, says five is the most accurate number (1942, 1954, 1968, 2002, 2014). And we say, let's take a look at the extenuating circumstances of those days when we lived in a happy pluralistic universe where, on any given year, a half-dozen national titles might be handed out.

Next, a contemplation of what happened to the "football factory," the appellation under which Ohio State academics labored so unhappily back in the day. Andy Geiger, the former athletics director at the turn of the century, famously said that Ohio State wished to be one of the best public universities in the country, and the best public universities had the best athletics programs. His president, William Kirwan (their tenures overlapped), had other thoughts. "We've reached a point where big-time intercollegiate athletics is undermining the integrity of our institutions," he said, "diverting presidents and institutions from their main purpose." He *didn't*, however, say that while he was still at Ohio State (he said it later).

History suggests it was easier to develop an athletic program than an academic one, but over time Ohio State's academic side caught up: Ohio State has become the major teaching and research institution in Ohio and one of the most comprehensive universities in the country. It was now secure in both reputations, the difference being that few of its 167 majors played weekly before a hundred thousand people.

The transient virtues of No. 1

Poll-ish sausage and Ohio State

THE ARRIVAL OF THE COLLEGE FOOTBALL PLAYOFF IN 2014 PUT AN END to some of the whimsy over the No. 1 spot, although not all. There was still dissent, for in 2018, the University of Central Florida claimed the No. 1 spot (and the national championship) based upon its undefeated record and the fact that the two teams who played for the sanctioned title—Alabama and Georgia—both lost to Auburn, and CFP had beaten Auburn. (Central Florida's players got national championship rings and their coaches got national championship bonuses.) By and large, though, the argument moved downward to the No. 5 and 6 spots: those who *didn't* get in.

The No. 1 argument had the weight of tradition, and it was older than football itself. (Historically-inclined readers will recall that the Romans were once No. 1, then the Christians—by virtue of several good drafts—superseded them for the top spot.) In the formative years of American football, though, the conversation was held mainly in the East, where the game began. There, in the marginal formulations of the time, the Ivy League held sway for almost all of football's first half century, persisting on into the 1920s and even beyond, with pollster Richard Poling choosing a 9–0 Princeton team as national champion in 1950. This, in the old days, was the rub: the sheer number of selectors and the variety of their methodology, with titleholders chosen by everything from mathematical models like Poling's to the throwing of chicken bones.

Early in the century, there was nothing but a couple of old boys who picked the likeliest Ivy League school and pronounced it "champion." Wrote the inestimable Dan Jenkins back in 1967, "Nobody argued about it, preoccupied as most people were with striking for an eight-hour work day and wondering where Khartoum was. Nobody even cared. You told a man that your school was No. 1 some eighty years ago and all he said was, 'That's swell but, excuse me, I got to go invent the airplane.'"

THE FIRST POLL TO USE A MATHEMATICAL FORMULA WAS THE DICKINSON SYSTEM, devised in 1926 by Frank Dickinson, an economics professor at the University of Illinois who started it to amuse himself. At first, he rated teams in his conference, and when word got out, he was persuaded to go national. There wasn't much to it, for Dickinson simply awarded points for wins, losses, and ties based on the quality of each opponent, then divided the total by the number of games played. There was even "a sectional variant" to account for teams from different parts of the country (although, in the eyes of his critics, not enough of a variant). His poll was the first to acquire widespread acceptance, even as some of his choices were labeled ridiculous.

But "quality," like the term "consensus," was in the eye of the pollster, and while Dickinson's math never got very far into number theory, it held sway with fans up until 1940. By then, there were other systems—Houlgate, Boand, and Dunkel, for instance—as well as the poll that would soon dominate the discussion: the Associated Press poll. The Houlgate System was actually created in response to Dickinson's system. It statistically favored strength-of-scheduling to counter what Deke Houlgate called Dickinson's "Midwest sectionalism," and it had its own cachet through the 1950s, continued even today by Houlgate's grandson.

The original Houlgate was a publicist from Los Angeles who raised his profile by inventing something he called the Futility Bowl, which matched his picks for the worst two college teams in a hypothetical postseason game to be played in Death Valley. In 1945, he mused over his choices before picking Worcester Polytechnic Institute and Ohio's College of Wooster to "fumble it out."

He noted that in the previous year, Wooster had won one game and Worcester two. But in 1945, Wooster finished its season in a blaze of uselessness, losing to Western Michigan, 66-0, and both Houlgate's picks—Wooster and Worcester—had "magnificent records of inefficacy." If the game were actually to be played, he said, there should be no admission, meaning no one should be allowed to watch.

BECAUSE OF THE ASSOCIATED PRESS'S REACH—BACK IN THE DAY WHEN NEWSPRINT STILL EXISTED—its ratings made it to the masses, and it's likely we have the national newswire to thank for our modern preoccupation with numbered lists that confer status upon everything from football to unicycle hockey. Stewart Mandel of *Sports Illustrated* blamed it on Casey Kasem. "So many generations of pimply-faced American teenagers grew up listening to the host of *America's Top 40* tell us where our favorite Bee Gees song was on the charts that week that now we crave rankings for every aspect of our lives," Mandel wrote. (A brief survey of the internet shows that we now have a ranking of the twenty-five strangest things ever seen on a subway, as well as one rating the oddest last meal requests from Death Row.)

Casey Kasem notwithstanding, the person responsible for all this was actually AP's sports editor, Alan J. Gould, who in the middle of the 1935 season began making up his own ratings and sending them to AP subscribers. Called by *Time* magazine "a slight, bow-tied, cigar-chomping newsman," the amazingly forthright Mr.

Gould said his work was "just another exercise in hoopla." The next season, he began soliciting information from his AP-member sports editors, and so began the polling era. The AP's poll was ascendant largely because it ran in all the newspapers, and for the rest of the century, it conferred what was generally regarded as college football's national championship.

As other pollsters came out of the woodwork, many worked backward and retroactively conferred their own championships. One of the earliest retroactive polls was done by Parke H. Davis, in the 1933 edition of *Spalding's Football Guide*. Not dwelling on the niceties of the game, Davis simply looked over the schedules and results and marked his champions, including the Lafayette team he coached in 1896. (The fact that he died a few months later may or may not be a critique on his methodology.)

It was a splendid element of democracy that saw—after the fact, of course—*five* teams being named national champion in 1920. (If Ohio State had simply stayed home and not played in the Rose Bowl—which it lost—someone would certainly have awarded the Buckeyes a title as well.) While the pollsters became a little more unified over time, there were still five-title years into the 1980s. By this time, the NCAA had a list of what it called "major selectors," which did little to clarify championships, leaving the AP—and United Press International, which started its Coaches Poll in 1950—as the *major* major selectors. (By 2017, some 249 national champions declared by one poll or another since Dickinson's first, an offering so pluralistic as to satisfy almost everyone.)

The NCAA's list, it seemed, was put together sometime in the 1980s by a Michigan guy named Bob Rosick who named nearly forty selectors. (The NCAA, however, disavows any affiliation and says the list is "simply for historical purposes," while adding, "it can be a bit spotty.") Kent Stephens, the Cincinnatian who's the long-time curator of the College Football Hall of Fame, explained it as Rosick simply listing as many pollsters as he could find, with no attempt to specify who was legitimate and who was not.

This magnanimity of polling has led Alabama to claim seventeen titles for itself while being listed in various polls a total of twenty-two times. (That the school doesn't recognize the remaining five titles is considered an act of great forbearance on the part of the Crimson Tide, even though its "official" list is still something like the prettiest girl in the senior class counting valentines from underclassmen.) Says Stephens, "Alabama has retired the trophy in this field." He notes that some schools have actually kept their standards high. "I'm not a Irish fan," he says, "but I respect the fact they have not lowered their standards, as others have done, as to what a national title is. If they went 'Bama on us they could claim nearly twenty."

Ohio State has demonstrated a clear sense of decorum by claiming only eight national championships, merely half of the sixteen polls that awarded national titles to the Buckeyes in one season or another. The eight—considered inviolate by Buckeye fans—are 1942, 1954, 1957, 1961, 1968, 1970, 2002, and 2014. Yet the fair-minded onlooker, under oath, would surely hang an asterisk on at least a couple of those seasons.

The Buckeyes first showed up as a national championship team in 1933, when the Dunkel Index chose Sam Willaman's 7–1 team. Unfortunately, everyone else chose Michigan, which made particular sense because Michigan beat Ohio State that year, 13–0. Willaman won more than he lost, but he didn't beat Michigan enough, and his teams were thought to be "underperforming." His coaching career had begun at Cleveland's East High where he had flunked Benny Friedman. Sam wanted big guys, which Benny wasn't, except for his hands. So Benny went over to Glenville High where Sam told the Glenville coach, "Bet you a dinner for all the high school coaches in Cleveland you'll never make a football player out of Benny Friedman." (Friedman took Glenville to what was then regarded as the national high school championship and went on to become one of the greatest quarterbacks ever—high school, college, and pros. History has failed to record where the coaches' dinner was held.)

So not even Ohio State would claim a title that had been won after losing to Michigan. Richard Dunkel, who started with a stack of index cards, went on to become one of the reputable pollsters. He said his statistical formula enveloped all variables affecting a team but in 1933, as much as Buckeye fans would have liked to embrace him, even they remained skeptical.

Ohio State's first consensus titles came in 1942 and 1954, both courtesy of the Associated Press, which by this time was the accepted dean of the national ratings. (When the NCAA discussed "consensus," any dictionary definition of the word went out the window; it simply meant that here was a pick a whole bunch of people liked and the selector seemed to have no criminal record.)

In between came the 1944 season in which Carroll Widdoes's unbeaten Buckeyes produced their first Heisman winner, Les Horvath, and finished behind an imposing Army team that—scoring 56 points a game—might have beaten the old Cleveland Rams of the NFL. No one pays much attention to Ohio State's 1944 team, but it's not only a title-contender (both the Sagarin Poll and the National Championship Foundation chose the Buckeyes, even if retroactively), it's an even better story.

IN 1944, SIX OF THE TOP TEN TEAMS WERE SERVICE TEAMS OR ACADEMIES, and of the top six, the only non-military school was No. 2 Ohio State. The war had created an uneven playing field on which the service teams romped to every advantage. The war department didn't affect West Point training, so it didn't lose its players—and Earl "Red" Blaik, a former Miami of Ohio assistant and now Army coach, employed the country's best recruiting system: he used West Point grads as his scouts and when he had identified the best players, various Congressmen—regarding it as their patriotic duty—appointed them to the academy.

Blaik was by this time known as "the ogre of wartime football," and he had All-Americans who never saw active duty (other than game days), nor even finished the academy. Blaik never talked about his "system," and as historian Murray Sperber wrote, "because of the media and public reverence for wartime heroes, no one pressed him on it." Thus, Sperber pointed out, "the classic ideal stayed intact."

The college game in 1944 was on welfare. Thousands of players found themselves, as one writer put it, "serving Uncle Sam instead of their alma maters." Nearly two hundred colleges quit football altogether in 1943, while others fielded teams of boys who had just gotten home from their high school proms. (It was worse for the fledgling NFL; at the end of its 1943 season, more than half the league was in service.) Colleges were left, essentially, with freshmen—Ohio State in 1944 had thirty-one of them—or older players who were 4F. Three freshmen were in Widdoes's starting backfield. Elsewhere, Utah State was reported to have had a guard named Anderson who was pushing 35, and Michigan had two players with the same surname (which, one suspicious observer thought, were probably father and son).

Widdoes's boys didn't play Army's tougher schedule, but they didn't have the Army manpower, either, and no other "civilian" team seemed close to the Buckeyes. (Their nearest college competition was Michigan, whom they beat 18–14, and the Wolverines ended the season at No. 8.) Consider for a moment the college landscape, which had been eclipsed by the services who drafted—literally—their choice of players. It was the equivalent of Army being allowed to pick its team from the pages of the 1944 *Street & Smith's College Football Yearbook*. There was a service team champion that year, which was Army, but Ohio State won what historian Jack Park in his *Ohio State Football Encyclopedia* called "the National Civilian Championship." The asterisk this time doesn't go to Ohio State; it goes to Army.

The 1942 and the 1954 titles weren't without their controversy, either. The Georgia Bulldogs claimed "the consensus national title" in 1942, the Dawgs contending their win over UCLA in the Rose Bowl made them title-worthy—a splendid point, by the way—although they were applying one that didn't exist in 1942 when bowl games were largely thought of as "exhibitions."

Here's what happened: on November 21, Georgia lost to unranked Auburn, dropping the Dawgs from No. 1 to No. 5—and they never recovered, at least in the polls. For on that same day, a No. 5 Ohio State beat No. 4 Michigan, then on Thanksgiving weekend, having risen to No. 3, the Buckeyes beat the Iowa Pre-Flight Seahawks to finish 9-1 and ranked No. 1 by the Associated Press—which counted then as the national title.

In the commerce of the gridiron day, Georgia's demolishing of No. 2 Georgia Tech, 34–0, that same weekend, then beating UCLA in the Rose Bowl was considered of little import. And a late loss even today can still be difficult to overcome (Ohio State's only loss—to Wisconsin— had occurred a month earlier). There was another factor favoring the Buckeyes in their quest for the national title: back in the day, the preponderance of poll voters came from the Great Lakes and the East, a fact often to the detriment of Southern teams. (While it was considered as more Yankee skullduggery, there seemed to be at least a small resemblance to Lincoln's Civil War strategy of blockading the South.)

Still and all, it was good that the Buckeye defense didn't have to face Georgia's backfield of Charley Trippi and Frank Sinkwich (the Croatian kid whom Georgia had somehow stolen out of Youngstown, Ohio). Sinkwich was the 1942 Heisman winner, and both he and Trippi would be Hall of Fame backs.

THE 1954 TEAM, IN REALITY, SHARED THE TITLE WITH UCLA, EVEN AS OKLAHOMA ALSO REMAINED UNBEATEN. (Oklahoma wasn't much in the discussion because the major polls considered the Sooners' schedule untitle-worthy, and they hadn't played well against the few good teams they faced.) Ohio State finished the season as AP's No. 1, but UCLA was first in the UP Coaches Poll. The Buckeyes went off to play in the Rose Bowl where the daft "no-repeat" rule gave them Southern Cal as their opponent instead of No. 2 UCLA (who had just beaten Southern Cal, 34–0). The Rose Bowl thus missed a grand opportunity to host what would have been in the minds of most people a genuine national title game (disregarding, of course, the Sooners). The Bruins' defense was insanely good, allowing an average of 4.4 points a game, but Ohio State played a tougher schedule, beating six ranked teams, including then-No. 2 Wisconsin. Advantage: Ohio State.

THE 1957 TITLE IS A MORE DIFFICULT CALL. This time, the polls were reversed: Ohio State was picked by the UP Coaches Poll, and Auburn by the AP. Others weighed in, of course: The Football Writers Association picked Ohio State, and so did the International News Service, while the Poling System chose Auburn, as did several of the other math-based polls such as Sagarin and Billingsley, whose choices were made retroactively.

(The Coaches Poll had its own detractors: Stewart Mandel at *Sports Illustrated* said that often the coaches didn't even do their own ratings; like the sportswriters, they were too busy with their own games. It was also a poll, he said, "where biases and agendas not only go uncorrected but are almost par for the course." Even some of the coaches agreed. "It's a popularity contest," said one, testifying less to the nature of polls and more to the human condition.)

The Poling System, begun in 1935 by Richard Poling, a former football player at Ohio Wesleyan, was a mathematical rating system considered one of the more accurate polls of its day, as is the Sagarin Poll today, created by a guy named Jeff Sagarin, a ratings wonk who started ranking teams when he was in the fifth grade. Studying theoretical math at MIT—and a stint in graduate school at Ohio State—helped him with his avocation, and in 1972 when *Pro Football Weekly* bought his ratings, it became his vocation. Sagarin won't specify how his ratings are compiled, only that he looks at victory margins, home field advantage, and schedule difficulty (which mean that an unbeaten team isn't always at the top of his charts). His system is highly regarded, so much so that he has been called "one of the most influential people in U.S. sports." Still, Sagarin understands the quotient of whimsy behind all games, saying, "Real life is under no obligation to conform to mathematical models made by human beings."

Auburn did have a championship caliber team in 1957—it shut out six opponents and didn't give up a rushing touchdown all season—but the school was on probation for giving a pair of high school recruits $1,000. Although the Tigers were banned from a bowl appearance, in those benighted years they could still be considered for the national title—a rule that was soon changed. And Auburn stuffed the AP ballot box, which wasn't permitted again, either. There was a little-known rule permitting *any* AP subscriber a vote, so Auburn's savvy sports publicist curried the favor of every small-town newspaper and radio station he could, and the Tigers were a shoo-in with 210 first-place votes to Ohio State's 71.

All in all, the 1957 championship seems like a split title, depending upon one's quality of forgiveness, of course. It would have been a good year for a playoff, pitting Ohio State's running offense (and its burly soon-to-be-All-American fullback, Bob White) against Auburn's No. 1 defense. (There were reports from Alabama that Auburn had a drill placing the ball on the two-yard line with the second team given four tries to score against the starters—which happened just once all season.)

Then there's Ohio State's 8-0-1 season in 1961. That year, the Buckeyes stumbled at the gate, tying Texas Christian in the opening game before rolling off eight straight wins. Meanwhile, the TCU Horned Frogs had what might be called the greatest losing season in college football history: they knocked No. 8 Kansas into the ranks of the unranked; blemished the No. 3 Buckeyes; then dropped No. 1 Texas three spots down in the polls, which prompted Texas coach Darrell Royal's immortal quip about TCU: "They're like a bunch of cockroaches. It's not what they eat and tote off, it's what they fall into and mess up that hurts." (All this from a team that finished the season at 3-5-2.)

At Thanksgiving, things were shaping up nicely in Pasadena. The Rose Bowl organizers were anticipating an Ohio State-Alabama matchup—the top two teams in America playing for what surely would have been another *de jure* national title. Bear Bryant's Crimson Tide beat Georgia Tech on November 18 to stay undefeated, and the game was covered by the great—sometimes caustic—*Los Angeles Times*'s sports columnist, Jim Murray, whose reports on segregation (he'd been appalled by the "white only" drinking fountains in the airport) helped cause a verbal Appomattox. Students at UCLA said they'd protest the Rose Bowl if a segregated Alabama team showed up, and Murray summarized their stance as, "We won't play with those white folks until they come to the twentieth century."

A few days later, Ohio State was having its own embroilment. The Buckeyes finished their regular season on Thanksgiving weekend in Ann Arbor, devastating Michigan, 50–20, and looking forward to the Rose Bowl. Then the trip west was nixed by the university's faculty council, a majority of whom contended football was being over-emphasized. That decision made national headlines, too, including one from the *Fresno Bee-Republican* that read, "Faculty Nips Ohio State Roses in Bud."

Amid its controversy, Alabama chose to stay close to home and played in the Sugar Bowl where the Tide beat Arkansas, 10–3. (Murray called it "The White Supremacy Bowl.") Ohio State, meanwhile, simply stayed home. Fate being what it is, the Rose Bowl lost what would have been one of its greatest matchups, in which—for once—a true national champion might have emerged. What Bear referred to as his "itty-bitty boys"—they averaged less than two hundred pounds—would not get to meet Ohio State's great African American running back, Bob Ferguson, in a game where racial equality might have gotten an accurate rehearsal.

The AP named Alabama No. 1. (The championship, wrote historian Andrew Doyle, "was undeniable proof of achievement and legitimacy for a state that historically led the nation only in adult illiteracy and infant mortality.") Ditto the UPI Coaches Poll. Both were close votes over No. 2 Ohio State. The Football Writers Association of America chose the Buckeyes, thus Ohio State—ignoring the metaphorical asterisk—claimed 1961 as one of its eight championships.

Ohio State's 1968 season was a no-brainer for the pollsters, as it was challenged only marginally by an 11-0 Penn State. Because of its inferior schedule (described as made up largely of eastern opponents who were the equivalent of mid-majors), Penn State didn't receive a nod from even the math-based polls. The 1968 Buckeyes of "super sophomore" fame are recognized as one of the great all-time college football teams, and their failure to live up to expectations in the next two seasons where two losses kept them from a possible three consecutive titles, is, in the eyes of the fan base, still one of the great Ohio tragedies, ranking with the great 1937 Ohio River flood and the Xenia tornado of 1974.

THE BUCKEYES OF 1970—CLAIMED BY THE UNIVERSITY AS ANOTHER NATIONAL CHAMPIONSHIP TEAM—also came with an asterisk, but one that was fully understood. It was the "Super Soph" team as seniors, sentimental favorites to go unbeaten for three seasons, and they almost did. The year ended with three unbeaten teams at the top of the polls—Texas, Ohio State, and Nebraska, ranked 1-2-3. (Nebraska's record was marred only by an early season tie with then-No. 3 USC). The UPI coaches were not yet embarrassed by their No. 1 title-holders turning in lesser-number bowl performances, and they picked Texas as their No. 1. It was almost as good a pick as Ohio State, for Texas was the defending national champion, and riding a 30-game win streak. (Right behind, in the same period, was Ohio State at 28-1.)

So what happened? Texas lost to Notre Dame in the Cotton Bowl, 24–11, and the Buckeyes barely showed up in Pasadena where they were beaten by a three-loss Stanford team. Nebraska, meanwhile, defeated No. 5 LSU in the Orange Bowl, getting the title nod from, among others, the Associated Press and the Football Writers Association. Given that Nebraska was working on a 31-game win streak of its own—and another title in 1971 (being as close to consensus as you could get in those days), the post-bowl polls seemed wholly upright. Hence the Ohio State asterisk.

The decade of the 1970s is, indeed, the asterisk decade, because the Buckeyes were in the title hunt each of the Archie Griffin years (1972–1975) when they lost two regular season games in four years, both to Michigan State. They tied Michigan in 1973 and beat USC in the Rose Bowl, but the tie cost them a title: AP and the Football Writers chose 11-0 Notre Dame as No. 1; UPI picked a one-loss Alabama, who traipsed off to the Sugar Bowl and lost to Notre Dame. (The National Championship Foundation selectors chose Ohio State as its No. 1 in 1973, but the NCF also picked Michigan—after all, the two teams had tied on the field—while pollsters Richard Poling and Jeff Sagarin both chose Ohio State.) In 1974 and 1975, Ohio State picked up No. 1 votes from math-based polls, but both years ultimately belonged to Barry Switzer's great Oklahoma teams, who were AP's No. 1 choice.

OHIO STATE GOT A BARE MENTION IN 1998 WHEN THE SAGARIN POLL CHOSE JOHN COOPER's powerful 11-1 team, which was No. 1 for nine weeks before being upset by Michigan State. Everyone else, though, chose Tennessee's unbeaten Volunteers. (Sagarin, remember, was the guy who liked strength-of-schedule and sometimes chose teams that might have a loss somewhere along the way.) It was also the first year of the Bowl Championship Series, which put the top two teams against one another in something that looked like a playoff but was in reality an extension of the bowl season.

Both AP and the Coaches Poll had Tennessee (12-0) and Florida State (11-1) at No. 1 and No. 2, and that was that. Afterward, *Sporting News* fantasized about a Tennessee-Ohio State final and had the Vols winning that game, too. (Joe Germaine was intercepted on the final drive, Tennessee 24-20, although a simulation by buckeyewire.com pitted the 1998 team against Urban Meyer's 2012 one, using sports-reference.com's Simple Rating System and had it beating Meyer's undefeated—but postseason ineligible—team, 41-19.)

Under any analysis, Ohio State 1998—which some still consider the greatest Buckeye team of all—was a final four one without a playoff. It was the kind of thing that led to belligerent criticism of the Bowl Championship Series, which *Sports Illustrated* called "the most divisive creation in the history of American spectator sports." In terms of bureaucracy, there wasn't much to the BCS, which was a three-person staff headquartered in the director's

Kansas City house. "I don't give out my address," he said once, "because I don't want someone egging my house."

Its conclusions became, in time, relatively simple: two-thirds human opinion, one-third an average of six independent computer rankings, or as one of the pollsters said, "two-thirds art, one-third science." The pollsters (who came and went over the BCS's sixteen years) included old standbys Jeff Sagarin and Richard Billingsley, the former minister and fan who'd been around since the 1960s. Billingsley's polling began when he used an old Olivetti hand-crank adding machine and gave copies of his results to friends. He was such a Poindexter with numbers that he sorted through the records of every D-I football team, spent years clearing up discrepancies, and turned up 792 disputed game results, causing a friend to say, "You're either the most dedicated college football fan or you lead the most pathetic life of any man alive." There was, at one point, the Dunkel Index, still around after seventy years (it could now, by the way, not only rank football teams but predict the weather, which meant you not only got a game result but knew if you should take an umbrella.)

Controversy, however, remained alive and well. And, of course, Ohio State featured in it. One dispute had nothing to do with the polls, and the other one did. University of Miami fans, for instance, were incensed over Ohio State's double-overtime win in the 2002 title game. Considered one of the most exciting games in history, it turned on a questionable fourth-down pass interference call that kept the Buckeyes alive and led to the end of Miami's dynasty. Both the Big 12 and the Big Ten backed the call and *Referee Magazine* listed it among its "eighteen best calls in officiating history." Hurricane fans regarded it as wholesale larceny.

In 2006, the controversy belonged to Florida, who got into the title game over Michigan, whose only loss was the 42–39 barnburner with Ohio State. (With OSU and Michigan No. 1 and No. 2, the game was, as Stewart Mandel reported, "the de facto national championship playoff," and it had the highest regular-season television ratings in thirteen years.) Before the final weekend, the polls agreed: Ohio State, USC, Michigan, Florida, in that order. But after second-ranked USC was upset by UCLA in its final game, no one other than Ohio State and Michigan fans wanted an Ohio State-Michigan replay for the national title. Urban Meyer's Florida team then vindicated the BCS polls by lambasting the Buckeyes, 41–14, in the championship game, thus initiating the SEC's run of seven straight BCS titles, and elevating the notion of SEC superiority over the Big Ten.

In 2007, after Ohio State's meager outing against LSU in the title game won by the Tigers, 38–24, there were questions about why Ohio State was *in* the title game. (Even if only barely.) But then there were questions about why LSU was there, too. LSU had lost two triple-overtime games, although its coach, Les Miles, pointed out the Tigers had remained undefeated "in regulation." Finally, there wasn't much to say about a season in which top ten teams lost twenty-nine times.

One commentator pronounced the season, which began with I-AA Appalachian State upsetting No. 5 Michigan—in Ann Arbor, no less—"comically strange." Another said it was "a year of festive arson and freewheeling nonsense." He also said Ohio State was doomed from the start because the Buckeyes "ran on a clock and 2007 was too surreal for anything but melting pocket watches."

Before the Buckeyes returned to their next title game, in 2014, there was a new platform in town—the College Football Playoff (the monetary value of which surpassed half a billion dollars, according to *Forbes*, most of which went to the Power Five teams). There was actually a four-team playoff, and the computers were no longer involved. Instead, there was a thirteen-member committee. One of the BCS pollsters, Peter Wolfe, an infectious disease doctor, lost his lofty vantage point but said there was an upside because drunks no longer sent him emails written in all caps. (His ratings went online.)

Soon, the new four-team format was incurring its own criticism. The *Los Angeles Daily News* said it was even more polarizing than the BCS, comparing the CFP committee to the old Soviet Union Politburo, "a supreme ruling body that's unelected and unaccountable." Ohio State helped furnish the CFP's initial playoff controversy with the Buckeyes' No. 4 position in the gridiron fundament again being called into question.

Baylor and TCU fans, with what they felt were their equal chances at the No. 4 spot, fell to an unjust No. 5 and 6. "The shift to the playoff system was an attempt to alleviate controversy," said the *Washington Post*, "but instead it seems to have merely shifted the angst from the No. 2 and No. 3 teams to those occupying the No. 4 and No. 5 slots." (The *Post* called it "the cutoff that divided exultation in Ohio from the tears in Texas.")

This complaint from what was called "the melancholy fringe," however, was drowned by the Buckeyes' formidable, if unpredictable, march through the playoffs. Their title demonstrated how easy it was to overlook the best team in the field, who might have lost a game somewhere along the way, and emphasized the new importance of being No. 4.

In 2016, a one-loss Ohio State team made the CFP against the odds—and over the Big Ten champ Penn State who'd beaten the Buckeyes in Happy Valley back in October. (The Buckeye validation was that they'd played a tougher schedule and beaten three top ten teams.) Unfortunately, the double-overtime 30–27 win against Michigan seemed to have left Ohio State like one of those old Hayes-Schembechler teams who, after their own season-ending conflagration, were too dazed to play a bowl game. The Buckeyes lost to Clemson in the CFP semifinal, 31–0, only their second bowl shutout in ninety-five years.

There was more controversy again in 2017 when the Bucks *didn't* make the field. That, of course, was the season of their 55–24 drubbing by Iowa. They had recovered from their early loss to Oklahoma, and even after Iowa, had risen from No. 12 to No. 5. But Alabama had dominated its weaker schedule, and the Bucks were haunted by that unholy afternoon in Iowa City. Oddly, Alabama was *not* haunted by either its loss to Auburn on November 25 or its failure to win its conference.

"Alabama slid into the Playoff this weekend by doing nothing," reported *USA Today*. "So, if I'm Urban Meyer, I'm wondering today why I scheduled Oklahoma in Week 2 rather than Akron." *SBNation.com* attributed the debate to "two deeply flawed résumés," saying Ohio State shouldn't have lost but once—and it was probably best if one of those hadn't been a 31-pointer against a 7-5 team.

Like the Buckeyes in 2014, Alabama went on to win the national title from the No. 4 spot. "You're never going to eliminate controversy," said Roy Kramer, the onetime SEC commissioner credited with inventing the old BCS. "If you have an eight-team playoff, fans of the No. 9 team will be unhappy. If you have a sixteen-team playoff, No. 17 is going to be unhappy." (The Colley Matrix, another NCAA-recognized selector, awarded the No. 1 spot to the University of Central Florida, who had remained undefeated but played in the lowly American Athletic Conference, which was not one of the "power" conferences. UCF players referred to them as "the cartel.")

IT WAS A TESTAMENT TO THE INSATIABLE APPETITE OF THE FANS WHO WANTED IT ALL, which is ultimately the appetite that will give D-I football an eight-team playoff—breaking, no doubt at all, the heart of every No. 9 fan. (D-II has a twenty-eight-team playoff, while D-III's is a thirty-two-team field.)

The pollsters, meanwhile, weren't physically present in the throne room anymore, but there'd always been a kind of maverick quality to them—gearheads who emerged blinking into the sunlight after a weekend in a dark room processing numbers. They were, by and large, devout hobbyists led by a small cohort of sophisticated guys (polling is essentially a guy-thing) such as the one-time Ohio State grad student Jeff Sagarin who actually made a living at polling. (Gamblers used Sagarin for "Power Rankings," invaluable in figuring the spread.)

The internet, meanwhile, had room for them all (including a transplanted Dane, now physics professor at the University of Tennessee, named Soren Sorensen who cautioned fans that his polls weren't readily understood by people who weren't conversant in linear algebra). The fans followed them as they always had, argued with them like they did their own rancorous uncles, and—whether they recognized it or not—were informed by the polling pronouncements. In their subliminal presence through each autumn, they were still guiding our decisions.

Internal wars on the home field

In which the other side of the campus offers game

Difficult to imagine in Columbus, but football wasn't a thought when the doors of the Ohio Agricultural and Mechanical College opened in 1873 in the cornfields north of the city. That fledgling operation was a beneficiary of the Morrill Land Grant College Act, by which federal land was sold to finance institutions of higher education. The act emphasized practicality and most notably aimed at the education of farmers and mechanics. Especially, said its architect, Justin Smith Morrill, "the sons of toil." This might be considered the first small note referencing football players at what would, in time, become the third-largest university campus in the country—and a perennial football power.

The Grantland Quarterly, only somewhat tongue-in-cheek, called Morrill "the unsung father of American college football," pointing out how many schools might be lost to Division I without the Morrill funding. Among AP's top ten in 2019, seven were land grant colleges. (The absence of land grant schools might be welcome news for Michigan, though, for the Big Ten would then consist of only itself, Iowa, Indiana, and Northwestern.)

Morrill's act has been called one of the country's greatest pieces of legislation, for it redistributed some eleven million acres of land that were then sold to underwrite dozens of new schools. In the process, colleges and universities—whose thrust was previously classical—adopted the study of agriculture and mechanics (hence the name: *Ohio Agricultural and Mechanical College*). This resulted in the democratization of education, burgeoning technical education, and, ultimately, widespread economic growth.

The unfortunate underside of the Morrill Act, however, is that it was "a wealth transfer disguised as a donation," the description by Tristan Ahtone, a respected journalist with the additional qualification of being a Kiowa tribesman. Because the land was taken—with little or no pay—from Indigenous people and handed out as endowments for new universities. The topic is now entered into the various academic discussions of "reconciliation" but unlikely to arouse much sentiment in the citadels of athletic power, at least not until Oglala Lakota College, say, fields a football team.

None of this was much on the minds of the Ohio State masters in the early years, although they were debating those emerging definitions. President Edward Orton didn't want to produce only "the narrow and conceited specialist" but students with a broad liberal education. The agricultural teacher on the six-member teaching staff, Norton Townshend, wanted the liberal part of the curriculum—English and ancient languages—dropped in favor of "the practical." (Townshend was no philistine; he was, in fact, an agricultural scientist and one of the best, wholly given to bringing a scientific education to Ohio's farmers. He simply thought Ohio State should be an institution for them, with a program serving their needs when other institutions did not. He'd studied Latin, encouraged one of his sons to study classical languages, and in short time began to praise Ohio State's broad curriculum.)

So liberal education won out—barely—and the victory resulted in a change of the school's name in 1878: henceforth, it would be known as "The Ohio State University." President Orton's small victory didn't end the discussion, though; it marked only its beginning. It also meant that Ohio State was going to be exclusive; its students would be required to prove their worthiness by passing an entrance exam. If this meant not everyone would be admitted, then so be it. "High school graduates who found the university's entrance exams too difficult should attend Miami or Ohio Universities," Orton said.

Exclusivity, however, came with a caveat—because it was a land grant college, the argument went, Ohio State should get by without additional state support. Orton disagreed, citing Cornell and the University of Illinois as examples of well-supported land-grant institutions. But by 1880, in order to bring in enough bodies to balance the books, nearly all entrance requirements beyond a high school diploma were dropped. Ohio State had become an open admissions university, and exclusivity would have to find another route.

So the university opened itself to the masses, all the while maintaining its vision of being the state's flagship school, as evidenced by its name, *The* Ohio State University. "The emphasis is on the first three letters: *t-h-e*," explained former university archivist Raimund Goerler. "We take pride in being *The*. We see ourselves as the foremost in Ohio and one of the foremost in the United States. If anybody is deserving of support, we are."

This notion has been heartily adopted by Ohio State's graduates (and near-graduates) as they applaud themselves for their triumphs, even though denizens of the state's other schools tend see it as presumptuous, as if they were being relegated to their obscure little outposts in the variously uncelebrated parts of Ohio.

Historically, the university had difficulty being "The University," witness such testimony as that offered in 1902 by Mr. Ralph Mershon, seeking admission to the University Club of New York City but turned away because the club did not recognize degrees conferred by Ohio State. (Only in Columbus was it "The University.") In 1909, the Carnegie Foundation refused to put the university on its list of accepted institutions and, furthermore, chastened the Ohio legislature for creating three public institutions—Miami University, Ohio University, and Ohio State—which the report said pitted each against the other in "the sheer competition for survival." All of them, said foundation president Henry Pritchett, "were burdened with students who should have been required to stay in high school."

The foundation's complaint was that the Ohio legislature, instead of endowing one really good school, was supporting three also-rans. Ohio State was not Wisconsin or Michigan, nor had it excelled with a more limited curriculum, as Purdue had. "For those founders and leaders who had expected Ohio State to be a great university patterned after Cornell," wrote Pritchett, "the disappointment was hard to bear." He thought state universities could only grow strong by becoming "selective admissions institutions," an idea that wouldn't return fully to Ohio State until late in the century.

In reviewing the sparse documentation of Ohio State's early decades, we are left with journalism professor James Pollard's succinct note: "It is hard to imagine the primitive beginnings." The school was still remote from Columbus—the idea was to shelter students from the city's various dens of iniquity—and its ambition remained largely in the minds of a small group of perseverant men. One of these was its fifth president, a former Presbyterian minister named William Oxley Thompson who brought OSU into the Western Conference. This move separated OSU from the other Ohio schools athletically, and it raised the university's academic profile by its association with other important Midwestern schools. A great university required powerful friends, Thompson said, and with the Western Conference, it now had them.

The first great foreordained event stating Ohio State's upwardly mobile intent was the building of Ohio Stadium. The Ivy League luminaries—Harvard, Princeton, Yale—had built large stadia before WWI, and Ohio State wanted to breathe that same rarified air. It would lead the way with a stadium that could do something no new chemistry building could: be an overarching symbol of the school's progress and prestige. Thompson called it "the largest single enterprise which the university has ever undertaken."

It signaled the emergence of the university into an institution of first rank, and like the medieval town announcing its greatness by building a cathedral which seemed to rise out of the wheat fields toward heaven, the stadium rose from the banks of the Olentangy. It would be a symbol of not just athletics but of the university as a whole, announcing its aspirations in the classroom, as well as on the playing field. It would be *The* Ohio State University.

And here began—wholly *without* intention—the abiding dissension between athletics and academics that would plague the university for most of the century. For this great university symbol would be increasingly seen as an *athletic* one. First, it was mightily visible, especially during the autumn when it was the backstory for the games themselves. (Hundreds of thousands of people, for instance, did *not* tour weekly the chemistry lab nor read of its triumphs.) The stadium, as university historians pointed out, gave Columbus—and much of Ohio—"a proprietary interest in the campus it never had before," an interest that was, by and large, football. It also advanced the notion that athletics might be easier to advance than academics.

Through the mid-century, the uneasy truce between the two sides of the campus held. Then 1961 ended it. That was, of course, when the faculty council denied one of Woody Hayes's best teams a trip to the Rose Bowl. Still, it was only a Pyrrhic victory. For never again would that body exercise such power over athletics. It didn't mean, however, that the academic side didn't push back. For much of the decade, football seemed a subdued part of the Columbus campus, and even that colorful organ of macho bravura, *Sports Illustrated*, reported in 1967 that "the stern demands of modern academics signify the passing of a frenzied football era at Ohio State." Or as John Bonner, dean of student relations at OSU, said, "Today's students put academic proficiency squarely in the center of their collegiate universe."

If athletics seemed subdued, it was perhaps because campuses across the country were ablaze (sometimes quite literally) with the accumulated grievances of an untidy century. Protests cumulated in the spring of 1970 with what became known as the Kent State Massacre, when four students were killed by National Guardsmen. And that debacle overshadowed the Ohio State riots where, a few days earlier, National Guardsmen in Columbus dispersed a crowd of some 4,000 protesters with tear gas. (Its highlight was a stellar off-the-field moment for Woody when the old firebrand walked calmly into the protest to talk with the students. The fact that he was unsuccessful in talking them down was secondary to his valiant attempt, and it was thought he'd been the only member of the school administration to actually speak directly to the protesters.)

Even with such a backdrop, *Sports Illustrated*'s reports of the death of football in Columbus proved to be—as any real fan already knew—overly hyperbolized. The old magician had pulled 1968 out of his hat, and then he recruited Archie Griffin. In Columbus, at least, football was still the majority culture. Even so, football didn't dominate all of the student body. OSU was a big place with an explosion of clubs, organizations, and interests where one could carve out his or her own space and even have some left for football. What often passed for apathy was just divided—rather than single-minded—attention. "Football here is an important Midwestern cultural event," said one young professor. "It is not primarily a college matter."

There was an intemperate moment in the 1960s when it was predicted that high academic standards would break up the Big Ten, but like a good defense adjusting to a new offense, the athletic departments adjusted. Academic councilors helped the student/athlete navigate the deeper waters of the school's academic landscape, even as top programs erected firewalls admitting only top students.

Conversely, athletes could be steered into programs that wouldn't encroach on *their* main mission, which was football. (In defense of the jock, "exercise science" was less about exercise and more about science, and *Scientific American* reported that students with the highest aerobic capacity and lowest body fat tended to do well in the classroom.)

As the various departments retreated to their campus fiefdoms, the grumbling became largely muted. What emerged was a new truce, a kind of parity in which one side of the campus respected (in varying measure) its odd counterpart on the other side. (Think Aaron Burr and Alexander Hamilton before the politics and the fatal stomach wound.)

In 1987, Ohio State took a huge academic step when then-president Edward Jennings switched from an open admissions policy to a selective one. On the academic side, it was comparable—at least in theory—to something football coaches had been doing for decades, which was selective recruiting. The move almost immediately raised Ohio State's academic profile. (Perhaps Jennings had heard President Thompson's voice from early in the century saying, "The superior student should be given an opportunity to reach his goal unhindered by the drag of average mediocrity in his classmates.")

The real long-term struggle was that the academic advocates didn't want to lose their hard-won gains, and they remained nervous about the university's reputation as a "football factory." In 1991, there was the rift between Big Ten freshman-of-the-year running back Robert Smith and his own coaches, a curious episode in which a football player suddenly became the academic standard-bearer.

Smith left the team after he said the coaches, notably assistant Elliot Uzelac, an intense old-school autocrat, mistreated players and maligned academics. Smith said Uzelac told him he was taking his studies too seriously and that he'd return to the team only if Uzelac was gone. Uzelac wasn't and Smith didn't. He sat out the season, Ohio State struggled to 8-4, and lost to Michigan again. The upshot was that Uzelac suffered through angioplasty at University Hospital and a lost job, while the school suffered a black eye.

Just before the Michigan game in 1991, Jennings's successor, Gordon Gee, extended coach John Cooper's contract, even though Cooper had a negative trifecta against Michigan: three losses. Athletic director Jim Jones said the contract, coming as it did just before The Game, ensured that no one could say a win over

Michigan had saved Cooper's job (and, conversely, the implication was that a loss wouldn't cost him the job). "We are pleased with the direction our program is going," Jones said, "and with the effort of our student-athletes on the field and in the classroom." Gee and Jones were clearly in concert, and their decision was a clarification of what they saw as "institutional values." (Even if Cooper did get a nudge from the tumultuous Earle Bruce firing of four years before. No one wanted *that* again.)

It was still courageous, for the fan base wasn't happy about it, especially as Cooper, new contract in hand, took a 31–3 drubbing from Michigan. This was also the game in which Desmond Howard set a Michigan record by running back a punt 93 yards, then struck a Heisman pose in the end zone. To add insult to injury, Howard was a *Cleveland* kid, one who'd gotten away, even if he did eat tofu and carry a briefcase to class while wearing a coat and tie.

It was the kind of behavior that led one OSU fan to later say, "I despise Desmond Howard with the burning intensity of a thousand suns." Needless to say, Cooper was at the moment more popular in Michigan than in Ohio and there were rumors he'd been smuggled back into Columbus in an equipment trunk.

To President Gee, football was a venue for showcasing the entirety of the school—and for fund-raising. "A great university is not built on the record of a winning team," he said, "but a winning team can be built on the reputation of a great university." In early December, the normally jovial Gee, sounding unusually peevish, told *Dispatch* sports editor George Strode, "Once and for all, Ohio State had to shed its image as a football school and has to assume what it is—a great university. And, by God, that's what's going to happen!"

Being the best academically, however—even with the mighty presence of *U.S. News and World Report*'s annual ratings—was something of a subjective judgment. (Witness *U.S. News*'s influence: Arizona State linked its president's salary to ASU's place in *U.S. News*'s ratings.) But as its own historians pointed out, Ohio State was the major teaching and research institution in Ohio—and one of the most comprehensive universities in the country. Yet for much of the public, the university was defined primarily by football.

When Gee addressed private functions, he told his audiences that strong athletics and strong academics were inclusive of one another, not exclusive—"symbiotic." He explained that Ohio State might annually receive $350 million more for its own academics—if funded at Michigan's level of tuition and state support. Then he'd ask: would Ohioans stand for such a discrepancy between the two schools in their football expenditures?

It appeared simpler to Gee's athletic director, Andy Geiger: "Ohio State wants to be one of the best public universities in the country, and the best public universities in the country have the best athletics programs in the country."

When Edward Jennings returned as interim president early in the century, he said the debate over the character of Ohio State—"Should this be a national research university with the very best students and faculty, or should this be everyman's university"—which began in his earlier term was over. It was now the age of public universities, he said, and for the first time "we can concentrate our resources on the quality of the institution."

By most markers, Ohio State had become a Top 25 school, although the 2003 academic plan admitted that "we will never be a truly great university without dramatically enhancing the reality and perception of the teaching and learning and research and scholarship we do." And: "Although much as been accomplished in recent years, our academic reputation has not appreciably improved."

In 2012, referencing Ohio State, *The New York Times*'s Laura Pappano wrote that "for good or ill, big-time football is the public face of the university, the brand that admissions offices sell, and a public-relations machine…" Pappano pointed out that Ohio State had "seventeen members of the American Academy of Arts and Sciences, three Nobel laureates, eight Pulitzer Prize winners, thirty-five Guggenheim Fellows, and a MacArthur winner. But sports rule."

Then she quoted Gordon Aubrecht, an Ohio State physics professor, who said, "It's not, 'Oh, yeah, Ohio State, that wonderful physics department.' It's football."

In the 1990s, a longtime Columbus journalist, Jane Ware, wrote *An Ohio State Profile: A Year in the Life of America's Biggest Campus*. Its virtue was what Ware called the University's "wondrous scope." It encompassed nooks and crannies of knowledge, she said, such as earth rotation, parasitic mites, and the study of Urdu, as well as a budget of near a billion dollars (now over seven times that), 8,500 courses, and "people who come from and go to every place on Earth." Ware's book described offerings so wide and diverse, with the university's various participants spread across such an imposing intellectual range that taken together they'd surely fill a stadium of their own.

Ware ended with summer commencement and the resounding cheers when the president said, "I congratulate you and welcome you to the company of educated men and women." It was not the familiar din of Ohio Stadium, but it was cheering nonetheless: the other side of the campus had game, too.

Bibliography

One
Football's crazy uncle

Austin, Brad, *Democratic Sports: Men's and Women's College Athletics During the Great Depression*, Fayetteville: University of Arkansas Press, 2015

Blanchette, John, "Schmidt adds spice to UI's tale," *The Spokane Spokesman-Review*, November 6, 2009

Brondfield, Jerry, *Woody Hayes and the 100-yard War*, New York: Random House, 1974

Brooks, Philip L., *Forward Pass: The Play That Saved Football,* Yardley, Pennsylvania: Westholme Publishing, 2008

Brown, Paul, *The Paul Brown Story*, New York: Atheneum, 1979

"Chatting with McKinnon," *Columbus Dispatch*, November 26, 1940

Danzig, Allison, "81,000 see Notre Dame upset Ohio State," *The New York Times*, November 3, 1935

Hunter, Bob, *Saint Woody, The History and Fanaticism of Ohio State Football*, Potomac Books: Washington, D.C., 2012

Perkins, Bret, *Frantic Francis, How One Coach's Madness Changed Football*, Lincoln: University of Nebraska Press, 2009

Schmidt, Francis, and Harold Fitzgerald, "The new open game," *Saturday Evening Post*, October 5, 1935

Two
Creation story

Anderson, Lars, *The First Star: Red Grange and the Barnstorming Tour That Launched the NFL,* New York: Random House, 2009

Austin, Brad, *Democratic Sports: Men's and Women's College Athletics during the Great Depression*, Fayetteville: University of Arkansas Press, 2015

Bohn, Michael K., *Heroes & Ballyhoo: How the Golden Age of the 1920s Transformed American Sports,* Dulles, Virginia: Potomac Books, 2009
Brandt, Nat, *When Oberlin was King of the Gridiron: The Heisman Years*, Kent, Ohio: Kent State University Press, 2001
Brooks, Philip L., *Forward Pass: The Play That Saved Football,* Yardley, Pennsylvania: Westholme Publishing, 2008
"College football not on wane, Hoover research group reports," *The New York Times*, January 5, 1933
Daley, Arthur, "Football: thrills, frenzy, drama, upsets," *The New York Times*, October 7, 1945
Danzig, Allison, *The History of American Football: Its Great Teams, Players, and Coaches,* Englewood Cliffs, New Jersey: Prentice-Hall, 1956
Deford, Frank, "I do love the football," *Sports Illustrated*, November 23, 1981
Glier, Ray, *How the SEC Became Goliath: The Making of College Football's Most Dominant Conference,* New York: Howard Books, 2012
Heisman, John M., and Mark Schlabach, *Heisman: The Man Behind the Trophy,* New York: Simon & Schuster, 2012
Kieran, John, "Sports of the Times," *The New York Times,* November 2, 1928
"The 1919 college football national championship," *TipTop25.com*
"Ohio State books Tigers," *The New York Times,* December 27, 1924
Oriard, Michael, *King Football: Sport & Spectacle in the Golden Age of Radio & Newsreels, Movies & Magazines, the Weekly & the Daily Press,* Chapel Hill: The University of North Carolina Press, 2001
———, *Reading Football: How the Popular Press Created an American Spectacle,* Chapel Hill: The University of North Carolina Press, 1993
Parrish, Michael E., *Anxious Decades: America in Prosperity and Depression, 1920–1941*, New York: W.W. Norton & Company, 1992
Podolski, Mark, "College football: Oberlin College still savors historic win over Ohio State in 1921," *Lorain Morning Journal*, September 22, 2014
Pollard, James E., *Ohio State Athletics, 1879–1959*, Columbus: Athletic Department of Ohio State University, 1959
Sayre, Joel, "Frenzied football," *Life* magazine, November 1, 1948
"Unusual year for college elevens," *The New York Times,* December 17, 1916
Watterson, John Sayle, *College Football: History, Spectacle, Controversy,* Baltimore: Johns Hopkins University Press, 2000
Reilly, Lucas, "222–0: The worst blowout in football history," *Mental Floss*, November 18, 2016
Roberts, Howard, *The Big Nine: The Story of Football in the Western Conference,* New York: G.P. Putnam's Sons, 1948
Roman, Robert J., *Ohio State Football: The Forgotten Dawn*, Akron: University of Akron Press, 2017
Schmidt, Ray, "Changing tides: college football 1919–1930, parts 1–3," *College Football Historical Society Newsletter*, July-September, 2000
———, "Some 1920s Disputes," *College Football Historical Society Newsletter*, February, 2001
———, *Shaping College Football: The Transformation of an American Sport, 1919–1930*, Syracuse: Syracuse University Press, 2007
Smith, Melvin I., *Evolvements of Early American Foot Ball,* Bloomington, Indiana: Author House, 2008

Umphlett, Wiley Lee, *Creating the Big Game: John W. Heisman and the Invention of American Football*, Westport, Connecticut: Greenwood Press, 1992
Wallace, Francis, "This football business," *Saturday Evening Post*, September 29, 1929
Watterson, John Sayle, *College Football: History, Spectacle, Controversy*, Baltimore: Johns Hopkins University Press, 2000
"Wilce uses psychology," *The New York Times,* October 18, 1923
"Western officials gather," *The New York Times,* December 5, 1924

Three
The Cathedral

French, Thomas E., *A Manual of Engineering Drawing for Students and Draftsmen*, New York: McGraw-Hill Book Company, Inc., 1929
"Give out football ticket prices for fall games," *The Lantern*, August 25, 1922
"John Wilce, former OSU grid coach, is dead at 75," *The Salem (Ohio) News*, May 18, 1963
"No changes in prices of football tickets," *The Lantern*, July 18, 1923
Mason, Daniel S., Marvin Washington, and Ernest A. N. Blist, "Signaling status through stadiums: the discourses of comparison within a hierarchy," *Journal of Sports Management*, September, 2015
Poole, Gary, "Classic stadiums, classic memories: on a tour in the Midwest, where college football is big, and so are the stadiums," *New York Times,* October 21, 2005
"Rome's Colosseum outdone by our football bowls," *The New York Times*, November 5, 1922
Wilce, J. W., Dr., "Dedication Day," *The Ohio State Monthly*, October 1922

Four
Brown's town

Brown, Paul, *The Paul Brown Story*, New York: Atheneum, 1979
Natali, Alan, *Brown's Town: Twenty Famous Browns Talk Amongst Themselves*, Orange Frazer Press: Wilmington, Ohio, 2001
O'Toole, Andrew, *Paul Brown: The Rise and Fall and Rose Again of Football's Most Innovative Coach*, Clerisy Press: Cincinnati, 2008

Five
Ohio State's lost dynasty

Clary, Jack, "Paul Brown," *The Coffin Corner*, Vol. 14, No. 1, 1992 *http://www.profootballresearchers.org/archives/Website_Files/Coffin_Corner/14-01-446.pdf*
Lombardo, John, *A Fire to Win, The Life and Times of Woody Hayes*, St. Martin's Press: New York, 2005
Natali, Alan, *Woody's Boys, Twenty Famous Buckeyes Talk Amongst Themselves*, Orange Frazer Press: Wilmington, Ohio, 1995
O'Toole, Andrew, *Paul Brown: The Rise and Fall and Rose Again of Football's Most Innovative Coach*, Clerisy Press: Cincinnati, 2008
Rhoden, William C., "On pro football: when Paul Brown smashed the color barrier," *The New York Times*. September 25, 1997.
Rosenberg, Michael, *War as They Knew It: Woody Hayes, Bo Schembechler, and America in a Time of Unrest*, Grand Central Publishing: New York, 2008

Sherman, Ed, "How Michigan State's Duffy Daugherty helped integrate college football," *Chicago Tribune*, February 16, 2015 *http://www.chicagotribune.com/sports/college/chi-duffy-daugherty-michigan-state-integration-20150216-story.html*

Young, A.S. (Doc), "The Black Athlete Makes His Mark," *Ebony*, May 1969

Six

James Thurber, PR man

Bernstein, Burton, *Thurber: A Biography*, New York: Dodd, Mead & Company, 1975

Holmes, Charles S., *The Clocks of Columbus*, New York: Atheneum, 1972

Kinney, Harrison, *James Thurber: His Life and Times*, New York: Henry Holt & Company, 1995

Tanner, Stephen L., "James Thurber and the Midwest," *American Studies*, Vol. 33, No. 2 (Fall, 1992) 61-72

Thomson, Tom, "Thurber Connection," *Short North Gazette*, *http://www.shortnorth.com/ThurberConnection.html*

Thurber, James, "If you ask me," *P.M.*, October 22, 1940

———, "You could look it up," *Saturday Evening Post*, April 5, 1941

Seven

Passing fancy

Brown, Paul, *The Paul Brown Story*, New York: Atheneum, 1979

Forbes, Dick, "Sid Gillman resurrected UC football," *Cincinnati Enquirer*, 1989

Herskowitz, Mickey, *The Quarterbacks: Uncensored Truth about the Men in the Pocket,* William Morrow and Company: New York

Lawson, Earl, "Football's man without mercy," *Saturday Evening Post*, October 8, 1955

Oremland, Brad, "The NFL coaching tree," *Sports Central* (February 22, 2008)

Pasquarelli, Len, "An offense by any other name …" *ESPN.com*, October 25, 2007

Quinn, T.J., "True West: the story Behind the NFL's high-octane offense," *New York Daily News*, January 11, 2003

Seed, Shawna, "Sid Gillman: airing it out," *ESPN.com,* June 10, 2013

Zimmerman, Paul, "Screen gem," *Sports Illustrated*, September 2, 2001

Zimmerman, Paul, "When Sid was Caesar," *Sports Illustrated*, February 1, 1988

Eight

The day the weather changed history

Blount, Jim, "1950 'blizzard bowls' had lasting impact on football," *Hamilton Journal-News*, November 27, 2002

Bruce, Earle, with George and Darcy Lehner, *Earle: A Coach's Life*, Orange Frazer Press: Wilmington, Ohio, 2000

Daley, Arthur, "Strictly guesswork." *The New York Times*, November 24, 1950

———, "Monday Morning Quarterback," *The New York Times*, November 27, 1950

Emmanuel, Greg, *The 100-Yard War: Inside the 100-year-old Michigan-Ohio State Football Rivalry*, John Wiley & Sons, Inc.: Hoboken, 2004

Felton, Dick, "Snow Bowl didn't blur memories of Janowicz," *Columbus Dispatch,* February 29, 1996

———, "Snow Bowl heroes recall bitter chill," *Columbus Dispatch*, November 18, 1990
Forste, Wally, "Fast field sure when UC, Miami play Saturday, *Cincinnati Post*, November, 23, 1950
Greenberg, Steve, and Dale Ratermann, *I Remember Woody: Recollections of the Man They Called Coach Hayes,* Triumph Books: Chicago, 1997
Hayes, Woody, *You Win with People*, Typographic Printing Company: Columbus, Ohio, 1973
Katzowitz, Josh, *Sid Gillman: Father of the Passing Game*, Clerisy Press: Covington, Kentucky, 2012
Keysor, Jim, "The white hurricane of 1913," *The Climate Observer*, November 14, 2013
Lawson, Earl, "Miami wearing MSC crown and smile of victor after conquest of Gillman's Bearcat eleven," *Cincinnati Times Star*, November 27, 1950
Lombardo, John, *A Fire to Win: the Life and Times of Woody Hayes*, St. Martin's Press: New York, 2005
McCambridge, Michael, ed., *ESPN College Football Encyclopedia*, ESPN Books: New York, 2005
McNulty, John, "Our footloose correspondents," *The New Yorker*, December 16, 1950
"Michigan defeats Ohio State, 9–3," *The New York Times*, November 26, 1950
Oller, Rob, "Snow Bowl legends accumulate—fifty years later, folks are trying to separate fact from fiction," *Columbus Dispatch*, Friday 17, 2000
Pickenpaugh, Roger, *Buckeye Blizzard: Ohio and the 1950 Thanksgiving Storm*, Gateway Press, Inc: Baltimore, 2001
"Redskins surprise Bearcats," *Cincinnati Enquirer*, November 26, 1950
Schmidlin, Thomas W., and Jeanne Appelhans Schmidlin, *Thunder in the Heartland: A Chronicle of Outstanding Weather Events in Ohio*, Kent State University Press: Kent, Ohio, 1996
Strode, George, "OSU ticket man was 'firm but not abrupt,' *Columbus Dispatch*, July 28, 1985
Woolford, Dave, "1950 Snow Bowl: a game for all time frozen in history," *Toledo Blade,* November 15, 2000

Nine
Woody and his culture

Allen, Frederick Lewis, *Only Yesterday: An Informal History of the 1920s*, New York: Harper & Row, 1931
Austin, Brad, *Democratic Sports: Men and Women's College Athletics during the Great Depression*, Fayetteville: University of Arkansas Press, 2015
Brendon, Piers, *The Dark Valley: A Panorama of the 1930s*, New York: Alfred A. Knopf, 2001
Briley, Ron, review of *With Amusement for All: A History of American Popular Culture since 1830* by LeRoy Ashby, *Journal of Sport History*, Fall, 2007
Clotfelter, Charles, "Big-time college athletics 80 years later," *Duke Today*, October 27, 2009
DeCarlo, Leisa, "Ohio State homecoming has long history of drama," *The Lantern*, October 17, 2014
Dyreson, Mark, "The emergence of consumer culture and the transformation of physical culture: American sport in the 1920s," *Journal of Sports History*, Winter 1989

Hanley, Lawrence F., *Radical Revision: Rereading 1930s Culture*, Urbana: University of Illinois Press, 1996
Lombardo, John, *A Fire to Win: The Life and Times of Woody Hayes*, New York: Thomas Dunne Books, 2005
Miller, Patrick B., *The Sporting World of the Modern South*, Urbana: University of Illinois Press, 2002
Oriard, Michael, *Dreaming of Heroes: American Sports Fiction, 1868-1980*, Chicago: Nelson-Hall Inc., 1962
———, *King Football: Sport & Spectacle in the Golden Age of Radio & Newsreels, Movies & Magazines, the Weekly & the Daily Press,* Chapel Hill: The University of North Carolina Press, 2001
Simmons, John S., "John R. Tunis and the sports novels for adolescents: a little ahead of his time," *The Alan Review*, Fall 2001
Vare, Robert, *Buckeye: A Study of Coach Woody Hayes and the Ohio State Football Machine*, Popular Library: New York, 1974
"Wes Fesler says he'll deemphasize O.S.U. football," *The Marion Star,* April 2, 1947

Ten

The dynasty begins

"Cassady's run thru Badgers voted No. 1 football thrill," *Chicago Daily Tribune*, December 9, 1954
Dyer, Braven, "Sports Parade," *Los Angeles Times*, November 27, 1954
Hayes, Woody, *Football at Ohio State*, 1957
"In the Rose Bowl: Ohio State Coach Hayes calls Leggett's play unbelievable," *Washington Post and Times Herald*, January 3, 1955
Levy, Bill, *Three Yards and a Cloud of Dust*, World Publishing Company: Cleveland, 1966
Lombardo, John, *A Fire to Win: The Life and Times of Woody Hayes*, St. Martin's Press: New York, 2006
"1919 Model T Car Brings Four to Rose Bowl Game," *Harford Courant*, December 24, 1954
"Ohio coach says five Big 10 elevens outclass Trojans," *Chicago Daily Tribune*, January 2, 1955
Povich, Shirley, "This Morning," *Washington Post and Times Herald*, November 22, 1954.
Shaplen, Robert, "The Ohio State story: win or else," *Sports Illustrated*, October 24,1955
Ward, Arch, "In the wake of the news," *Chicago Daily Tribune*, December 8, 1954
Weigel, J. Timothy, *The Buckeyes: Ohio State Football*, Henry Regnery Company, Chicago, 1974
Wild, James E., "Sunlight on Sports," *The Sun*, November 8, 1954
Wolf, Al, "Sportraits," *Los Angeles Times,* November 8, 1954

Eleven

The end of innocence

Freeman, William H., *Physical Education, Exercise and Sport Science in a Changing Society,* Jones & Barlett Learning: Sudbury, Mass., 2012

Kemper, Kurt Edward, "Struggling for the Soul of the Cold War University," *College Football and the American Culture in the Cold War Era*, University of Illinois Press: Chicago, 2009
Marshall, Bruce, "When the Buckeyes bucked the Rose Bowl," *Goldsheet.com*
Martin, Charles H., "Commentary: beer, parking, and football, *Journal of Sport History*, Fall, 2007
Odenkirk, James, "The Eighth Wonder of the World: Ohio State University's rejection of a Rose Bowl bid in 1961," *North American Society for Sport History*, fall, 2007
"Ohio State Students Demonstrate," *Washington Post Times Herald*, November 30, 1961
Scanlon, John, "The scent of roses," *Saturday Review*, April 21, 1962
Shaplen, Robert, "The Ohio State story: win or else," *Sports Illustrated*, October 24, 1955
"10,000 Buckeyes march in protest," *Los Angeles Times*, November 29, 1961
Vare, Robert, *Buckeye: A Study of Coach Woody Hayes and the Ohio State Football Machine*, New York: Popular Library, 1974
Watterson, John Sayle, *College Football: History, Spectacle, Controversy*, The Johns Hopkins University Press: Baltimore and London, 2000
Zimmerman, Paul, "Sportscripts," *Los Angeles Times*, December 12, 1954

Twelve
Rules of the game

Byers, Walter, with Charles Hammer, *Unsportsmanlike Conduct: Exploiting College Athletes*, Ann Arbor: the University of Michigan Press, 1995
"Coaches disagree on new rules," *Chicago Daily Tribune*, January 14, 1963
"College football gets a moderate sub rule," *Chicago Daily Tribune,* January 14, 1960
Daley, Arthur, "Return of the Mobs," *The New York Times*, January 21, 1963
Danzig, Allison, *The History of American Football,* Edgewood Cliffs, New Jersey: Prentice-Hall, 1956
"Kill platoon system in college football," *Chicago Daily Tribune*, January 15, 1953
Looney, Douglas S., "One is more like it," *Sports Illustrated*, September 3, 1990
Munn, Clarence, "Thumbs down on the one platoon," *Sports Illustrated*, November 29, 1954
Nelson, David M., *Anatomy of a Gam,* Associated University Presses, Inc.: Cranbury, New Jersey. 1994
Rosner, Scott R., and Kenneth L. Shropshire, editors, *The Business of Sports*, Boston: Jones and Bartlett Publishers, 2004
Russin, Joseph M., "NCAA passes liberal substitution rule, *The Harvard Crimson*, January 14, 1964
Smith, Robert, *Play-by-Play: Radio, Television, and Big-Time College Sport*, Baltimore: The Johns Hopkins University Press, 2001
Smith, Wilfrid, "Football A to Z: the substitution rule explained," *Chicago Tribune.* October 22, 1963
Sperber, Murray, *Onward to Victory: The Crisis That Shaped College Sports*, New York: Henry Holt and Company, 1998
"Two-unit football team planned by Ohio State," *New York Times,* January 23, 1954

Watterson, John Sayle, *College Football: History, Spectacle, Controversy*, The Johns Hopkins University Press: Baltimore and London, 2000
"West coaches rap return of old sub rule," *Chicago Daily Tribune,* January 15, 1963
White, Gordon S., "N.C.A.A. is expected to permit return of unlimited substitution, *New York Times*, January 11, 1965
Whicker, Mark, "Clemson crashing the party of elite football," *Los Angeles Daily News*, August 28, 2017
Zimmerman, Paul, "Complaints grow: baffling sub rule doomed?" *Los Angeles Times*, October 27, 1963
———, Paul, "Here's an upset: Buckeyes are passing now," *Los Angeles Times*. October 16, 1963

Thirteen
Top of the national heap

Cantwell, Robert, "Say it isn't so, Woody," *Sports Illustrated*, September 11, 1967
Hyde, David, *1968: The Year That Saved Ohio State Football*, Orange Frazer Press: Wilmington, 2008
Hyman, Mervin, "Just keep cool, baby, and run those fat tackles," *Sports Illustrated*, October 21, 1968
Lombardo, John, *A Fire to Win: The Life and Times of Woody Hayes*, St. Martin's Press: New York, 2005
Natali, Alan, *Woody's Boys: Twenty Famous Buckeyes Talk Amongst Themselves*, Orange Frazer Press: Wilmington, Ohio, 1995

Fourteen
Tiger, Tiger, burning bright

Brown, Chris B., *The Art of Smart Football*, 2015
———, *The Essential Smart Football*, 2012
Dresow, Keegan, *Offensive Football Systems*
Ellison, Glenn "Tiger," *Run-and-Shoot Football: Offense of the Future,* Parker Publishing Company: West Nyack, New York, 1965
Gwynne, S.C., *The Perfect Pass: American Genius and the Reinvention of Football*, New York: Scribner, 2017
Hyde, David *1968*; *The Year that Saved Ohio State Football*, Orange Frazer Press: Wilmington, Ohio, 2008
Jaworski, Ron, *The Games that Changes the Game*, Ballantine Books: New York, 2010
Layden, Tim, *Blood Sweat and Chalk*, Sports Illustrated Books: New York, 2011
Martin, Buddy, *Urban's Way: Urban Meyer, the Florida Gators, and His Plan to Win*, Thomas Dunne Books: St. Martin's Press: New York, 2008

Fifteen
The sophomores grow up

Emmanuel, Greg, *The 100-Yard War: Inside the 100-Year-old Michigan-Ohio State Football Rivalry*, John Wiley & Sons, Hoboken, 2004
Hyde, David, *1968: The Year That Saved Ohio State Football*, Orange Frazer Press: Wilmington, 2008
Jenkins, Dan, "Revival and revenge," *Sports Illustrated*, November 30, 1970
Kessler, Kaye, "Bye, bye, No. 1," *Sports Illustrated*, December 1, 1969

Menzer, Joe, *Buckeye Madness: The Glorious, Tumultuous, Behind-the-Scenes Story of Ohio State Football*, Simon & Schuster: New York, 2005
Natali, Alan, *Woody's Boys: 20 Famous Buckeyes Talk Amongst Themselves*, Orange Frazer Press: Wilmington, Ohio, 1995
Rosenberg, Michael, *War as They Knew It: Woody Hayes, Bo Schembechler, and America in a Time of Unrest*, Grand Central Publishing: New York, 2008
http://www.stack.com/a/loudest-college-football-stadiums

Sixteen
Archie comes running

Allen, Nate, "Ex-Hogs coach can't forget Buckeyes," *Arkansas Democrat-Gazette*, December 29, 2010
Football Game Box Scores/Play-by-Plays, 1938-1978, Bentley Historical Library, U of M Athletic Department Records, *http://www.umich.edu/~bhlumrec/athdept/fbstats*
Hogg, J.T., "Mating in Bighorn Sheep: multiple creative male strategies," *Science*, September, 1984
Jenkins, Dan, "No doubt about who's champ," *Sports Illustrated*, January 8, 1973
Natali, Alan, *Woody's Boys: 20 Famous Buckeyes Talk Amongst Themselves*, Orange Frazer Press: Wilmington, Ohio, 1995
Rosenberg, Michael, *War as They Knew It: Woody Hayes, Bo Schembechler, and America in a Time of Unrest*, Grand Central Publishing: New York, 2008
"Schembechler's the name. Football's his game," *Sports Illustrated*, Douglas Looney, September 14, 1981
Solari, Chris, "MSU-Ohio State 1974: Spartans, Buckeyes relive the chaos," *Lansing State Journal* November 15, 2014
Sylvester, Curt, "Bye, Roses! M loses, 14–11: Goal-line stands send OSU to bowl," *Detroit Free Press*, November 26, 1972
Vare, Robert, *Buckeye: A Study of Coach Woody Hayes and the Ohio State Football Machine*, Popular Library: New York, 1974

Seventeen
Split decisions

Byers, Walter, with Charles Hammer, *Unsportsmanlike Conduct: Exploiting College Athletes*, Ann Arbor: University of Michigan Press, 1995
Greenberg, Steve, and Larry Zelina, *Ohio State '68: All the Way to the Top*," Champaign, Illinois: Sports Publishing Inc., 1998
Hayes, W. Woodrow, *Football at Ohio State*, 1957
Hoffer, Richard, "Football, Ohio style: a sportswriter and his state saw themselves in stoic, grind-it-out terms," *Sports Illustrated*, August 4, 2003
Hyde, David, *1968: The Year That Saved Ohio State Football*, Orange Frazer Press: Wilmington, 2008
Jenkins, Dan, "Who Gets the Oscar?" *Sports Illustrated*, November 10, 1969
Nelson, David M., *The Anatomy of a Game: Football, the Rules, and the Men Who Made the Game,* Newark: University of Delaware Press, 1994
Telander, Rick, "Defining a Grid Legend, *Sports Illustrated*, March 23, 1987

Eighteen
The oldest rivalry

Arledge, Roone,. *Roone: A Memoir*, Harper Collins: New York, 2003

Emmanuel, Greg, *The 100-Yard War: Inside the 100-year-old Michigan-Ohio State Football Rivalry*, John Wiley & Sons, Inc.: Hoboken, 2004
Hunter, Bob, *Saint Woody, The History and Fanaticism of Ohio State Football*, Potomac Books: Washington, D.C., 2012
Hyman, Mervin D. & Gordon S. White, Jr., *Big Ten Football: Its Life and Times, Great Coaches, Players and Games*, Macmillan: New York. 1977
Litman, Laken, "Jim Tressel looks back on the unintentional guarantee that flipped Michigan–Ohio State," *Sports Illustrated*, November 21, 2018
Looney, Don, "Schembechler's the name. Football's his game," *Sports Illustrated*, September 14, 1981
"The 10 greatest rivalries," ESPN.com, January 3, 2000
Powers, Ron, *Supertube: The Rise of Television Sports*, Coward-McCann: New York, 1984
Rosenberg, Michael, *War as They Knew It: Woody Hayes, Bo Schembechler, and America in a Time of Unrest*, Grand Central Publishing: New York, 2008
———, "Why the Michigan–Ohio State rivalry badly needs a Wolverines win," *Sports Illustrated*, November 23, 2018
Schembechler, Bo, and Mitch Albom, *Bo: Life, Laughs, and Lessons of a College Football Legend*, Warner Books, Inc.: New York, 1989
Tracy, Marc, "Michigan tries to steady that big chip on Ohio State's shoulder," *The New York Times*, November 21, 2018

Nineteen
The last grand eccentric

Brondfield, Jerry, *Woody Hayes and the 100-Yard War*, New York: Random House, 1974
Dufresne, Chris, "Simple fist of fate," *Los Angeles Times*, December 29, 2003
Fox, Bucky, "Woody Hayes stormed to football glory at Ohio State," *Investor's Business Daily*, December 28, 2015
Garrett, Betty, "Lion in autumn," *Ohio Magazine*, October 1978
Hayes, Woody, *You Win with People*, Columbus, Ohio, 1973
Hyde, David, *1968: The Year That Saved Ohio State Football*, Orange Frazer Press: Wilmington, 2008
Interview, Tony Lamke, former Wilmington High School coach, 2018
Jenkins, Dan, "62–0," *Sports Illustrated*, October 6, 1969
Lombardo, John, *A Fire to Win: The Life and Times of Woody Hayes*, St. Martin's Press: New York, 2005
Natali, Alan, *Woody's Boys: Twenty Famous Buckeyes Talk Amongst Themselves*, Wilmington, Ohio: Orange Frazer Press, 1995
Rosenberg, Michael, *War as They Knew It: Woody Hayes, Bo Schembechler, and America in a Time of Unrest*, Grand Central Publishing: New York, 2008
———, Michael, "Woody's last stand," *Sports Illustrated*, December 23, 2016
Severo, Richard, "Maestro of the singalong dies at 99," *The New York Times*, August 2, 2010
Telander, Rick, "Defining a grid legend," *Sports Illustrated*, March 23, 1987
Terrell, Roy, "You love Woody or hate him," *Sports Illustrated*, September 24, 1962
Thomas, Robert, Jr., "Woody Hayes is dead at 74; tempestuous football coach," *The New York Times*, March 13, 1987
Torry, Jack, "Woody Hayes: the man, the legend," *Columbus Monthly*, May 1986

Vare, Robert, *Buckeye: A Study of Coach Woody Hayes and the Ohio State Football Machine*, New York: Popular Library, 1974

Twenty
End game

Baskin, John, and Lonnie Wheeler, *Legends*, Wilmington, Ohio: Orange Frazer Press, 2009

Carter, Cris, with Jeffri Chadiha, *Going Deep: How Wide Receivers Became the Most Compelling Figures in Pro Sports*, New York: Hyperion, 2013

"Chris Carter, Hall of Fame wide receiver: the clutch, difficult catches set him apart," *Associated Press*, August 1, 2013

Feller, Jason, "History shows it can be risky to trade great players for picks," *NFL.com*, May 4, 2009
http://www.nfl.com/draft/story/09000d5d8101bfd7/article/history-shows-it-can-be-risky-to-trade-great-players-for-picks

Grossi, Tony, *Tales from the Brown's Sideline,* Champaign, Illinois: Sports Publishing L.L.C., 2004

Keim, John, *Legends by the Lake*, Akron: University of Akron Press, 1999

Lieber, Jill, "A sad goodbye to Columbus," *Sports Illustrated*, August 3, 1987

Menzer, Joe, *Buckeye Madness: The Glorious, Tumultuous, Behind-the-Scenes Story of Ohio State Football*, imon & Schuster: New York, 2005

Neff, Craig, "Agents of turmoil," *Sports Illustrated*, August 3, 1987

Oller, Rob, "Ohio State football—Q&A with former Buckeye Paul Warfield," *Columbus Dispatch,* September 3, 2015.

Pluto, Terry*, When All the World was Browns Town: Cleveland's Browns and the Championship Season of '64,* New York: Simon and Schuster, 1997

Stensrud, Matthew, "Charting Cris Carter's journey from hardship to the Hall of Fame," *bleacherreport.com*, February 18, 2013
h*ttp://bleacherreport.com/articles/1531416-charting-cris-carters-journey-from-hardship-to-the-hall-of-fame*

Stuart, Chase, "Yards per catch kings," *Football Perspective.com*, June 18, 2016
http://www.footballperspective.com/yards-per-catch-kings-paul-warfield-stanley-morgan-james-lofton-and-more/

Thompson, Hunter S., *The Great Shark Hunt: Strange Tales from a Strange Time*, New York: Simon & Schuster, 1979

Twenty-one
The man who followed The Legend

Berkow, Ira, "No tuxedo for Earle Bruce," *The New York Times*, November 28, 1987

Bruce, Earle, with George and Darcy Lehner, *Earle: A Coach's Life*, Orange Frazer Press: Wilmington, 2000

Hersch, Hank, "Short on style, But plenty long on substance," *Sports Illustrated*, December 01, 1986

Livingston, Bill, "Bruce dismissal shames Ohio State," *Plain Dealer*, November 17, 1987

Looney, Douglas S., "A beautiful Rose, even for 'Bama," *Sports Illustrated*, January 14, 1980

———, and Armen Keteyian, unpublished article on Earle Bruce, written for *Sports Illustrated*, December 5, 1987

Paprocki, Ray, "The week the town went crazy," *Columbus Monthly*, January 1988
Schlichter, Art, *Busted: The Rise and Fall of Art Schlichter*, Orange Frazer Press: Wilmington, 2009
Sharkey, Mary Anne, "OSU in furor over Bruce firing," *Plain Dealer*, November 18, 1987
Underwood, John, "A breath of fresh air after a heavy Hayes," *Sports Illustrated*, April 9, 1979
Wojciechowski, Gene, "The mystery of Earle Bruce," *Los Angeles Times*, January 17, 1988

Twenty-two
The outsider

"Brian Griese comes off the bench, guides underdog Wolverines past Buckeyes, 13–9," *Plain Dealer*, November 24, 1996
Callahan, Gerry, "Cooper's Town," *Sports Illustrated*, September 8, 1997
Daugherty, Paul, "Cooper can't win with Buckeye fans," *Cincinnati Enquirer*, November 22, 1994
Hartman, Marcus, "By the numbers: John Cooper's OSU recruiting," *Buckeye Sports.com*, February 19, 2014 *https://scout.com/college/ohio-state/Article/By-The-Numbers-John-Coopers-OSU-Recruiting-105075827*
Lauderback, Chris, "The complicated legacy of John Cooper, *Eleven Warriors*, June 18, 2013 *https://www.elevenwarriors.com/2013/06/22916/ohio-state-football-the-complicated-legacy-of-john-cooper*
Livingston, Bill, "Bond with players missing at OSU," *Plain Dealer*, November 9, 1998
———, "Cooper finds fit among the elite," *Plain Dealer*, September 29, 1997
———, "Cooper makes wine from critics' whine," *Plain Dealer*, January 1, 1997
———, "From folksy to failure: Cooper's faulty legacy," *Plain Dealer*, January 3, 2001
Menzer, Joe, *Buckeye Madness: The Glorious, Tumultuous, Behind-the-Scenes Story of Ohio State Football*, Simon & Schuster: New York, 2005
Murphy, Austin, "Piling it on once again," *Sports Illustrated*, October, 11, 1993
Person, Joseph, "Fans delight in stories of USC's Brewer's big game against Ohio State," The (Columbia) *State*, December 24, 2008
"The pressure of Ohio State," *Sporting News*, January 15, 2001
Reilly, Rick, "Class struggle at Ohio State," *Sports Illustrated*, August 31, 1998.
Sullivan, Tim, "Reaction to Cooper not all rosy, *Cincinnati Enquirer*, December 3, 1994
Telander, Rick, "In Woody's shadow," *Sports Illustrated*, August 22, 1988
Vinella, Susan, "Ohio State Football: Big Kat gets extra heat on studies," *Dayton Daily News,* August 26, 1998.
Wertheim, Jon L., "Picked off," *Sports Illustrated*, November 16, 1998

Twenty-three
Titletown, U.S.A.

Chengelis, Angelique S., "Rowdy behavior is on the rise," *Detroit News*, November 25, 2002

Daugherty, Paul, "Bucks delivered thrills, title—as promised," *Cincinnati Enquirer*, January 4, 2003
Emmanuel, Greg, *The 100-Yard War: Inside the 100-Year-old Michigan-Ohio State Football Rivalry*, John Wiley & Sons, Hoboken, 2004
Hunter, Bob, "This was OSU football as so many remember it," *Columbus Dispatch*, January 4, 2003
King, Kelley, "Winning ugly," *Sports Illustrated*, November 25, 2002
Layden, Tim, "A beautiful mind: Craig Krenzel, national champion quarterback and molecular genetics major, wields the most imposing weapon in the game," *Sports Illustrated*, August 11, 2003
Livingston, Bill, "A magic season," *Plain Dealer*, January 5, 2003
May, Tim, *A Season to Remember*, Sports Publishing LLC, 2003
Miller, Joshua A., "UC vs. OSU: Looking back, looking forward, *Cincinnati Magazine*, September 25, 2014
Miller, Rusty, "Ohio State will pay 3 visitors over $2m," *Associated Press*, April 7, 2014
Murphy, Austin, "Next stop: Fiesta Bowl," *Sports Illustrated*, December 2, 2002.
———, "Still standing: a whopping eight teams enter November without a loss," *Sports Illustrated*, November 4, 2002
Oates, Tom, "Today's game a grudge match? Go figure," *Wisconsin State Journal,/* October 19, 2002
Ocker, Sheldon, "Impenetrable Tressel's influence is illuminated," *Akron Beacon Journal*, November 24, 2002
Opper, Matt, "Gino Guidugli: the enigmatic one," *SBNation*, June 12, 2011 *https://www.downthedrive.com/pages/gino-guidugli-the-enegmatic-one*
Parker, Jeff, "The night the town stood still," *Columbus Monthly*, March 2003
Svoboda, Jeff, "Grant did a little bit of everything," *Buckeye Sports Bulletin*, December 2012
Tinley, Scott, "An oral history of the 2003 Fiesta Bowl between Miami, Ohio State," *Sports Illustrated*, January 4, 2013
Tressel, Jim (with Chris Fabry), *The Winners Manual: For the Game of Life*, Carol Stream, Illinois: Tyndale House, 2008
Tracy, Marc, "College football playoff," *The New York Times*, December 3, 2017

Twenty-four
Tresselball

Brennan, Christine, "Jim Tressel's mystique gone; now, he's just another coach," *USA Today*, March 10, 2011
Bird, Michael, "Yep, USC has a 7-game winning streak over Ohio State that dates back to 1975," *SBNation*, Dec 29, 2017
Daugherty, Paul, "Jim Tressel sold us image he wasn't," *Cincinnati Enquirer*, May. 30, 2011
———, "Worst part of Tressel's NCAA saga? Discovering he's just like us," *Cincinnati Enquirer*, April 28, 2011
Dohrmann, George, with David Epstein, "SI investigation reveals eight-year pattern of violations under Tressel," *Sports Illustrated*, June 6, 2011
Hunter, Bob, "Controversy? In the end, fans see Tressel as winner," *Columbus Dispatch*, September 19, 2015
———, *Saint Woody, The History and Fanaticism of Ohio State Football*, Potomac Books: Washington, D.C., 2012

Low, Chris, "Timeline: Jim Tressel's fall," *ESPN.com*, May 30, 2011 *http://www.espn.com/college-football/news/story?id=6607982*

Livingston, Bill, "Can anyone win the Clarett affair?" *Plain Dealer*, November 17, 2004

———, "Dad passes down rivalry to son," *Plain Dealer*, November 14, 2006

———, "Five years after tattoo scandal," *Plain Dealer*, September 18, 2015

———, "Forget his buttoned-down look, 'the game' is Tressel's strong suit," *Plain Dealer*, December 29, 2005

———, "From fairy-tale beginning to smacked by Gator tails," *Plain Dealer*, January 9, 2007

———, "From I-AA YSU, Bucks found A-1 leader," *Plain Dealer*, September 01, 2007

———, "In title bout, Tressel's lore gets bruised, *Plain Dealer*, January 10, 2007

———, "Ohio State coach Jim Tressel burnishes legacy in The Game," *Plain Dealer*, November 26, 2010

———, "Ohio State coach Jim Tressel should not be defined solely by his wrongdoings," *Plain Dealer*, March 27, 2011

Longman, Jeré, "The two sides of Jim Tressel," *The New York Times*, January 3, 2007

Markovich, Jeremy, "President Tressel," *CBSSports.com*, December 29, 2015 *https://www.cbssports.com/collegefootball/feature/25431105/president-tressel*

Newton, David, "Is Panthers WR Ted Ginn Jr the fastest player in the NFL?" *ESPN*, December 15, 2015 *http://www.espn.com/blog/carolina-panthers/post/_/id/17918/is-panthers-wr-ted-ginn-jr-the-fastest-player-in-the-nfl*

Rea, Mark, *"The Curious Case Against Ohio State Football,"* wordpress.com, August, 2011 *https://markrea.wordpress.com/2011/08/*

Thamel, Pete, "Tressel is a reminder of why rules blur," *The New York Times*, March 9, 2011

Tracy, Marc, "Five years after scandal, Jim Tressel is still a Buckeye," *The New York Times*, November 23, 2016

Twenty-five
The miracle of 2014

Culpepper, Chuck, "Ohio State beats Alabama, 42-35, to advance to title game, *Washington Post*, January 2, 2015

Dahlberg, Tim, "In Vegas, Ohio State isn't a team worthy of Top 4," *Associated Press,* December 8, 2014

"81st annual Sugar Bowl, January 1, 2015, College Football Playoff Semifinal," *allstatesugarbowl.org*

Grega, Jr., James, "Ohio State unable to 'got on a roll offensively' in loss to Hokies," *The Lantern*, September 7, 2014

Kalland, Bobby, "Ohio State's 2014 national title trophy says 'TUN'," instead of Michigan," *cbssports.com*, September 17, 2015

Livingston, Bill, "Fastball offense and Ohio State's rush to the future," *Cleveland Plain Dealer*, January 1, 2015

———, "The Ohio State Buckeyes' Cardale Jones has surprised many, but not coach who recruited him," *The Plain Dealer,* January 6, 2015

Rabinowitz, Bill, *The Chase: How Ohio State Captured the First College Football Playoff,* Chicago: Triumph Books, 2015

Rohan, Tim, "A No. 3 Quarterback Topples No. 1 Alabama," *The New York Times*, January 2, 2015

———, "At Ohio State, an overabundance lines up under center," *The New York Times*, December 31, 2014

———, "For the Buckeyes, a win and a loss," *The New York Times*, November 29, 2014

Rosenberg, Michael, "Ohio State's win over Michigan State proves Buckeyes are here to stay," *Sports Illustrated*, November 9, 2014

Staples, Andy, "Party Crashers," *Sports Illustrated*, January 19, 2015

Thamel, Pete, "Cardale Jones has never struggled on the field—only off it," *Sports Illustrated*, December 29, 2014

———, "Ohio State finds itself in good hands behind ebullient QB Cardale Jones," *Sports Illustrated*, December 22, 2014

———, "We're No. 4!" *Sports Illustrated*, December 15, 2014

Wasserman, Ari, "If talent alone decided the game, Tide would roll," *The Plain Dealer*, December 24, 2014

———, "Inside the night Ohio State QB Cardale Jones went from third-string afterthought to Buckeye savior," *Cleveland.com*, December 7, 2014

Twenty-six
Lost man—the disappearing fullback

Bird, Hayden, "The rise of the NFL tight end and fall of the fullback, part II," *NFL History*, January 22, 2012

Briggs, David, "Ohio State captain Boren seeks to add leadership to thin linebacker position," *Toledo Blade*, October 20, 2012

———, "Ohio State coaches tab Boren at linebacker, *Toledo Blade*, October 14, 2012

Brooks, Bucky, "Fullbacks continue to fight off blockers, extinction in modern NFL," *nfl.com*, June 7, 2009

"Dave Francis, Buckeyes' fullbacks run over Wolverines, 28-0," *The Plain Dealer*, February 28, 2012

Harmon, Pat, "New style at Ohio State," *Cincinnati Post*, November 6, 1968

———, "Weed exudes enthusiasm," *Cincinnati Post*, December 2, 1957

Heisman Memorial Award Issue, *Journal of the Downtown Athletic Club*, December 1973

Heitner, Darren, "What is the future for the NFL fullback?" *Forbes*, September 5, 2013

Livingston, Bill, "Ohio State's Zach Boren not taking his senior season for granted," *The Plain Dealer*, November 12, 2002

Tate, Loren, "Position all but forgotten," *The News-Gazette* (Champaign-Urbana), November 9, 2009

Morris, Gary, "Football 101: Is the fullback back, or will the decline continue? *SBNATION*, June 25, 2014

Natali, Alan, *Woody's Boys*, Wilmington, Ohio: Orange Frazer Press, 1995

Olson, Eric, "NCAA college football fullbacks are alive and well in Big Ten," *www.collegefootball.ap.org*

Piotrowicz, Nicholas, "Initiation is the sincerest form of flattery for OSU," *The Blade*, December 28, 2016

Rabinowitz, Bill, *Buckeye Rebirth*, Chicago: Triumph Books, 2013

Stuart, Chase, "Wherefore art thou fullback? *football perspective.com*, May 22, 2013

Trotter, Jim, "The NFL," *Sports Illustrated*, October 22, 2007
Walsh, Bill, "How I evaluate each position: fullback," *PSX Draft Insider Special*
Williams, Charean, "Fullbacks: vanishing breed," *Chicago Tribune,* September 24, 2006
Wright, Alfred, "Two big decisions," *Sports Illustrated*, November 13, 1961

Twenty-seven
The football library

Danzig, Allison, *The History of American Football*, Englewood Cliffs, New Jersey: Prentice-Hall, 1956
Ellison, Glenn "Tiger," *Run-and-Shoot Football: Offense of the Future,* West Nyack, New York: Parker Publishing Company, 1965
Grobani, Anton, *Guide to Football Literature*, Detroit: Gale Research Company, 1975
Gustkey, Earl, "Lou Holtz's coaching in no joke but he can sure tell one," *Los Angeles Times*, November 23, 1988
Hayes, W. Woodrow, *Football at Ohio State*, 1957
———, *Hotline to Victory*, 1969
Jones, Gomer, and Bud Wilkinson, *Modern Defensive Football*, Prentice-Hall: New York, 1957
Jones, Gomer, *Offensive and Defensive Line Play,* Prentice-Hall: Englewood Cliffs, New Jersey, 1961
Perkins, Brett, *Frantic Francis: How One Coach's Madness Changed Football*, Lincoln & London: University of Nebraska Press, 2009
Tramel, Berry, "A Sooner forever," *The Oklahoman*, November 11, 1994
"Wilce discusses modern football," *The New York Times,* July 21, 1922
Wilce, John Woodworth, *Football: How to Play It and How to Understand It*, New York: Charles. Scribner's Sons, 1923

Twenty-eight
Urban's legend

Bacon, John U., *Fourth and Long: the Fight for the Soul of College Football*, New York: Simon & Schuster, 2013
Bishop, Greg, "Hernandez among many who found trouble at Florida in the Meyer years," *The New York Times*, July 6, 2013
Bradley, Thomas, "Breaking it down," *thelantern.com*, June 3, 2012
Culpepper, Chuck, "Like Urban Meyer or not, college football will miss him when he's gone," *Washington Post*, November 23, 2018
———, "Tension pays Ohio State a visit along with Penn State," *The Washington Post*, November 23, 2019
———, "2015 Sugar Bowl: Ohio State beats Alabama, 42–35, to advance to title game," *The Washington Post*, January 2, 2015
Fitzsimmons, Emma G., and Marc Tracy, "After Urban Meyer suspension, some at Ohio State see a culture of sports above all," *The New York Times*, August 29, 2018
Fulton, Ross, "An interview with Urban Meyer," *www.eleven warriors.com*, August 2, 2012
Hutchins, Andy, "On why Urban-Meyer-to-Ohio-State rumors will come true," *alligatorarmy.com*, June 1, 2011

Lesmerises, Doug, "Why Ohio State football has broken the College Football Playoff—but can make it easy this year," *cleveland.com*, November 8, 2019
Litman, Luke, "Ohio State gets the battle it needed," *Sports Illustrated*, November 23, 2019
Livingston, Bill, "Cotton Bowl 2017: J.T. Barrett's farewell was a win, but not a statement," *The Plain Dealer*, December 30, 2017
———, "Ohio State's Urban Meyer and the birth of the spread offense," *The Plain Dealer*, August 29, 2016
Low, Chris, "Urban Meyer, Ohio State continue domination of Michigan," *espn.com*, November 24, 2019
Maese, Rick, "With Ohio State facing latest sex abuse case, attorney says May report 'barely scratches the surface,'" *The Washington Post*, November 7, 2019
Meyer, Urban (with Wayne Coffey), *Above the Line: Lessons in Leadership and Life from a Championship Program*, New York: Penguin Press, 2016
Price, S.L., "Urban Meyer," *Sports Illustrated*, December 7, 2009
Rabinowitz, Bill, *Buckeye Rebirth: Urban Meyer, an Inspired Team, and a New Era at Ohio State*, Chicago: Triumph Books, 2013
———, *The Chase: How Ohio State Captured the First College Football Playoff*, Chicago: Triumph Books, 2015
Sallee, Barrett, "Ohio State coach Urban Meyer announces retirement," *bssports.com*, December 4, 2018
Thamel, Pete, "The legend of Joe Burrow," *Yahoo Sports*, November 6, 2019
———, "Playmaker," *Sports Illustrated*, September 21, 2015
Thompson, Wright, *The Cost of These Dreams: Sports Stories and Other Serious Business*, New York: Penguin Books, 2019
Tracy, Marc, "As Big Ten declines, homegrown talent flees," *The New York Times*, October 3, 2014
———, Michigan tries to steady that big chip on Ohio State's shoulder, *The New York Times*, November 21, 2018
———, Ohio State overwhelms Michigan, again," *The New York Times*, November 24, 2018
———, "Urban Meyer to retire from Ohio State following tumultuous season," *The New York Times*, December 4, 2018
Wilson, Mitch, "Full lineup: 22nd Florida football player arrested under Urban Meyer regime," *bleacherreport.com*, February 24, 2009
Witz, Billy, "Ohio State passes its first test of the season by beating Penn State," *The New York Times,* November 23, 2019

Twenty-nine
New Day dawning

Adelson, Andrea, "The committee remains disappointingly predictable," *espn.com*, December 20, 2020
Albom, Mitch, "Michigan football's sickening reality: Ohio State is just better," *Detroit Free Press*, December 1, 2019
Arnold, Jeff, "Justin Fields has 'Heisman moment' in Ohio State's win over Michigan," *The New York Times*, November 30, 2019
Connelly, Bill, "Clemson, Ohio State and the making of a College Football Playoff classic," *espn.com*, December 30, 2019
Culpepper, Chuck, Gene Wang and Glynn A. Hill, "Clemson has Trevor Lawrence this time," *The Washington Post*, December 19, 2020

Culpepper, Chuck, and Jacob Bogage, "In thrilling Fiesta Bowl semifinal, the gain goes to Clemson, the pain to Ohio State, *The Washington Post*, December 29, 2019
———, "LSU, behind the power of purple, makes its case as this year's superteam," *The Washington Post*, December 7, 2019
———,"Notre Dame's problem against the Alabamas of the world is also college football's problem," *The Washington Post*, December 31, 2020
——— ,"Ryan Day's unlikely path to Ohio State shows how miraculous it is to find the right coach," *The Washington Post*, January 4, 2021
———, "Tension pays Ohio State a visit along with Penn State but both are turned away," *The Washington Post*, November 23, 2019
———, "With Ohio State soaring, Michigan can only look up," *The Washington Post*, November 30, 2019
Davidson, John Daniel, "The suspension of Ohio State's Chase Young is everything that's wrong with the NCAA," *The Federalist*, November 13, 2019
Dodd, Dennis, "Chase Young's dominant play makes Ohio State the most complete team in the nation," *cbssports.com*, October 26, 2019
Eisner, George, "THE state of Ohio State football, Part 1: was the 2019 season a success?" *www.landgrantholyland,com*, January 20, 2020
Lesmerises, Doug, "By beating Michigan, Ohio State's Ryan Day becomes one of 11, and is brought to tears," *Cleveland.com*, November 30, 2019
———, Ohio State football decided a Big Ten Championship mattered, even if this win cost the Buckeyes a playoff seed," *The Plain Dealer*, December 8, 2019
———, "What Ohio State's blowout loss to Alabama tells you about the Buckeyes," *Cleveland.com*, January 11, 2021
Litman, Laken, "Organically and subtly, Ryan Day is making Ohio State football his own," *Sports Illustrated*, November 21, 2019
———, "Ohio State gets the battle it needed," *Sports Illustrated*, November 23, 2019
Mathis-Lilley, Ben, "The College Football Playoff is great and makes everyone sad," *slate.com*, November 7, 2019
Means, Stephen, "What was America like last time Cincinnati beat Ohio State?, *cleveland.com*, September 3, 2019
Newberry, Paul, "Another boring blowout in the era of super teams in college football," *Associated Press*, January 12, 2021
Olson, Andrew, "THE application denied: Ohio State's trademark request rejected," *saturdaydownsouth.com*, September 11, 2019
Planos, Josh, "Ohio State is always facing high expectations—scandal or not," *fivethirtyeight.com*, August 31, 2018
Rosenberg, Michael, "Ohio State blows past Michigan in latest chapter of a rivalry that's been anything but even," *Sports Illustrated*, November 30, 2019
Sabin, Rainer, "The seeds of Michigan football's loss to Ohio State sown on recruiting trail," *Detroit Free Press*, November 30, 2019
Svrluga, Barry, "After all the disruption in college football, it was all domination for Alabama, *The Washington Post*, January 12, 2021
———, "Justin Fields put No. 1 Alabama—and the NFL—on notice with masterful Sugar Bowl, *The Washington Post*, January 2, 2021
Tamanini, Matt, "Ohio State opens as 6-5-point underdog for Nov. game vs. Michigan, *landgrantholyland.com*, March 19, 2019
———, "The five biggest things we learned from Ohio State's obliteration of Maryland," *landgrantholyland.com*, November 10, 2019

Thamel, Pete, "Ohio State squanders CFP semifinal shot: 'It's the worst feeling in the world,'" *Yahoo Sports*, December 29, 2019
———, "The legend of Joe Burrow: from overlooked at Ohio State to Heisman frontrunner at LSU," *Yahoo Sports*, November 6, 2019
Witz, Billy, "Ohio State passes its first test of the season by beating Penn State," *The New York Times*, November 23, 2019
Zimmerman, Luke, "Former Ohio State assistant Nick Saban talks Woody Hayes," *landgrantholyland.com*, April 8, 2013

Thirty
The transient virtue of being No. 1

Culpepper, Chuck, "College Football Playoff field set but controversy linger with Ohio State in, TCU snubbed," *Washington Post*, December 7, 2014
Danzig, Allison, *The History of American Football: Its Great Teams, Players, and Coaches*, Englewood Cliffs, New Jersey: Prentice-Hall, 1956
Doyle, Andrew, "Bear Bryant: symbol for an embattled South," *Colby Quarterly*, Volume 32, March, 1996
"College football national championships in NCAA Division I FBS," *https://en.wikipedia.org/wiki/College_football_national_championships_in_NCAA_Division_I_FBS*
Einstein, Charles, "When football went to war," *Sports Illustrated*, December 6, 1971
"Faculty Nips Ohio State Roses In Bud," *The Fresno Bee-Republican,* November 29, 1961
"Football Bowl Subdivision Records," *http://fs.ncaa.org/Docs/stats/football_records/2018/FBS.pdf*
Hadley, Mitchell, "Behind the close-up: the 1962 Rose Bowl," *It's About TV*, December 27, 2012
Jenkins, Dan, "This year the fight will be in the open," *Sports Illustrated*, September 11, 1967
Jonietz, Erika, "Computing athletics," *MIT Technology Review*, November 1, 2002
Kirk, Jason, "The all-time 'consensus' college football national championships list," *SBNation*, January 22, 2018
Lesmerises, Doug, "Is it six or eight national championships for Ohio State?" *Plain Dealer*, January 24, 2015
Mandel, Stewart, *Bowls, Polls, & Tattered Souls*, Hoboken: John Wiley & Sons, 2007
Mather, Victor, "College football rankers by the dozen ask the No. 1 question," *The New York Times*, October 23, 2012
Moore, Jack, "The bizarre, confusing ways college football has picked its champion," *vocativ.com*, January 12, 2016
Murray, Jim, 'Bama and Ol' Bear," *Los Angeles Times*, November 19, 1961
———, "Bedsheets and 'Bama," *Los Angeles Times*, November 20, 1961
Niesen, Joan, "The computer poll uprising: creators of the BCS's most controversial component look back," *Sports Illustrated,* July 11, 2018
Ridpath, David, "The College Football Playoff and other NCAA revenues are an exposé of selfish interest," *Forbes*, January 17, 2017
Snow, Blake, "Game of numbers: How the BCS rules college football," *Wired*, December 3, 2010

Trex, Ethan, "Fuzzy math: how college football's champs were chosen," *Mental Floss*, December 8, 2010

Walsh, Christopher J., *Who's #1: 100-Plus Years of Controversial National Champions in College Football*, Lanham, Maryland: Taylor Trade Publishing, 2007

Wilken, Dan, "Committee blew it with Alabama," *USA Today*, December 4, 2017

Thirty-one
The internal wars

Baroway, Malcom S., A *History of the Ohio State University: The Gee Years, 1990–1997*, Columbus: The Ohio State University Press, 2003

Cantwell, Robert, "Say It Isn't So, Woody," *Sports Illustrated*, September 11, 1967

"College profiles," *https://www.collegedata.com/cs/data/college/college_pg03_tmpl.jhtml?schoolId=379*

Everman, Lisa, "Jennings relishes return to old role, *The Lantern*, July 10, 2002

Freedman, Morris, "Ohio State not best model for College Park," *The Baltimore Sun*, February 5, 1998

"Honest Independence": The Life of Norton Strange Townshend, *https://clements.umich.edu/exhibit/townshend/,* William L. Clements Library, University of Michigan

Hooper, Osman Castle, *History of Ohio State University, Volume II*, Columbus: The Ohio State University Press, 1926

Mendenhall, Thomas C., editor, *History of the Ohio State University*, Vol. II, Columbus: The Ohio University Press, 1926

The Ohio State University Academic Plan Second-Year Report, September, 2003

The Ohio State University Academic Plan 2006 Update, November, 2006

Pappano, Laura, "How big-time sports ate college life," *The New York Times*, January 20, 2012

Pollard, James E., *History of Ohio State University: The Story of Its First Seventy-five Years, 1873–1948*, Columbus: The Ohio University Press, 1952

Rea, Mark, "Things weren't so rosy for Bucks in 1991," *419sports.com*, July 12, 2016

Suggs, Welch, "How gears turn at a sports factory," *The Chronicle of Higher Education*, Vol. 4, issue 14, November 29, 2002

Weaver, Karen, "Media Deals, College Football, and Governance: Who's in Charge?" *Change, The Magazine of Higher Learning*, July, 2013

Wojciechowski, Gene, "Look who's talking, again: running back Robert Smith has been taken back by the Ohio State football team, but hasn't taken back what he said," *Los Angeles Times*, August 31, 1992

Index

John Baskin was the first player from his South Carolina high school to make a college varsity, a gratuitous and little-known fact he earned largely by default—and the fact that Hillcrest High's stellar fullback, Baskin's classmate, became so homesick he left his Wingate College camp where he was contending for a starting position, took a bus back to Greenville, then walked twelve miles home carrying two suitcases. Baskin's finest moments seemed to occur in either spring practice or twenty years later in the annual Mars Hill College varsity-alumni game where he was awarded the only athletic trophy of his life, which, he later learned, was awarded to anyone who was over forty and dumb enough to suit up against the varsity.

Mike O'Bryant played on Mason High's first football team where his finest moment came as a senior, after his 70-yard scoring scamper—Wing Right, Right 22—in the season opener was called back. Two plays later, he did it again, this time for 50 yards and a righteous score. O'Bryant graduated after winning the league in the 100-, 220-, and 440-yard dashes. He had a brief fling at running back with the semipro Cincinnati Blue Devils but doesn't remember much about it because beer was served on the sidelines. He scouted for Purcell coach Tom Lichtenberg, helping radio sports personality Dan Patrick's dad, Jack, who worked in the University of Dayton's computer department, to develop the first computerized scouting reports in the city. He went on to coach at Mason for twenty years.

Todd Kale was never a keen participant in team sports, thanks to most of his coordination being limited to his drawing hand. Nevertheless, he was drawn in (pun intended) by the Columbus football tales, from the ambitious creation of the Horseshoe to the evolution of Ohio coaching. And years ago, in a grade school English class, Kale was introduced to James Thurber, never forgetting the unique line work in Thurber's cartoons, a characteristic central to Kale's own art.